THE TONGUES OF MEN
Hegel and Hamann on
Religious Language and History

American Academy of Religion
Dissertation Series

edited by
H. Ganse Little, Jr.

Number 27

THE TONGUES OF MEN
Hegel and Hamann on Religious Language
and History
by
Stephen N. Dunning

Stephen N. Dunning

The Tongues of Men

Scholars Press

Distributed by
Scholars Press
PO Box 5207
Missoula, Montana 59806

THE TONGUES OF MEN
Hegel and Hamann on Religious Language and History
Stephen N. Dunning
University of Pennsylvania, Philadelphia, Pennsylvania

Library of Congress Cataloging in Publication Data

Dunning, Stephen Northrup.
    The tongues of men.

    (Dissertation series - American Academy of Religion ;
27 ISSN 0145-272X)
    Bibliography: p.
    1.Christianity and language. 2. History (Theology)
3. Hamann, Johann Georg, 1730-1788. 4. Hegel, Georg
Wilhelm Friedrich, 1770-1831—Religion. I. Title.
II. Series: American Academy of Religion. Dissertation
series - American Academy of Religion ; 27.
BR115.L25D86   901   79-10729
ISBN 0-89130-283-2
ISBN 0-89130-302-2 pbk.

53,282

Printed in the United States of America
1 2 3 4 5

Edwards Brothers, Inc.
Ann Arbor, MI 48104

FOR ROXY

If I speak in the tongues of men
and of angels, but have not love,
I am a noisy gong or a clanging
cymbal.

1 Cor. 13:1

CONTENTS

ACKNOWLEDGEMENTS

I would like to take this opportunity to express my gratitude to just a few of those who have helped make this project possible: to the Deutscher Akademischer Austauschdienst (DAAD) for generous financial support, 1974-1976; to Professors Karlfried Gründer, Otto Pöggeler, and Oswald Bayer of Ruhr Universität, Bochum, for advice and encouragement; to Professor George Rupp of Harvard Divinity School for his discerning criticisms of successive drafts of the dissertation; to Professor Gordon Kaufman of Harvard Divinity School, who has taught me that there is no substitute for patient study of difficult texts; and to my wife, Roxy, whose unfailing intellectual, emotional, and spiritual support insured that what began as a providential conception finally achieved tangible expression.

NOTE ON SCRIPTURE QUOTATIONS

In general, passages quoted from the Bible follow the Revised Standard Version (Old Testament, 1952; New Testament, Second Edition, 1971), as authorized by the Division of Christian Education of the National Council of the Churches of Christ in the United States of America. I also occasionally use renderings from: the King James Authorized Version (1611); The New American Bible (1970), sponsored by the Bishops' Committee of the Confraternity of Christian Doctrine; and the New International Version of the New Testament (1973), prepared under the auspices of the New York Bible Society International.

PREFACE

As a study in historical meaning and biblical language, this essay deals with problems of theological method. I have been led to write it by a very particular sequence of circumstances. The first of these was my realization that contemporary theologians are virtually unanimous in their assumption that, at least with regard to the interpretation of history, faith and theology must accommodate themselves to secular knowledge. This realization did not involve a highly technical understanding of such terms as "faith" and "secular." The opposition I perceived was simply one in which the language of secular history and the language of faith are set against each other, and the former is accepted while the latter is considered problematical. The resulting dilemma for contemporary theology is that it has to choose between defining faith as an enemy or as an ally of secular historical reason. The fixed point is the presupposition of secular knowledge, and faith is adjusted, if not explicitly subordinated, to it.

The second event was my conclusion that G. W. F. Hegel's philosophy of religion does not live up to its promise to do justice to faith within the context of philosophical reason. For some time I had been impressed by Hegel's effort to develop a philosophical language which could reconcile Christian faith with rational, autonomous knowledge. As I studied that language in terms of its own unfolding system, I was often amazed at how comprehensive and many-sided -- even kaleidoscopic -- Hegel's thought is. One problem, however, continued to disturb me. The more I came to "know" God in Hegelian categories, the less I had any sense of the presence of God. In other words, the God of speculative philosophy did not seem to bear any relation to the God of the Bible, who is portrayed as speaking to men and personally guiding their lives. Instead of expressing the truth of faith as it is experienced by individual Christians, Hegel appeared rather to have an impersonal and merely conceptual understanding of God.

1

The third and decisive event was my discovery that J. G. Hamann, a friend and fellow-Königsberger of Kant, offers a radical alternative to the options I had encountered in contemporary theology and Hegel. Hamann's thought -- about the world no less than about God -- is cast in biblical language. In the second half of the twentieth century, such an approach may sound anachronistic or even comical. Nevertheless, Hamann's understanding of history, language and faith illustrates a clear alternative to contemporary theological methods. However unacceptable it may be to secular theologians, it cannot be dismissed as irrational, pietistic, or, in the term which appears frequently in American discussions, "fundamentalistic." The language of the Bible, as interpreted by Hamann, offers far greater resources for understanding the world than most modern theologians acknowledge. One of my purposes in writing this essay is to substantiate that claim.

Because of the particular sequence of these events, this study is and remains a reflection upon the major issues involved in a comparison of Hegel with Hamann. As an area of great interest to them both, and one where they each have exercised a great deal of influence, the interpretation of history provides a point of departure for the essay. In the course of investigating their respective understandings of history, the question of the language in which such an enterprise should be pursued emerges. Finally, the implications of their different approaches to history and language for the life of Christian faith clarify what is at stake in choosing between them.

Despite the significance of Hegel and Hamann for other thinkers, the method of analysis I employ in this essay is systematic rather than historical. In order to deal as thoroughly as possible with the question before me, I have limited myself in terms of both primary and secondary texts. I do not aim to be "comprehensive" with regard to either Hegel or Hamann or their interpreters. To do so would be to risk superficiality or to write several volumes instead of one. Hegel is one of the most prolific writers in the German language, and Hamann one of the most elusive. The scholarly literature about them is often more difficult to follow than their own writings. Therefore, this essay is limited, for the most part, to close analysis of

several texts by Hegel and only one by Hamann. It is my hope
that this approach will increase the accuracy of my interpretations and sharpen my line of argument, without in any way
impairing the relevance of my conclusions to contemporary
discussion about theological method.

CHAPTER I

INTRODUCTION

The thesis of this dissertation is that contemporary Protestant theology of history faces a dilemma which can be illuminated by a comparison of the thought of G. W. F. Hegel (1770-1831) and J. G. Hamann (1730-1788). That dilemma is the conflict between the secular language in which modern man normally understands the meaning of history and the biblical and confessional language of traditional Christian faith. My argument is that Hegel's program of secularization jeopardizes the integrity of the personal faith of individual Christians, whereas Hamann's effort to interpret history in biblical terms provides faith with a coherent self-understanding.

In this chapter I sketch the development of the conflict between secular and religious language in the theologies of history of selected major twentieth century theologians. My conclusion is that, despite the very real differences in their efforts to deal with this conflict, all of those surveyed share the assumption that the theological task is to redefine faith in relation to secular historical knowledge. Karl Barth and Rudolf Bultmann argue (in very different ways) that faith must be protected from the encroachments of secular historical methods. H. Richard Niebuhr and Richard R. Niebuhr claim to portray Christian and secular interpretations of history as reciprocally related. And Van Harvey and Wolfhart Pannenberg return to the conviction of Ernst Troeltsch that secular knowledge can provide a firm foundation for the major historical claims of Christianity. For all their differences, however, these theologians are united in presupposing that secular historical knowledge is valid and authoritative as the means for understanding secular history, and that the theological question is how to define the historical dimension of faith in relation to such knowledge.

Hegel was a major philosophical defender of secular language as the best medium for understanding not only world history but also Christianity. In his view, the philosophy of

5

history has deep theological roots, and its task is to develop those roots into their secular articulation and application in order to reach an adequate comprehension of them. His carefully worked out position is helpful for understanding the claim that theology and secular knowledge can unite in the philosophy of history. It also shows that such a union can reduce Christian faith from a way of life to a conceptual stage in the development of speculative philosophy.

In contrast to Hegel, Hamann's understanding of history is cast in biblical language and in terms of Christianity as seen from the perspective of the concrete faith of individual believers. As such, it is unusual in modern theology, and is consequently often misunderstood. Hegel published the first major interpretation of Hamann's thought, which he tried to understand in secular rather than biblical categories (a tendency which goes back to J. G. Herder and F. N. Jacobi, who were Hamann's direct disciples). In spite of such misinterpretation, Hamann's biblical method is relevant to contemporary theology, for it offers a coherent alternative to both the dichotomy between faith and secular history suggested by Barth and Bultmann and also to the secularization of faith advocated by Hegel and those who follow in his footsteps.

In addition to exploring the systematic issue of secular *versus* biblical language for the understanding of history, this essay makes two other contributions to existing scholarship. To my knowledge, it is the first thorough study of Hegel's article on Hamann, which is unique in the Hegelian corpus for its detailed attention to the life and thought of an individual Christian. In contrast to the abstractions and generalities which characterize Hegel's most famous and influential works, his review of Hamann's writings deals in depth with a particular person whose thought is also available to us in his own works. Thus it is an unusual opportunity to see how Hegel deals with the faith of a devout individual Christian. The other contribution concerns Hamann scholarship. Although extremely advanced in recent years by scholars writing in German and Dutch, there are only a few books and articles on Hamann in English. This study adds to those works the first translation and interpretation in English of Hamann's last

major work, the *Golgotha and Scheblimini*. It is also the first
effort in English to demonstrate the influence of biblical
language on Hamann's thought and style, and the relation he sees
between biblical language and the interpretation of history.

The Dilemma of Contemporary Theology

In October, 1901, Ernst Troeltsch delivered a lecture which
illustrates the dilemma of contemporary theology as I understand
it. Entitled "The Absoluteness of Christianity and the History
of Religions," this lecture is an explicit effort to articulate
the relation between the claim that Christianity is absolute
truth and the secular methods of analysis of religions as human,
historical phenomena. In this lecture, which he published in a
somewhat revised form, Troeltsch makes clear that the truth of
Christianity cannot be accepted as normative in the same sense
that secular historical understanding is, for him, normative.
Rather, he looks to secular understanding to provide a firm
foundation and justification for the claims of Christian faith:

> All that the Christian needs, therefore, is the
> certainty that within the Christian orientation of
> life there is an authentic revelation of God and that
> nowhere is a greater revelation to be found. This
> certainty he can discover even in a purely historical
> consideration of Christianity. In such a considera-
> tion the faith in God that animated Jesus and his
> followers encounters him with a power that is irre-
> sistably transforming, profoundly moving, and binding
> in the highest degree. With complete composure he
> can consign to the world to come the absolute religion
> that represents not struggling faith but changeless
> and certain knowledge of the truth.[1]

Troeltsch's statement shows that he is by no means a pure
secularist: his faith in the power of Jesus to transform lives
is profound, and he is thoroughly committed to the religious
truth of Christianity. Nevertheless, he does not understand
and defend his faith in the language of the Bible or Christian
doctrine. Instead, he appeals to "a purely historical consideration" as the means of justifying the truth of the Christian
message. This consideration will, he believes, bring about an
encounter with the faith of Jesus and the first Christians, and
thus make the seeker's faith a "changeless and certain knowledge
of the truth." But it will not do so by virtue of religious

presuppositions. It will approach the biblical accounts with
the tools and vocabulary of modern historical interpretation,
and on this basis alone it will encounter and understand the
truth. This secular language is presupposed as valid, and as
the authority by which the language and claims of the Bible are
to be affirmed.

The optimism Troeltsch expresses in this passage was not
naive. In the next paragraph he qualified this statement with
the admission that "only the future would bring complete deliv-
erance, perfect knowledge, and permanent victory."[2] What the
immediate future brought, however, was World War I. Suddenly
European theologians found that secular history could produce
barbarism just as easily as civilization, a barbarism never
even imagined by the secular historians of the time. The justification by secular interpretation sought after by Troeltsch no
longer seemed as attractive as it had. Economic collapse and
World War II intensified this sense of insecurity and disillu-
sionment with the course of world history and its interpreters.

The development of Protestant theology of history in the
twentieth century can be interpreted as a sudden and sharp
movement away from Troeltsch's pre-war position and then a long
and arduous struggle to return to it, in hopes of reconstructing
it upon more adequate grounds. World War I provided the crucible
in which the early theologies of Karl Barth and Rudolf Bultmann
were forged. More mature works, written in the 1940's, still
reflect their desire to keep the understanding of Christian
faith free from the authority of secular methods of understanding history. Yet neither, for all this scepticism, questions
the truth and value of secular methods in their own right.
Rather, their effort is to find another language for the explanation of Christian faith and the events upon which it is based,
and thereby to isolate Christianity from the sceptical relativism
of secular historical thinking.

This divorce is clearest in Bultmann, whose work as an
historian of early Christianity proceeds on the basis of entirely
different methods than does his work as a Christian theologian.
His programmatic essay of 1941, "New Testament and Mythology,"[3]
provides a succinct statement of this dichotomy. In Bultmann's
view, the New Testament combines an historical account of the

life of Jesus with mythological interpretations of the significance of his life.[4] In contrast to Troeltsch, who proposed
validating the significance to which this mythological language
points on the basis of an historical understanding of Jesus,
Bultmann considers both languages equally problematical for
faith. Mythological language, he says, is unintelligible to
modern man: it is obsolete and wrong. To insist upon a blind
acceptance of it would be an arbitrary position which bases
faith upon works. It cannot be believed literally, for Christ
never returned and the mythical eschaton never happened.[5] To
eliminate all mythological language in favor of historical
language, however, simply distorts Christianity. Attacking
Harnack in particular, Bultmann declares that history has only
"academic interest, but never...paramount importance for
religion."[6]

The solution to this conflict between mythological language,
which is unintelligible, and historical language, which elimi-
nates the "kerygma" (proclamation of Christ), is, according to
Bultmann, to "demythologize" the biblical accounts into existentialist language.[7] Whereas both mythological and historical
language are an effort, by ancients and moderns respectively,
to give the appearance of objective truth to their spiritual
experience, existentialist language is the straightforward
means by which modern man can express subjective truth in his
own terms. To use the crucifixion of Jesus as an example, it
should not be made an object of faith, for it is neither an
event of mythological redemption nor an act of historical
heroism.[8] Rather, it is an existentialist portrayal of the
truth that every Christian must be "crucified" in his heart.
When understood in this subjective manner, says Bultmann, the
crucifixion ceases to be either a timeless mythological truth
or an event limited to the historical past. Rather, it is
grasped as an "eschatological event *in and beyond* time, in so
far as it (understood in its significance, that is, for faith)
is an everpresent reality."[9]

Through all of this runs the presupposition that "eschatological" events such as the resurrection of Jesus are not historical events, and that therefore "the historical problem is
not of interest to Christian belief in the resurrection."[10]

There is no historical evidence which could strengthen or challenge the Christian's faith in the resurrection. This aloofness
of faith from the problematic of history is demonstrated by
Bultmann's view of the church. As the eschatological Body of
Christ, it is an existential reality which "is not just a phenomenon of secular history, it is phenomenon [sic!] of significant
history, in the sense that it realizes itself in history."[11]

By disengaging faith so completely from the historical
realm, Bultmann succeeds only in bringing it into utter bondage
to the present. The sole criterion of truth in his view is
contemporary self-understanding. He starts with existentialist
subjectivity, and he ends up there. Bultmann's unwillingness
to endorse the historical claims of the Bible as historical,
and his outright rejection of all mythological language, leave
him with no foundation for faith other than his own existentialist self-understanding.

Karl Barth applauds Bultmann's emphasis upon such kerygmatic
events as the resurrection, but rejects his effort to dehistori-
cize their significance: "Faith in the risen Lord springs from
His historical manifestation, and from this as such, not from
the rise of faith in Him."[12] This criticism occurs in Barth's
long article on "Man in his Time" (1948), throughout which he
argues for the historical basis of Christian faith. In the
last analysis, however, it is difficult to see how Barth's
kerygma rests upon historical evidence any more than Bultmann's.
Rejection of the claim that some historical events recorded in
the Bible are only myths does not in itself constitute an
argument for them as history. Even in this late -- and relatively moderate -- section of his *Church Dogmatics*, Barth is
very concerned to maintain the distance between biblical and
secular history:

> The narratives are not meant to be taken as 'history'
> in our sense of the word. Even 1 Cor. 15:3-8 is
> treated in a strangely abstract way if it is regarded
> as a citation of witnesses for the purpose of histori-
> cal proof. True, these accounts read very differently
> from myths. The Easter story is differentiated from
> myth, both formally and materially, by the fact that
> it is all about a real man of flesh and blood. But
> the stories are couched in the imaginative, poetic
> style of historical saga, and are therefore marked by
> the corresponding obscurity. For they are describing
> an event beyond the reach of historical research or

depiction. Hence we have no right to try to analyse
or harmonise them. This is to do violence to the
whole character of the event in question....each of
the narratives must be read for its own sake just as
it stands.13

This passage shows what is -- and it not -- meant by Barth's
announcement that Christian faith in Jesus "springs from His
historical manifestation, and from this as such." The resurrection of Christ is not, as Bultmann maintains, merely myth.
Jesus walked the face of the earth as "a real man of flesh and
blood." Barth seems to assume that myths must, by definition,
be about imaginary people. Since no one disputes that Jesus
really lived, the stories about him circulated by the early
church cannot be dismissed as myth.

These stories cannot, however, be subjected to historical
scrutiny. They are "not meant to be taken as 'history' in our
sense of the word." They are, rather, "historical saga," which
does not aim at "historical proof" or at dispelling all "obscurity." They describe events which are "beyond the reach of
historical research or depiction." Here Barth makes clear that,
however much he may argue that the events of Christianity are
inaccessible to secular historical investigation, the methods
of secular interpretation of history are normative for the study
of all other events. Indeed, in order to protect the historical
claims of Christian faith from secular interpretation, he borrows the term "historical saga" from a non-Christian theory of
types of historical literature. In contrast with Troeltsch,
who uses secular, historical language to vindicate Christianity,
and Bultmann, who uses secular non-historical (existentialist)
language for the same purpose, Barth tries to use secular, historical language to justify the claim that Christianity is both
historical and not available to historical research!

The paradox of Barth's use of secular language to disavow
the relevance of that language to faith is paralleled by his
use of biblical language. Without doubt he is one of the most
brilliant exegetical theologians of modern times. His sense
of the radically historical nature of the events which constitute Christianity pervades all his thought. Nevertheless,
although he considers the historical claims of the Bible to be
normative for Christian faith, he does not understand them in

the *historical* sense in which they are presented in the biblical witness. To use just one example, taken from the argument in the paragraph quoted above: Barth says that 1 Cor. 15:3-8 should not be "regarded as a citation of witnesses for the purpose of historical proof." By this he seems to mean that the narratives of the appearances of Christ remain "strangely abstract" if each one is not read "for its own sake just as it stands." In other words, the stories of Jesus' appearances after his death cannot be treated generically, as different illustrations of the same truth. Each one has its own place in Scripture and teaches a truth that is distinct. Barth discourages taking Paul's catalogue of appearances to Cephas (Peter), James and himself as a justification for "abstract" historical induction from the several accounts. In so doing, he overlooks a main thrust of Paul's appeal, which is merely one example of a theme that is constant in the New Testament. Paul cites the various appearances not as isolated historical data, but as different confirmations of the fact that Jesus had fulfilled the Old Testament prophecies about the Messiah. This means that the appearances are not events to be interpreted by theological or secular methods which are developed later, but are to be understood through the historical prophecies of them which had come centuries earlier. Thus Paul affirms that "Christ died for our sins in accordance with the scriptures" (1 Cor. 15:3-4). The historical claims of Christianity, when understood in the language of the Bible, are interpreted neither through secular, historical research nor through theories about historical saga, but through the correlation between prophecies given at one historical moment in time and the events which fulfill them at another historical moment in time. For all his "Biblicism" and rejection of modern historical methods in relation to Christianity, Barth fails to appreciate the biblical view of historical interpretation and judgment. This failure may be inevitable for one who accepts the authority of secular historical methods for understanding non-biblical history. The Bible itself knows no such limit. For Barth to use it and only it as a lens on history would mean for him to interpret even the events of the contemporary secular world "biblically." I shall return to this matter in my discussion of Hamann's theology of history.

With H. Richard Niebuhr, twentieth century theology of history enters a new stage. Convinced that the positions of both
Troeltsch and Barth contain valuable truths, he proposes a way
to reconcile the need for secular historical interpretation with
the historical convictions of Christian faith. This reconciliation is based upon the claim that they constitute two distinct
approaches to history which are both valid and necessary for a
balanced understanding. In *The Meaning of Revelation* (1941),
Niebuhr devotes an entire chapter to explaining the differences
and relation between what he calls "internal history" and "external history."[14] Internal history, he says, is the past as personally appropriated by a believer, the revealed past of faith,
and the past of the community with which a person identifies
himself and whose symbols and values are his symbols and values.
All men have an identity of this sort, and with it an internal
history that shapes their entire perception of the past. In
contrast, external history is a way of understanding the past
from a disinterested and impersonal perspective. Here the relation between history and historian is one not of faith but of
secular methods of interpretation, so that, in theory at least,
the individual identity of the historian is not a factor.[15]

According to Niebuhr, Christians have only themselves to
blame for the conflict between their internal understanding and
secular, external understanding of church history. Their error
was that they attempted (like Barth) to "isolate sacred from
secular history." This effort, says Niebuhr, led to "fruitless
quarrels" with those who did not agree with their idea of a
sacred history of revelation as distinct from the mundane history of the world. It also produced the theological "inconsistency" of substituting "belief in the occurrence of miraculous
events for faith in God."[16]

Niebuhr's conviction is that internal history is a matter
of selves discovering who they are in a community of other
selves, and that the Christian's confession must be of his own
experience rather than of the experience and history of the
early church, which is beyond his personal knowledge. On the
basis of this theory of historical understanding as a function
of the self, Niebuhr claims that internal and external history
are really "two aspects" of or perspectives on the same past,

since both are approaches which every self can and must employ.
In this way he tries to avoid the "extreme dualism" of pitting
sacred against secular and internal against external in the
interpretation of history.[17]

Up to this point, the language of Niebuhr's analysis has
been drawn largely from the secular sciences of historical and
social-psychological analysis, without reference to traditional
Christian terminology. At the close of the chapter, however,
he argues that the unity of the "two aspects" of knowledge of
one past is very much like the paradoxical unity of God and man
in Christ. This is a reference to the Council of Chalcedon of
451, at which the bishops declared that in the one person of
Jesus Christ there existed two natures, one divine and the other
human, which were in no way mixed or confused despite their
unity in one person. Niebuhr's argument is that Christians
today must accept the paradoxical unity of internal and external
history in the same way that fifth century Christians accepted
the paradoxical unity of the divine and human natures in Christ:

> External history is the medium in which internal
> history exists and comes to life. Hence knowledge
> of its external history is a duty of the church.
> In all this we have only repeated the paradox
> of Chalcedonian Christology and of the two-world
> ethics of Christianity. But it is necessary to
> repeat it in our time, especially in view of the
> all too simple definitions of history and revela-
> tion that fail to take account of the duality in
> union which is the nature of Christian life and
> history.[18]

The irony here is that Niebuhr's theory of the relation of
internal to external history is implicitly contradicted by this
appeal to the Chalcedonian model. The Fathers understood the
unity of the divine with the human in Christ as an act performed
by God for the salvation of mankind. Although men were the
direct beneficiaries of this act, they took no active part in
it whatsoever. Human nature was perceived as in need of salvation by the divine, and as obligated to it. In no way were that
need and obligation portrayed as reciprocal.

For Niebuhr, however, the relation between the internal
history of faith in revelation and the external history of disinterested observation is one of reciprocity. Even though
internal history corresponds to the divine nature in the

Chalcedonian model, Niebuhr says that the church is responsible for the enmity between them. To apply this logic to the model would be to say that God is as responsible as man for the fact of sin! Likewise, whereas God has no need of man nor any duties to him, Niebuhr says that external history is "the medium in which internal history exists and comes to life," and that therefore the church is obligated to strive for an "external knowledge" of itself.

The claim to reciprocity breaks down even further when we ask about the extent to which external history is equally in need of and obligated to internal history. Niebuhr refuses to grant to the church the same authority for secular historical understanding that he grants to secular understanding for the church. Although he affirms that every historian must have some internal history, this can occur only by a "leap" of faith.[19] The validity of external studies of Christian history is not contingent upon that leap and the self-identification of their authors with the Christian church. Christians are, it seems, to "confess" their faith, but never to judge other views on the basis of it.[20] Conversely, non-Christians may criticize Christians, and the church has a duty to hear and respond to those criticisms. In short, what started out as an argument for reciprocity between internal or Christian and external or secular understandings of history ends up as an argument for the authority of the secular over the Christian, and this argument is justified by an idiosyncratic if not patently false interpretation of the Chalcedonian christological model.

A more convincing argument for the reciprocity of internal and external approaches to history is put forward by Richard R. Niebuhr in *Resurrection and Historical Reason* (1957).[21] Niebuhr announces at the beginning of his book that "theology has come dangerously close to divorcing internal from external history."[22] As his title indicates, he does not shy away from the problem of the resurrection (as H. R. Niebuhr does); rather, he explicitly proposes that Jesus' resurrection can serve as the basis for a "critique of historical reason."[23] It succeeds as a paradigm for historical events, says Niebuhr, where Bultmann's concept of faith and Barth's concept of Christ both fail:[24]

The resurrection of Jesus Christ is an event in this kind of history, in which events must be treated for their own sake. The resurrection shares in the arbitrariness, irrationality and independence which characterize all events to some degree; and like them, it is problematic.[25]

Using a method very similar to that of H. R. Niebuhr, R. R. Niebuhr employs secular language to explain religious claims. Rather than presenting a theory of historical knowledge, however, he concentrates upon the nature of historical events. From their "arbitrariness, irrationality and independence," Niebuhr infers that all historical study must treat its subject as "problematic." On the basis of this argument, he concludes that secular knowledge should realize what an ideal paradigm for historical events the "problematic" resurrection of Jesus offers. Conversely, Christians should not reject the secular terms of his theory of historical events, for they offer the means for a deeper understanding of the resurrection. Explicitly affirming the need of Christians for self-understanding in secular language, Niebuhr says that "the church is dependent on the world, from which it likes to set itself apart, for the ability to find in Jesus Christ more than it has made of him with its categories."[26]

At the close of his book, Niebuhr illustrates what it would mean for the church to depend upon the world for a fuller understanding of Jesus Christ. In a brief discussion of the biblical accounts of the resurrection, he asserts that:

The outstanding feature of these passages is not their emphasis on the corporeal as such, but on identification and recognition, and hence on the flesh insofar as it is the medium of recognition.[27]

Niebuhr's purpose here is to correct the traditional debate over whether the resurrection of Jesus was corporeal or merely spiritual by arguing that the New Testament focuses on the recognition of Jesus by his disciples. This recognition involved both bodily and spiritual aspects, for the Risen Christ had to be spiritually present to the disciples as the bodily Jesus whom they could recognize. The implicit reciprocity between the corporeal and spiritual aspects of the resurrection becomes explicit in the secular categories of Niebuhr's theory of history: there is a "double relationship of the past to the present," he says, which is illustrated in the disciples' affirmation of Jesus' resurrection. Not only do they affirm his presence to them; they thereby also affirm "the historicity of the events, for independence and contingency, recollection and recognition are categories of history."[28] Once again, the biblical account of the resurrection becomes fully intelligible only in the language of a secular theory of history.

The real problem with understanding a Christian belief or doctrine in terms of a secular theory of history is, as we saw with both Barth and H. R. Niebuhr, that the interpretation of the Christian sources is often highly selective or even slanted toward the secular theory in question. R. R. Niebuhr's theory of recognition is meant to shift attention away from the "scandal" of bodily resurrection without "effacing" that tradition entirely.[29] Thus he claims that "the flesh" is emphasized only "insofar as it is the medium of recognition." A look at the New Testament, however, indicates that this is a very unbalanced reading of the texts. In only one of the accounts of Jesus' resurrection is his body not mentioned at all (Mt. 28:16ff.), and corporeality is very much emphasized in most of the others. (Like Niebuhr, I am not taking into account the appearances recorded in Mk. 16, due to the unreliability of the manuscript authorities.) In three accounts the flesh is, as Niebuhr says, a medium of recognition (Lk. 24:36ff.; Jn. 20:19ff.; and Jn. 20:24ff.). But in four other stories, three of which are the longest and most detailed descriptions of resurrection appearances, the corporeal emphasis either comes after the disciples recognize Jesus (Mt. 28:9) or it is clearly portrayed as inadequate for recognition. Thus the disciples on the road to Emmaus (Lk. 24:13ff.) did not recognize Jesus until he broke bread for them at dinner; Mary Magdalene thought he was a gardener until he called her name (Jn. 20:11ff.); and the disciples who were fishing did not recognize him by his appearance but by the fact that he gave them a miraculous catch of fish (Jn. 21:1ff.). In these cases, recognition that Jesus had been raised from the grave was contingent upon recognition of him by non-physical means. To minimize the role of the flesh, as Niebuhr does, on the grounds that it is only a "medium of recognition," is to distort the impression given by the total scriptural witness.

Whereas Bultmann explicitly denies the historical truth of
such "mythical" elements in the New Testament as the resurrection
and H. R. Niebuhr does not deal directly with it, Barth and
R. R. Niebuhr try to defend it in terms of a secular theory
about historical literature or events. Of these four, only
Bultmann seems to avoid misrepresenting traditional Christian
doctrine or the Bible in the interests of defending his own
theory. A similar willingness to espouse unequivocally the
authority of secular historical methods over those of faith,
and to reject biblical texts which cannot be translated into
secular language, characterizes the theology of Van A. Harvey.
In *The Historian and the Believer* (1966),[30] Harvey begins with
a very affirmative discussion of Troeltsch's methods and the
question, not explicitly dealt with by the other theologians,
of authority in historical knowledge. In his view, every historian has presuppositions or "warrants" by which he makes
historical judgments. These presuppositions, however, must be
scrutinized: "it is," he says, "misleading to assume that every
presupposition or warrant is as arbitrary as every other."[31]
One task of any adequate theology of history must be to examine
critically its own presuppositions and those of the sources on
which it depends.

When Harvey applies his critical method to the New Testament
picture of Jesus, he finds that there can be as many as four
meanings of the name "Jesus of Nazareth."[32] On the most fundamental level, there is the actual Jesus who lived in Palestine
almost two thousand years ago. This is "Jesus as he really
was," the famous "historical Jesus" who is out of reach of historical research, despite the efforts of scholars to recapture
him. As a result of those continuing efforts, however, a second
notion of Jesus has emerged, which is often not distinguished
from the first. This is "the Jesus that is now recoverable by
historical means," whom Harvey prefers to call "the historical
Jesus," for he believes that "there is some consensus among
historians who otherwise disagree," and that this consensus
constitutes a second approach to or understanding of Jesus.
The third Jesus portrayed in the New Testament is called by
Harvey the "memory-impression of Jesus," that is, the recol-
lections of those who actually knew and remembered him from

their own personal experience. This memory-impression, says
Harvey, is "highly selective" in the picture it presents of
Jesus. In some ways it corresponds to the "historical Jesus,"
but it differs in that it includes testimonies about Jesus which
cannot be verified by historical research. Finally, Harvey
designates "the transformation and alteration of the memory-
impression...by theological interpretation" as "the Biblical
Christ." These are stories about Jesus which he considers un-
historical; they are valuable not for their reporting of facts
but for what they reveal about the faith of the early church.
Examples which Harvey gives of such stories, which are partial
distortions of the historical truth rather than totally false,
are the birth and temptation narratives, "many of the miracles,"
all stories which "clearly reflect Old Testament prophecies,"
the resurrection and ascension, and the entire Fourth Gospel.
All of these, declares Harvey, despite some elements of the
memory-impression of Jesus, are highly theological and thus
historically questionable in their biblical form.

The point of this elaborate analysis is to establish a
basis for faith which does not require belief in the Biblical
Christ. Harvey wants to show that contemporary Christians can,
by means of the secular historical-critical method, sort out a
credible memory-impression of Jesus from the erroneous image of
the Biblical Christ. Thus modern scepticism about, for example,
miracles will in no way impede believing in the same Jesus whom
the first disciples knew and followed. Authentic faith entails
believing in his teaching, actions and crucifixion,[33] but not
in the accretions of later theological reflection:

> Christian faith is not belief in a miracle; it is
> the confidence that Jesus' witness is a true one.
> This faith is not made easier or more difficult by
> the occurrence of a miracle.... The resurrection-
> faith is that Jesus is, in fact, the Word, that
> this image does, in fact, provide the clue to the
> understanding of human life.[34]

Having undermined belief in miracles, the historical-
critical method of interpretaion is then in a position to establish faith in Jesus as "the Word" on a firmer foundation. In
Harvey's view, that foundation is the memory-impression image
of Jesus, for it can "provide the clue to the understanding of
human life." In itself, this phrase could mean nothing more

than that Christians come to understand their lives in the present better by virtue of their faith in the memory-impression
of Jesus. Freed from the need to believe in historical miracles,
they can have faith in the sense of the "confidence that Jesus'
witness is a true one." If this were the extent of Harvey's
meaning in using the word "image," then his claim to be defending Christianity as a belief in historical events and persons
might be legitimate.

That, however, is not the case. Realizing that his advocacy of distinguishing the memory-impression of Jesus from the
Biblical Christ risks proclaiming a different faith from that
which Christians have believed for centuries, and rejecting the
assertion of some contemporary theologians that a new proclamation is desirable, Harvey falls back on the position that the
two pictures of Jesus represent "two avenues, so to speak, to
the truth of faith," one based on history and the other on myth:

> The conclusion one is driven to is that the
> content of faith can as well be mediated through
> a historically false story *of a certain kind* as
> through a true one, through a myth as well as
> through history.[35]

When myth and history stand side by side as avenues to
faith, what is the ultimate warrant by which they are to be
judged? Harvey's emphasis that the myth must be "*of a certain
kind*" (the italics are his) indicates that he has a criterion
in mind that will apply to myths as well as to true historical
accounts. His admission that he is "driven" to this conclusion
seems honest enough: nothing in the preceding two hundred and
eighty pages indicates that, after vigorously defending secular
historical reason over against the authority of the Biblical
Christ, Harvey will re-open the door to mythical stories.
Furthermore, he cannot simply assert two avenues to faith without implying two different faiths, unless he can establish some
criterion as common to them both.

The warrant for faith which Harvey finally suggests is the
practical value of faith in the present: "Faith finds its cer-
titude, its confirmation, in the viability of the image for
relating one to present reality."[36] In short, it is not historical verification which has ultimate authority for faith,
any more than every sort of myth should be believed. The basis

on which faith finally rests is "the viability of the image for relating one to present reality." If an image proves to transform and direct one's life in a decisive way, then it deserves one's faith; if not, then it is not worthy of belief.

The difficulty with this appeal to "viability" in personal life is that it implies that the decisive warrants for Christian truth are to be found in subjective rather than objective judgments. Although it is obvious that faith must be subjectively appropriated to inspire a believer in the first place, Christians have traditionally understood authority in terms of the Bible, a creed or an ecclesiastical office, rather than in terms of merely personal and individual judgments. By falling back upon "viability," Harvey takes a position that is similar to Bultmann's program of existentialist demythologization, but which seems strangely at odds with the apparent purpose of his book -- to defend the historical-critical method in theological interpretations of the historical claims of faith. Having vigorously defended this method, Harvey finally denies it full authority for faith. If the "Biblical Christ" can lead to faith just as well as the "memory impression" of Jesus, and both are in turn subject to judgment on the grounds of their "viability," then the whole question of presuppositions and authority in the theology of history is more confused than clarified by Harvey's conclusion.

With this final step in his argument, Harvey demonstrates that he has failed to carry out Troeltsch's program of giving faith its certainty by means of a "purely historical consideration." That honor belongs to Wolfhart Pannenberg, who is the only major contemporary theologian to subordinate faith both formally and in fact to the judgment of secular historical methods. Pannenberg begins with the notion that revelation is God's self-revelation, an idea that goes back at least to Hegel; and with the concept of "eschatological" language, which has been a major item of discussion since the turn of the century. By the ingenious device of connecting these two ideas with each other, he radicalizes them beyond anything imagined by his predecessors. In his programmatic essay, "Revelation as History" (1960),[37] Pannenberg argues that, if God's revelation is of Himself, then the medium and content of revelation cannot be distinguished: God is revelation, and revelation is God. Likewise, if God's presence in the world is an "eschatological" presence, one that is known in and through history, then revelation must be understood "as" history. Furthermore, if revelation is history and God is revelation, then it can be said that God Himself is thoroughly historical and that history reveals the being of God. These claims lead to two rather startling conclusions, which together have made Pannenberg one of the better-known theologians of our time.

The first claim concerns the nature of this historical revelation of God. Since the historical process is not yet complete, all historical knowledge remains to some extent tentative and fragmentary. If the knowledge of God is thoroughly historical, then it, too, is tentative and fragmentary. This is exactly his position. Faith in God and knowledge of the meaning of history rest upon the same foundation in his view. That foundation is an ontology of the future:

> At present a being is "something," a unity in itself, only by anticipation of its unifying future. The future interprets the present and the past; all other interpretations are helpful only to the degree that they anticipate the future.[38]

This *sine qua non* of all being applies also to God, and Pannenberg refers frequently to God's "futurity," or present incompleteness. He bolsters this argument with an appeal to the teachings of Jesus about the Kingdom of God as that which is about to come, but is not yet fully here.

The futurity of God provides Pannenberg with a solution to the debate over history and myth. Following Bultmann, he understands myth as an attempt to represent God's being as fully immanent by means of analogies to the present-day world. But history is not just the modern way of achieving the same thing. Over against Bultmann, Pannenberg believes that history points toward the future and transcendence rather than the present and immanence. Thus it is "the catalyst which makes possible the movement from mythical religion to the proclamation of the Kingdom."[39] History, whether in the Bible or elsewhere, is what cuts through the mythical pictures of God and shows both His genuine presence in the world and the fact that He, and the

world, are not yet complete. History points to the future which
lies ahead, open and transcending the limitations of the present.

By identifying full ontological reality with the always-
arriving but never-here future, Pannenberg is trying to turn
Bultmann and Barth on their heads. For them, to identify God
with secular history is to deny His transcendence. If history
points toward the future, however, then it, rather than the
mythological language of the Bible (to which Barth in particular
clings), expresses the true transcendence of God. Thus the
familiar claims for biblical and secular language have been
reversed. Biblical language can reveal the immanence of God
but only secular history protects His transcendence.

The second claim which represents a startling departure
from the traditional positions in the debate is reminiscent of
R. R. Niebuhr's defense of the resurrection in terms of historical reason. Pannenberg, however, goes further than Niebuhr,
and affirms the resurrection not merely as a fitting paradigm
for historical events but as actually demonstrated by historical-
critical reconstruction. It is his conviction that careful
historical analysis of the apocalyptic traditions will demonstrate that the resurrection story is so unusual for its time
as to be explicable only by some extraordinary event. Since
the event itself, as historical, is beyond reach today, any
name for it will necessarily be metaphorical. Given the "demonstrated" extraordinary nature of the event, it does not seem
unjustified to follow the early church in calling it a "resurrection" from the dead.[40] In this way, Pannenberg proposes a
secular and historical understanding of the resurrection: Jesus
Christ is to be affirmed as the Risen Lord on the basis of historical evidence which is equally available to all men.

It is important to see the radical way in which Pannenberg
tries to embrace both aspects of historical knowledge. On the
one hand, biblical faith needs a secular understanding of history as future-oriented, or it will fall into mythological mis-
representations of God's immanence. Without a firm orientation
toward the future, faith would lose its eschatological dimension
and transcendent truth. On the other hand, secular history needs
faith, for its own historical analysis of the resurrection event
would remain incomplete and inadequate without the interpretive

metaphors of the first Christians. Thus biblical and secular languages for historical meaning constitute different aspects of eschatological language, which alone is adequate to point toward a future in which history, faith, and God will all be complete.

The difficulty with Pannenberg's program is, however, that the "eschatological language" which is meant to reconcile faith and secular history in fact only compromises them both. His claim that secular historians must accept the evidence for an extraordinary event which can be adequately expressed only by the metaphor of resurrection rests ultimately upon the alleged silence of the apocalyptic tradition about resurrection. Not only is any argument from silence suspect, but the frequent references in the New Testament to the belief of the Pharisees in resurrection make one wonder if Pannenberg is listening in the right direction. Moreover, this sort of explanation is not any more satisfactory to believers. The resurrection is far more intelligible for faith if it is expressed in the biblical language of prophecy and fulfillment rather than in secular terms of incomprehensible events which can only be symbolized by biblical metaphors. In short, Pannenberg is saying too much to claim the authority of secular history and too little to claim the authority of the Bible.

In his view of authority, Pannenberg provides conclusive evidence that his theology does not reconcile faith and secular historical understanding so much as it subordinates faith to non-Christian criteria. He not only tries to defend the resur-rection on the basis of such criteria and his "ontology of the future," which is worked out in terms of his secular philosophy of history; Pannenberg also explicitly denies that the Bible, as such, can have a comparable authority for faith: any "'theo-logy of the Word of God,'" he says, is "only the modern expres-sion" of "an authoritarian theology of revelation."[41] Thus the program of "revelation as history" does not overcome the dichotomy between faith and history which has so plagued twen-tieth century theology. By setting out to demonstrate the truth of the resurrection of Jesus by means of secular historical reason, Pannenberg's theological method subsumes faith under the rubric of history as a kind of historical knowledge which

can be validated only be secular investigation. In this way,
he ultimately denies to faith any independent truth and integrity.

In so doing, Pannenberg simply makes a common presupposition
of contemporary theologians the explicit starting-point of his
theological program. The presupposition is that the secular
interpretation of history is reliable and authoritative, a fixed
point and firm foundation for the understanding of history. In
the beginning of the century, Troeltsch expressed the hope that
it does not necessarily conflict with Christian faith, but can
be used to support and strengthen belief. Following World War I,
this optimism collapsed. Bultmann and Barth both reacted strongly against secular explanations of the historical claims of
Christianity. Bultmann was a master of secular historical methods, but declared them irrelevant to the existentialist understanding of the mixture of myths and history which makes up the
New Testament. Barth also granted to such methods full authority
in their own areas, but denied that the understanding of Christian faith is one of those areas. Both perceived a sharp dichotomy between myth and history, and both attempted to protect
faith from this dichotomy by finding a third category by which to
understand it. In the process, Bultmann fell into the position
of explaining the truth of faith by an appeal to existentialist
criteria. These are the product of modern, secular thinking, and
to all appearances only arbitrarily related to the historical
foundations of Christianity. Barth found himself so busy defending his theory of "historical saga" that he slanted his interpretation of biblical texts in favor of it. Neither really questioned the initial dichotomy between myth and history as a
legitimate hermeneutical principle.

In contrast with this retreat from secular interpretations
of faith, H. R. Niebuhr tried to connect myth and history in a
reciprocal relationship. He likened his theory of internal and
external history as two perspectives on the past to the Chalcedonian understanding of Christ. This appeal, however, involved
such a reversal of the Fathers' thinking that it was almost an
unwitting parody of the fate of traditional Christian faith in
the twentieth century. In the same way R. R. Niebuhr attempted
to defend his theory of the nature of historical events by appealing to the resurrection of Jesus as a paradigm for them.

His interpretation of the texts which deal with the resurrection
appearances was intended to show that the event is portrayed in
the New Testament as an event of recognition which requires a
corporeal dimension but does not emphasize it. This misses the
fact that the most detailed texts actually present the resurrection appearances of Jesus as events of corporeal *non*-recognition,
while stressing that, after their "spiritual" recognition of
Jesus, the disciples perceived that his body really had been
raised up from the grave. In short, the Niebuhrs' efforts to
understand the relation of the language of faith and the language
of secular history as one of reciprocity fail because that reciprocity is merely theoretical for them: their discussions of
the Chalcedonian doctrine and the bodily resurrection manifest
much less understanding and commitment with regard to Christian
language than with regard to the language of secular historical
interpretation.

    With Harvey and Pannenberg, the effort to return to
Troeltsch's explicit affirmation of secular history as the means
for justifying Christian claims is complete. Harvey identifies
the question of authority as central, and writes virtually his
entire book from the perspective of a modern, secular historian
who would like to remain a believer. In his conclusion, however,
he confuses that perspective by declaring that biblical myths
can be as legitimate a means to faith as historically reliable
texts, for the ultimate criterion for faith is neither its historical truth nor its biblical orthodoxy but its "viability" in
the life of the believer. Consequently, Harvey gives the impression of wanting to carry out Troeltsch's program but in fact
ending up close to Bultmann. In contrast, Pannenberg never
deviates from secular historical methods in his defense of the
resurrection claim. Nonetheless, he uses those methods in a
way that is unconvincing to secular historians, and explains
belief in the resurrection in a way that is unsatisfactory for
believing Christians. Neither theologian demonstrates that a
method based upon secular historical methods is an adequate
foundation and starting-point for a coherent theology of history.

The Contemporary Relevance of Hegel and Hamann

Given the apparent inability of contemporary Protestant theologians to defend successfully the historical claims of Christianity in relation to a secular theory of historical meaning -- without in some way misrepresenting those claims and jeopardizing the faith based on them -- the comparison of Hegel and Hamann can be of help in clarifying the issues and options involved in this problem of theological method. Hegel is the first great modern philosopher to explore systematically the relation of Christian theology to historical truth in terms of secular philosophy. Hamann is one of the few Christian writers in the modern period to criticize, and at the same time remain in close communication with, those who reject biblical authority. Thus Hegel articulates some of the philosophical and systematic convictions which have led to the contemporary dilemma; and Hamann suggests a theological method which could avoid it altogether. A close study of their thought can therefore illuminate the possible consequences of secularization in Christian theology, and compare those consequences with the implications of a theology which is based upon the Bible.

Due to the fact that Hamann's thought is generally secularized by his interpreters, among whom Hegel is one of the most prominent, his influence has been more evident in German literature than in theology. In contrast, Hegel's influence is everywhere apparent.[42] Despite their different styles and historical fates, the two thinkers agree upon the centrality of Christianity in any effort to understand the meaning of history. As I argue in Chapter II, the theoretical foundation which Hegel proposes in the Introduction to his *Lectures on the Philosophy of World History* (1822-1830)[43] is thoroughly theological: Hegel explicitly declares that Christianity is a condition for the knowledge of God's will for history.[44] In the development of his interpretation of history, however, Hegel argues that philosophical and political terms must supersede theological language. In the process of making this transition, he asserts that the subjects or agents of history are not individual men but states and institutions. In so doing, I argue, Hegel proposes a view of historical significance which makes engagement with the realm of political history virtually impossible for the individual Christian who is attempting to live a life based upon faith.

From this discussion of Hegel, I go on to Hamann for a radically different approach to the question of historical meaning. In Chapter III, I present his theology of history as one that is, in the view of its author, based upon the example and authority of the Bible. An analysis of the biblical language through which Hamann tries to understand history shows that, however anachronistic such language may seem today, it is at least capable of presenting historical significance as a coherent foundation for the life of faith. The text which I use for this analysis is Hamann's *Golgotha and Scheblimini* (1784).[45] This is a critique of Moses Mendelssohn's philosophy of religion,[46] in which Hamann defends biblical theology over against the rationalist methods and results of Enlightenment thought.

In his eighty-page article entitled "Hamann's Writings" (1828),[47] Hegel applauds Hamann's insightful criticisms of Enlightenment philosophy, and specifically endorses the *Golgotha* as "without doubt the most significant thing that he wrote."[48] Although often frustrated in his efforts to discern the meaning of Hamann's biblical allusions -- to the point of denouncing his style as mere "mystification" -- Hegel does not hesitate to interpret those allusions in terms of secular language, just as Hamann's disciples, Jacobi and Herder, had also secularized his thought. The tendency to read Hamann through a secular lens, and even as a precursor of Hegel, is still widely represented in philosophical, historical, and even theological literature.[49] In Chapter IV, I show through an analysis of both Hegel's article on Hamann and Hegel's own theory of religious language that, in addition to their wide divergence on the interpretation of history, their differences on language are so great that Hegel fails to comprehend Hamann's meaning, and ultimately imposes his own views upon him.

Even with regard to the matter of language, Hamann's understanding is cast in biblical terms. In Chapter V, I defend Hamann against Hegel's misinterpretations and criticisms of him on the grounds that he understands language and all human reason according to his interpretation of the language of the Bible. In so doing, I am building upon the conclusions of numerous German scholars of the past two generations, men whose works have constituted the much-trumpeted "Hamann Renaissance."[50]

The purpose of my analysis is not only to defend Hamann against Hegel but also to show the extent to which his theology of language supports and is supported by his theology of history. At the very least, his "biblical" language presents the relation of Christian faith to history in a way that is free of major internal self-contradictions.

In conclusion, I present a systematic summary and interpretation of the results of the preceding exegeses. My argument in Chapter VI is that biblical language cannot successfully be secularized if it is to retain its religious value and meaning for Christian faith. The alternative for Christians is to reject the modern presupposition of the authority of secular knowledge, and learn to understand the world and its history in the language of the Bible.

CHAPTER II

HEGEL'S SECULAR THEOLOGY OF HISTORY

There are three aspects of Hegel's philosophy of history
which are particularly relevant to this essay: his conviction
that the truth of Christianity provides the foundation for knowledge of the meaning of history; his way of working out this
theological knowledge in secular rather than religious language;
and his explicit denial that the meaning of history can be expressed in moral and personal terms such as those of traditional
Christian faith. The following investigation of these three
themes will be based as much as possible upon the notes which
Hegel himself wrote in preparing his lectures. Only when necessary will the notes of students who attended the lectures be
cited. This important distinction is possible thanks to the
excellent critical edition prepared by Johannes Hoffmeister
(1955).[1]

The Theological Foundations of Historical Meaning

At the beginning of his second draft (1830) of the lectures,
Hegel defines the philosophy of history as "the thoughtful consideration" of history.[2] He is aware that there is a possible
conflict or "dichotomy" between the philosophical commitments
of thought and the historical data which is "given" to it. History is the attempt to understand past events. It is not free
to manipulate those events to fit its own philosophical commitments.[3] The means by which Hegel attempts to reconcile this
apparent dichotomy between philosophical theory and historical
fact is the idea of reason:

> But the only thought which philosophy brings with it
> is the simple idea of *reason* -- the idea that reason
> governs the world, and that world history is therefore
> a rational process. From the point of view of history
> as such, this conviction and insight is a *presupposi-
> tion*. Within philosophy itself, however, it is not a
> presupposition; for it is *proved* in philosophy by
> speculative cognition that reason -- and we can adopt
> this expression for the moment without a detailed
> discussion of its relationship to God -- is *substance*
> and *infinite power*; it is itself the *infinite material*

31

of all natural and spiritual life, and the *infinite form* which activates this material content. It is *substance*, i.e. that through which and in which all reality has its being and subsistence; it is infinite *power*, for reason is sufficiently powerful to be able to create something more than just an ideal...; and it is infinite *content*, the essence and truth of everything, itself constituting the material on which it operates through its own activity....[4]

The only philosophical presupposition which Hegel proposes, then, is the idea that history is a rational process. This means essentially that history can be understood. Hegel is not proclaiming any mystical or hidden meanings in history. He is simply affirming the common sense observation that, if history can be understood at all, then it must be rational, for what is irrational is not subject to understanding. It is perfectly possible to ignore the rational order of history, and to declare it to be meaningless. But it is not possible to try to understand history without first believing that it can be understood: "Whoever looks at the world rationally will find that it in turn looks rational; the two exist in a reciprocal relationship."[5]

It is important to notice that Hegel is not claiming in advance that history has demonstrated its own rationality. The idea of reason is not a product of history, but of philosophy. With regard to history, it is merely a presupposition, the truth and value of which must be demonstrated by the actual ability of the philosopher to understand the world rationally. At this point, it is fair to say that history itself must either confirm or deny this initial presupposition. Contrary to a popular caricature of him, Hegel is not indifferent to the need for empirical verification of his philosophical theories.

It is also true, however, that "reason" is not an empty or formal term for Hegel. History cannot presuppose the rationality of the world without accepting from philosophy a definite notion of reason itself. The proof that this concept of reason is the true concept of reason is a philosophical matter, beyond the point of view of history as such. History, however, must accept this definite concept of reason and see how it develops an understanding of world history. History as such cannot plunge into the data of history without some such concept to guide it, even while it is testing that very concept in return.

The remainder of this paragraph is a summary of Hegel's concept of reason. It is here that a first indication is given of the theological foundation of historical knowledge, for the language in which Hegel describes reason is highly theological. Recognizing this, he delays discussion of the relation between reason and God until a later point. His purpose at the outset is simply to define reason itself. It is, he says, substance, infinite power, infinite material of all natural and spiritual life, and the infinite form of that material. As substance, it is that in which all reality exists. As power, it is creative force. As content, it is the essence or truth of everything.

These terms are all rich in allusions to Hegel's other works and philosophy in general.[6] They are also rich in allusions to theological understandings of God. The very use of the word "infinite" directs attention toward the divinity of reason. To describe reason as the substance "through which and in which all reality has its being" echoes Paul's appeal to the Athenians that God is that in which "we live and move and have our being" (Acts 17:28). Reason as "infinite power" alludes to God the Creator. This allusion is re-enforced by describing it further as the "infinite form which activates" the matter of creation, an image reminiscent of the Spirit of God "moving over the face of the waters" (Gen. 1:1-2). Finally, as "infinite content" of its own creative activity, reason does not need anything outside of itself. This aseity -- the ability to be totally self-supporting -- is what makes reason the "essence and truth of everything." In Christian theology, aseity is ascribed to God alone. To impute it to reason is, along with the other allusions, a clear indication that, in Hegel's view, there must be a theological basis for any adequate understanding of reason, and thus also for "rational" history.

A second indication of the connection between the philosophy of history and theology is Hegel's view of their parallel development.[7] In their early form, both reason and providence offered only an abstract understanding of the world. Both were expressions of the rejection of an Epicurean belief in chance and contingency, but both failed to develop their faith that the world is a *cosmos* (rational order) or that it is subject to God's will into concrete knowledge of the nature of that order or will.

Anaxagoras asserted the rationality of the world only to explain it by means of abstract definitions such as causality inhering in air, ether, water, etc. Religion taught that God is Lord over history only to undercut that teaching with the insistence that for humans to try to understand God's will is futile and presumptuous. In both cases, the inherent rationality of the world was perceived, but there was a failure to apply and develop that perception in order to understand the world.

In the same way that Socrates tried to relate the universal truth of reason taught by Anaxagoras to concrete reality, so Hegel would like to develop the concrete knowledge which the doctrine of God's providence implies. This is the third and most forceful demonstration of his theological approach to the interpretation of history. Hegel argues that the plan of divine providence can be comprehended, despite the "hardened prejudice" of theology in his time that it is impossible to have objective knowledge of God. Against such modern "subjectivism," Hegel cites the biblical teaching that Christians must know God as well as love Him, for, as Hegel paraphrases Paul, "the spirit leads into truth, searches all things, and penetrates even into the deep things of God" (1 Cor. 2:10).[8]

This mention of Scripture does not mean that Hegel is claiming its authority for his philosophy of history. He maintains that "the peculiar nature of the science of philosophy forbids us to attach authority to prior assumptions."[9] The use of Scripture is nothing more than a way of rebutting those who would denounce all efforts to understand the plan of providence on the basis of other passages in Scripture, such as the statement that God's ways and thoughts are higher than those of men (Is. 55:9). Hegel remarks with sadness and irony that "we have recently reached the point where philosophy has had to defend the content of religion against certain kinds of theology."[10] His way of doing this, however, is by an appeal not to the positive authority of the Bible but to the idea of revelation as a self-revelation of God's nature to human knowledge:

> God has revealed himself through the Christian
> religion; that is, he has granted mankind the
> possibility of recognizing his nature, so that
> he is no longer an impenetrable mystery. The
> fact that knowledge of God is possible also makes
> it our duty to know him, and that development of

the thinking spirit which the Christian revelation of God initiated must eventually produce a
situation where all that was at first present
only to the feeling and representing spirit can
also be comprehended by thought. Whether the
time has yet come for such knowledge will depend
on whether the ultimate end of the world has yet
been realised in a universally valid and conscious
manner.[11]

With the advent of Christianity, agnosticism about the
nature and will of God became obsolete. God Himself "granted"
knowledge of Himself in Christianity, a full revelation to complete and replace the mysteries of previous, partial revelations.
This is a step which God has taken toward mankind, not one which
mankind has achieved, as it were, on its own. Yet God's act of
self-revelation imposes on man a duty: to respond to this new
possibility affirmatively, that is, to seek to know God.

The implications of this self-revelation of God for philosophy and faith are nothing less than revolutionary. It means that
the goal of philosophy should be knowledge of God Himself. There
can no longer be a retreat from the Ultimate or Infinite as if
from an impenetrable mystery. Conversely, faith can no longer
content itself with a relationship with God which is limited to
subjective feeling and imagination. It is important to love
God, and faith will always be enriched by imaginative concentration upon images of and stories about God. But the challenge
which Christianity brings to faith is to *know* God in thought,
to engage in the hard work of reflection about Him, to accept
God's offer to understand His nature and will as both an offer
and a command.

In relation to the understanding of history, Hegel elabo-
rates on this theological basis in his unwritten remarks. He
says that Christians, as those who fully know God, are supplied
with "the key to world history. For here we have a definite
knowledge of providence and its plan."[12] The knowledge of Himself which God made available in Christianity is not simply an
abstract conception of His divine attributes. It is nothing
less than His will for the course of world history. The meaning
of history can be grasped only by Christians. Without the "key"
which they hold, history would remain a mystery, thwarting all
efforts to understand it. With that "key," the entire plan of
providence is unveiled and made accessible to knowledge.

Finally, Hegel suggests a fourth and final basis for under-standing the philosophy of history as a theological task. As the effort to understand the providential plan of God for world history, it is

> a theodicy, a justification of the ways of God.... It should enable us to comprehend all the ills of the world, including the existence of evil, so that the thinking spirit may be reconciled with the nega-tive aspects of existence; and it is in world history that we encounter the sum total of concrete evil.[13]

If history presents us with the spectre of evil, and God is known to be the author of history, then the task of philosophy of his-tory will be reconciling the evil of history with the goodness of God, that is, with His ultimate purposes for history. By understanding the place of evil events in the plan of providence, Hegel hopes to reconcile thought to those negative aspects of existence against which it rebels. In short, the task of the philosophy of history is to understand evil as no less God's will than the good. Nothing happens in history which does not reveal something about the nature of God. Hegel even remarks that "History is the unfolding of God's nature in a particular, determinate element."[14] When the nature of God is thus identi-fied with the entire course of history, so that all historical events are said to be not only permitted but also willed by Him, then the problem of "theodicy" becomes acute. Either God's transcendence over the evil aspects of history must be asserted, or the evil elements in the "historical" immanence of His nature must be justified as necessary means toward a greater end. Tra-ditional theologies normally take the former route, and puzzle over the relationship between God and the sinful world. Hegel takes the latter, identifying God's nature with all of world history, and puzzles over the ultimate purposes of evil. That is why his philosophy of history can accurately be described as a theodicy. It is the means by which Christians, in Hegel's view, can fully understand God's nature and presence in the world.

By his use of "theological" language to define reason, by historical parallels between reason and providence, by explicitly basing the possibility of understanding history upon the knowl-edge of God in His self-revelation in Christianity, and by his

identification of God's nature with the unfolding of all history,
Hegel demonstrates that the foundation for his philosophy of
history is thoroughly theological. In his development of the
general concept of historical meaning, however, he translates
the theological terms of that foundation into the secular languages of philosophy and political relations. This translation
must be understood in order to grasp the "reason" which Hegel
takes to be the meaning of all history.

The Secular Language of Historical Meaning

Hegel's analysis of "reason in history" involves a number
of general philosophical assertions. One is that history is a
"spiritual" process. Another is that the purpose of history is
freedom. A third declares that the subjects or agents of history are the "spirits" of nations and cultures as they progress
toward greater freedom.

> We must first of all note that the object we
> have before us, i.e. world history, belongs to the
> *realm of the spirit* [literally: marches forward on
> spiritual ground]. The world as a whole comprehends
> both physical and spiritual nature. Physical nature
> also plays a part in world history, and we shall cer-
> tainly include some initial remarks on the basic out-
> lines of this natural influence. But the spirit and
> the course of its development are the true substance
> of history. We do not have to consider nature here
> as a rational system in its own right...but only in
> relation to spirit.[15]

In Hegel's view, the opposition between spirit and nature
is fundamental for an understanding of history. The difference
between them can be stated simply: whereas the spirit progresses,
nature merely repeats itself. Transience, which constantly
destroys all that nature produces, becomes for the products of
the spirit the occasion for their own "transfiguration" into a
higher, freer form. This process is particularly evident for
Hegel in the succession of national spirits or cultures. As
each new culture is born out of the ruins of the old, it embodies
within it the truth of the old, and gives that truth a new place
as a part or "moment" within itself. In contrast, a tree produces fruit and seed which must take root and begin again from
the beginning. In nature, there is no carry-over, no progress
at all, whereas history is the story of the progress of the
spirit.[16]

The word "transfiguration" (*Verklärung*) recalls the theological language with which Hegel establishes the condition for the possibility of historical knowledge. The most crucial term in the passage discussed in the previous paragraph, however, is the German word, *aufheben*. The basic meaning of *aufheben*, which is a very common word in spoken German, is "to pick up." Each stage of the spirit, we could say, "picks up" the forms that have gone before it. A second meaning of *aufheben* is "to keep, to preserve." The previous stages are, says Hegel, preserved in the one which picks them up. Yet a third common meaning of *aufheben* is "to cancel, to abolish." Thus the term also implies that the old stages have been left behind, transcended, and replaced by the new.

Aufheben, as one word which expresses both preservation and abolition, describes the process and progress of the spirit. In the realm of nature, there is both preservation and perishing, but never of the same thing simultaneously. In the realm of the spirit, however, Hegel believes that such can be the case, and employs the word *aufheben* to signify both aspects at once. Clearly such a coincidence of two, apparently contradictory, meanings in one word is rich in possibilities for a speculative imagination. The problem is, how are we to translate such a term into English? Nisbet prefers "preserve," but never fails to give the German in a footnote for the wary reader. Other translators have adopted technical terms, such as "sublate" or "subsume," which completely lose the colloquial flavor of *aufheben*; or "transcend," which, like "preserve," captures one side of the meaning at the expense of the other.

This is not the place for a thorough discussion of the possible renderings of "aufheben." I have mentioned its many meanings because the systematic ambiguity of the word is crucial to Hegel's distinction between spirit and nature. Perhaps the closest English equivalent to Hegel's use of *aufheben* is "transform," a word which has the virtue of capturing all aspects of *aufheben* partially but does total justice to none of them. "Transformation" implies that something has both perished and been preserved. "*Aufhebung*," at least in Hegel's usage, says it explicitly. To say that history has meaning is to imply that historical changes, unlike changes in the cycle of nature, are transformations of something old into something new.

The process of the spirit is one of progressive self-transformation in history. In that same comparison with the natural process, Hegel remarks that this process of *Aufheben* is "an activity of thought."[17] This brings us to a second, fundamental ambiguity in his concept of spirit. In the context of so many theological allusions, it would be possible to interpret "spirit" as signifying an aspect or activity of God rather than man, much like the "Holy Spirit." In fact, however, Hegel uses *Geist* or "Spirit" for something which is both human and divine. It is, like thought, an activity of humans. It is also, like divine life, something which transcends its own apparent death. In short, *Geist* is that which has the capacity to *aufheben*, i.e. to transform itself, to perish and to preserve itself simultaneously. This capacity is, as it were, the divine depth of human existence. Thus *Geist* may be translated by "the Spirit," implying an aspect of the Godhead, and by "mind," implying the human activity of thought. Often "spirit" is the best compromise, for it has some of the same ambiguity found in *Geist*. It is common in English to speak of the human spirit no less than the Holy Spirit, although admittedly without the intellectualistic connotations of *Geist*.

This use of "spirit" to mean that which is, as it were, the "transformation" of the human and divine into a unity which preserves them both, is defended by Hegel in his unwritten remarks on history as belonging to "the realm of the spirit." He says:

> The province of the spirit is created by man himself; and whatever ideas we may form of the kingdom of God, it must always remain a spiritual kingdom which is realised in man and which man is expected to translate into actuality.[18]

Here, again, Hegel is pointing out an important difference which he sees between the realms of nature and spirit. Nature confronts man as something given, a world of objects which he has the power to manipulate but which he cannot simply create and destroy. He must observe nature, and conform to its laws, if he would succeed at all in his efforts to manipulate it. In contrast, spirit is not alien to him. It is his own life as created by himself. It is crucial to Hegel that we not let the "divinity" of the kingdom of God seduce us into thinking that it, or God, has some sort of alien transcendence. The kingdom

of God, which is His power, exists only insofar as it is realized
in man and by man. Only man can actualize God's power in the
world.

Spirit, then, is a self-transforming and divine-human
reality. Before further exploring this reality in its relation
to history, it may be helpful to clarify its relation to some
of the other terms Hegel has used, such as God, thought, and
nature. This is facilitated by Hegel's clear reference to the
triadic or "trinitarian" structure of his thought, a reference
which recalls his theological basis even as it illustrates his
view of the need to secularize religious language:

> Our business here is to consider world history
> in relation to its ultimate end; this ultimate end
> is the intention which underlies the world. We know
> that God is the most perfect being; he is therefore
> able to will only himself and that which is of the
> same nature as himself. God and the nature of the
> divine will are one and the same thing; it is what
> we call in philosophy the *Idea*. Thus it is the Idea
> in general which we have to consider, and particu-
> larly its operation within the medium of the human
> spirit; in more specific terms, it is the Idea of
> human freedom. The Idea reveals itself in its purest
> form in thought, and it is from this angle that logic
> approaches it. It expresses itself in another form
> in physical nature, and the third form which it assumes
> is that of spirit as such.[19]

A fundamental conviction which underlies all of Hegel's
thought on philosophy and religion is that they are two distinct languages for dealing with the same reality. Up to this
point, such parallels as reason and providence or the philosophy
of history and theodicy have been noted, but the basis on which
Hegel asserts their truth has not been made fully explicit. His
contention that Christianity is the revelation of full knowledge
of God is a religious expression of that basis. In the paragraph
just quoted, a precise philosophical justification is offered:
the word "God" is the religious designation for that which philosophers call the "Idea." Insofar as philosophy has the task of
translating religious insights into more precise philosophical
language, the philosopher must affirm that God *is* the Idea, and
that therefore the Idea has the triadic structure of the Christian
God. This "trinity" makes it possible for God to be both perfect
being and living will, for it enables Him, as it were, to will
Himself. In this sense, the perfect being which philosophy seeks

and the perfect will which faith worships are once again seen to be united in the Idea/God. Religion and philosophy are different languages for expressing the same truth.

The Idea, like God, is said by Hegel to be a triadic revelation of itself. Its "purest form" of self-revelation, corresponding to God the Father, is in thought. The logic of thought, unencumbered by the trappings of actual existence, is comparable to the mind of God itself. It is the entire pattern of possible relations, such as logic explores on a purely conceptual plane. The second way in which the Idea expresses itself is in physical nature. Religiously speaking, natural creation is the embodiment of the "Word" or *logos* of God. The third form in which the Idea reveals itself is spirit. Theologically, the Holy Spirit is often thought of as the unity or community of the Father and the Son. Similarly, spirit for Hegel is that reality in which the abstract truth of pure thought and the concreteness of the objects of nature are mutually transformed into a higher truth that embraces them both.

To say that history "belongs to the realm of spirit" is to affirm that it is the expression of this third aspect of the Idea/God. That is why Hegel declares that history is rational: one of its "moments" is the stage of pure thought, knowable by logic. Yet he also insists that his approach to history is empirical, for he has full respect for the second moment also, that aspect of history which, like nature, involves concrete facts. Spirit, as the unity of thought with nature, embraces both theoretical and empirical truth.

It would be misleading, however, to attempt to imagine that unity as in any way a static or finished one. History is, once again, a process. And spirit is fully expressed only as historical, as "in process." That is why Hegel began this paragraph with the announcement that history must be understood in terms of its "ultimate end." The purpose of history is what determines its direction. And, for a process as dynamic as history, direction determines and reveals its nature and truth. To understand the meaning of world history is, according to Hegel, to understand the purpose of the world.

This definition of the spirit as historical can be made even more precise. Spirit is, as we have seen, both divine and human. Its "divinity" could be said to consist in its relation to the Idea, as the unity of thought and nature. If this unity were merely divine, however, if it existed in and for a transcendent God but not in the world, then the human aspect of spirit would be lost. This is not the case. Hegel explicitly identifies history as the self-revelation ("operation" is a word supplied by Nisbet) of the Idea "within the medium of the human spirit." More specifically, he goes on, "it is the Idea of human freedom." World history is the process by which the Idea is revealing itself as that which is guiding history toward the goal of human freedom. It is in the realm of history as the progress of the Idea of human freedom that "the spirit attains its most concrete reality."[20]

The idea of history, according to Hegel, is the Idea of human freedom. Following the triadic structure of the Idea, Hegel divides world history into three phases, in what may be the most famous claim of these lectures:

> ...world history is the record of the spirit's efforts to attain *knowledge* of what it is *in itself*. The *Orientals* do not know that the spirit or man as such are free in themselves. And because they do not know this, they are not themselves free. They only know that One is free.... This One is therefore merely a despot, not a free man and a human being. The consciousness of freedom first awoke among the *Greeks*, and they were accordingly free; but, like the Romans, they only knew that *Some*, and not all men as such are free...; thus the Greeks not only had slaves,...but their very freedom itself was... undeveloped...and a harsh servitude of all that is humane and proper to man. The *Germanic* nations, with the rise of Christianity, were the first to realise that man is by nature free, and that freedom of the spirit is his very essence.[21]

Philosophy of history, searching for the pattern of meaning in the course of events, finds that the direction which they reveal runs from a very limited understanding of human freedom in the Orient to a highly developed notion of freedom in Northern Europe. Thus the empirical data confirm what philosophy had already suggested, that "freedom, by definition [*ihrem Begriffe nach*], is self-knowledge."[22] The essence of history is the progress of the self-knowledge of men.

This conforms to the theological basis of spirit as the unity of thought and nature. Whereas pure thought just thinks without any empirical object, and nature is a realm of objects

without thought, spirit is the "self-contemplation" in which the
Idea thinks about objects as identical with itself: "In other
words, the Spirit is the whole, and not just one or another of
the elements in isolation.... God is eternal love, whose nature
is to treat the other as its own."[23] The truth of history is
not to be found in a mere idea of history, nor in mere data; it
is to be found in the self-understanding of concrete, historical
human beings.

This does not mean, however, that freedom is subject to
arbitrary definition by individuals. Just as the course of freedom in history has been toward a more universal understanding of
it, to the point where freedom is now claimed to be "the very
essence" of man, so the consciousness of freedom must be possessed by a universal rather than a particular consciousness.
An oriental despot is "free" in such an external and arbitrary
sense that he is not really a free human being at all. The
Greeks and the Romans based their freedom upon the enslavement
of others, and found it (their own freedom) to be a "harsh servi-
tude." Only when freedom is affirmed as the universal nature of
man can any or all participate fully in it. Thus freedom is
never *from* the world, the totality of mankind; it is always in
and with the whole.

The realization of the collective nature of freedom, which
Hegel attributes to Christianity, corresponds to a collective
notion of personal fulfillment. Whereas personal freedom might
be assumed by many to be the capacity to identify oneself with
particular objects or causes, Hegel sees it the other way around:

> Consciousness of freedom consists in the fact that
> the individual comprehends himself as a person, i.e.
> that he sees himself in his distinct existence as
> inherently universal, as capable of abstraction from
> and renunciation of everything particular, and there-
> fore as inherently infinite.[24]

Thus the consciousness of freedom is a consciousness of being
able to renounce all particularity for the sake of one's identity
with the universal.

The universality of freedom as the essence of man, and the
necessary universality of any consciousness which would know itself as free, bring us to the problem of how the principle of
freedom can be applied in concrete history. Hegel makes it clear

that freedom came into the world as a universal principle only
with the advent of Christianity. In the Christian doctrine of
the Trinity of God the Idea is first revealed as *the* self-transforming, divine-human spiritual reality. Certain parallels between the Christian language for God and philosophical language
about the Idea can be traced. The two languages can be seen to
intersect in the notion of revelation as the self-knowledge of
God. But how can the principle of universal freedom, which
entered the world with Christianity, be said to provide a purpose for all world history? Hegel seems to be at a point where
he must either submit philosophical truth to the language and
criteria of its Christian origins or definitively free it from
them.

The choice Hegel makes is clear and unequivocal. The
dynamic of Christian faith is not only one of the revelation of
the truth of freedom; most important, there is a reciprocal and
necessary secularization of Christianity:

> This consciousness [of freedom] first dawned in
> religion, in the innermost region of the spirit;
> but to inco.porate the same principle into secular
> [*weltliche*] existence was a further problem, whose
> solution and application require long and arduous
> cultural exertions. For example, slavery did not
> immediately [come to an end] with the adoption of
> Christianity; still less did freedom at once pre-
> dominate in states, or governments and constitutions
> become rationally organised and founded upon the
> principle of freedom. This *application* of the prin-
> ciple to secular affairs, the penetration and thorough
> education [*Durchbildung*] of secular life by the prin-
> ciple of freedom, is the long process of which history
> itself [is made up].[25]

Freedom, in Hegel's understanding, entered the world with
Christianity, but, through its own spiritual dynamic, moved from
the sphere of religion into secular matters. The realm of full
expression of spirit is not that of religion; it is that of
states, governments and constitutions. "Reason in history"
means the increasingly rational organization of the secular
institutions of human relationships. The meaning of history
consists in the process of secularization whereby the freedom
attributed to God as Trinity is transformed into the freedom of
the Idea, which in turn is concretely realized as secular human
freedom. This is a long and difficult process, for it requires

nothing less than the appropriation of the freedom that has traditionally belonged to God alone by *all* who participate in history. Hegel's vision is of a world in which the religious
alienation of the self from the world, and of the world from
God, is transformed into a full consciousness of the unity of
God with His own self-unfolding in history. This is why the
language of historical meaning must be a secular language. The
full consciousness of freedom cannot be realized so long as freedom remains the exclusive property of Christianity. In order to
fulfill its own universality, freedom must be understood in a
secular language common to all mankind.

Three major aspects of Hegel's concept of freedom, then,
are self-knowledge, universality, and secularization. Freedom
exists only in the self-consciousness of the human spirit, only
insofar as it is understood as universal, and only be being
transformed from its religious, transcendent character into a
secular, immanent actuality. This transformation is the process
by which the purpose of history is being realized -- the Idea
of human freedom.

It is on the basis of this conviction concerning the necessity of secularization that Hegel casts his philosophy of history
in political language: "In world history," he writes, "the
individuals we are concerned with are nations, totalities,
states."[26] Neither individual persons nor God Himself are the
"material" of history. The historical "bodies," so to speak,
in which spirit works to realize its goal of human freedom are
states. Just as the individual's consciousness of freedom is
to be found in his capacity to renounce everything particular,
so his positive historical identity depends upon his commitment
to the state:

> This essential being, the unity of the subjective
> will and the universal, is the ethical whole, and
> its concrete manifestation is the *state*. The state
> is the reality within which the individual has and
> enjoys his freedom, but only insofar as he knows,
> believes in, and wills the universal.[27]

As "the unity of the subjective will and the universal,"
the state appears to be the presence or "body" of God in the
world. It alone is the "ethical whole" in which all alienation
has been overcome and transformed into a higher unity. Such

language has a theological ring which sets it apart from normal
usage of the word "state." Hegel remarks that the meaning of
"state" includes religion, science and art, for they are also
expressions of the historical age and area under consideration.
The state is a "whole" not only in an ethical but also in an
organic sense. It is the "spiritual individual, the nation --
in so far as it is internally differentiated to form an organic
whole."[28] Indeed, the truth of universality for Hegel is conditional upon its unity with all the particular wills and aspects
included within it. The universal must be internally differentiated in order to be a living and spiritual unity at all. An
obvious political implication of this idea is that freedom means
nothing except as the freedom of all the subjects in the state.
On a broader level, however, it also means that the political
health of a nation depends upon its religious, scientific and
artistic vitality.

Hegel discusses the immediate political implication first,
arguing against radical Romantic notions of a primitive state
of natural, universal freedom. Such views set the inherent
freedom of man against any and all restrictions imposed by
society upon the impulses and desires of individuals. To Hegel,
a state of nature without such restrictions is not freedom but
"rather a state of injustice, of violence, of uncontrolled
natural impulses, and of inhuman deeds and emotions." There is
no such immediate freedom, for "It still has to be earned and
won through the endless mediation of discipline acting upon the
powers of cognition and will."[29] When freedom is the historical purpose and accomplishment of the spirit through self-
knowledge, i.e. thought, there can be no identification of
freedom with arbitrary or emotional anarchy.

The appeal to thought also constitutes Hegel's argument
against reactionary traditionalists. Their appeal to patriarchy
and even theocracy also has emotional ties rather than self-
knowledge as its basis. The "patriarchal condition is based
upon the family relationship," in which all individual self-
consciousness is absorbed into a "unity [which] is essentially
one of feeling, and...remains on a purely natural plane."[30] The
achievement of freedom is possible only in the realm of thought,
not by mere emotion.

These two arguments are practical illustrations of what the "internal self-differentiation" of the state is *not*. It is not a state of nature in which every particular will is free from all restrictions. It is not a state in which the members are completely subordinated to the head of state. To be rational, free, and internally self-differentiated, a state must be the product of thought, which has as its goal the universalization and secularization of the consciousness of freedom.

In order to accomplish this goal, a state must be more than the set of political relations which we call "government." The state cannot fulfill itself except as a self-conscious spiritual individual. This is the second implication of the concept of true universality as internal self-differentiation:

> The national spirit is a determinate spirit....the foundation and content of the other forms of spiritual awareness.... The spirit is a *single* individual; in *religion*, its essential being is represented, revered, and assimilated as the divine being or God; in *art*, it is depicted as an image and intuition; and in *philosophy*, it is recognised and comprehended by thought. The forms which it assumes, because of the original identity of their substance, their content, and their object, are indivisibly united with the spirit of the state, so that *this* particular form of state can only exist in conjunction with a particular religion, and only this or that particular philosophy and art can exist within it.[31]

The national spirit is the true subject of history. It is the historical "identity" which is the expression of reason in any given age. Consistent with his program of secularization, Hegel understands the spirit of a nation as expressing itself in several languages. Religious language portrays it as God, as a divine being to be worshipped. Aesthetic language depicts it in sensible images. Whereas the truth of God is known to the worshipper in feeling, it is available in art to intuition. Only in philosophy is the national spirit *known* as such by the members of the nation. That spirit is identical with the God of religion and the images of art, but it is expressed in a form which can be fully recognized and comprehended. In the unity and identity of the national spirit resides the truth of any age. It alone determines the appropriate religion, art, and philosophy for that time.

Nevertheless, the state cannot remain an abstract set of religious, aesthetic, and philosophical relations. It is not merely a cult, artistic guild, or intellectual society. According to Hegel, the means by which the state insures that all that happens within it will be in accord with its nature as a national spirit is the constitution:

> The state itself is an abstraction which has its purely universal reality in the citizens who belong to it.... The need arises for some kind of government and political administration.... The state as an abstraction only acquires life and reality through the constitution....the constitution should be so organised that the minimum of obedience is required of the citizens and the minimum of arbitrariness is permitted to those who issue the commands.[32]

Without a constitution, the state remains an abstraction. By "constitution," Hegel means not a written document so much as the order or organization of the individuals who participate in the state. The state becomes real only in and through its citizens. Citizens live and work together by means of administrative organization which we call "government." The structure of a government, the principles by which it organizes itself from among the citizenry, is the constitution. The best constitution is the one which minimizes the alienation of those who rule and those who are ruled from one another.

In a short discussion of the various types of constitutions available to states, Hegel tries to discern which will most effectively permit the citizenry to govern themselves without jeopardizing the "vigour and strength" of the state as an "individual unity."[33] The constitution he defends is that of monarchy. Although aware of the danger of despotism, he sees total democracy as a threat to the unity of the state, when it is practiced, and as slipping inevitably toward aristocracy, when it is not. The aristocratic principle establishes the very structure of alienation of the governed from their governors that Hegel wants to avoid. Constitutional monarchy, however, can unite the order found in aristocracy with the freedom of democracy. Hegel implies that aristocracy is merely an unsatisfactory compromise between or false unity of despotism and anarchy, whereas a "monarchic constitution" preserves the truth of both the aristocratic and the democratic principles as "two moments within it."

Just as universality must be understood as "internal self-differentiation" within a totality, so monarchy, constituted as one "head" for many "members," embraces within itself a dialectic of unity-in-diversity.

Historical Meaning and the Life of Faith

The truth of Christianity is a condition for the philosophy of history. To understand the meaning of historical events is to understand God's self-manifestation in the world, and this is possible only if God has in fact revealed Himself as present and fully knowable in the historical world. The Christian belief that this has in fact happened is thus the foundation for all efforts to understand the meaning of history.

The meaning which Hegel finds in history, however, is secular and political rather than religious. The language in which he expresses it is drawn not from the Bible or Christian creeds or even from more recent theological reflection. All theological concepts are translated by him into secular equivalents. Thus God is discussed as the Idea and divine providence is understood as reason. The "bodies" of significance for the course of history are states, not churches. The goal toward which the history of states is progressing is human freedom in this world rather than human salvation in an eschatological world to come.

The juxtaposition of this theological foundation and its radically secular development leads to the question of how the individual Christian can understand himself, in Hegel's view, as an agent in history. Christian faith is a condition for the philosophy of history, but what is the relation between that faith and historical action itself? Does Christianity provide guidelines for understanding and acting in one's own immediate historical situation, or only for understanding history philosophically -- after the fact, as it were? Hegel's secular theology of history provides rich materials for the philosopher of history. But what does it offer to the individual who is faced with the task of fulfilling his potential as a "person," which Hegel has defined as understanding oneself as "inherently infinite" and as willing nothing but the universal?[34]

The ideal of self-identification with the universal appears
to call individuals to raise their consciousness above their own,
personal situations:

> ...when, for example, an individual in great per-
> plexity and distress receives unexpected help, we
> must not hold it against him if his gratitude at
> once leads him to see the hand of God at work. But
> the design of providence in such cases is of a
> limited nature; its content is merely the particular
> end of the individual in question. In world history,
> however, the individuals we are concerned with are
> nations, totalities, states. We cannot, therefore,
> be content with this faith in providence which, so
> to speak, trades in trivialities, any more than with
> a merely abstract and indeterminate faith which con-
> ceives in general terms of a ruling providence but
> refuses to apply it to determinate reality; on the
> contrary, we must tackle the problem seriously.[35]

The contrast which Hegel draws in this passage is between a
"limited" and a "serious" understanding of the work of providence. An individual who understands Christian faith in such
a way that he sees "the hand of God at work" in the situations
in which he finds himself in the world is not to be condemned.
Although Hegel's attitude is clearly disdainful, and he implies
that such personal interpretations of God's providence are simply the result of "great perplexity and distress," his purpose
is only to show how limited such an approach is, not to ridicule
it altogether. The problem with a personal understanding of
providence is that it limits the content of God's work in the
world to "the particular end of the individual in question."
That is, instead of striving to will the universal, the individual believes that God -- the universal -- is willing the
particular. In this sense Christian piety seems to Hegel to be
the reverse of self-fulfillment as consciousness of oneself as
"inherently infinite."

To "tackle the problem seriously," a person must identify
with the universal rather than the particular. A note of cau-
tion is sounded by Hegel, however. To rise above particularistic
"trading in trivialities" should not mean going to the opposite
extreme. Often those who disdain a personalistic understanding
of God's presence in the world adopt a "merely abstract and
indeterminate faith." Such a faith asserts its belief in providence, but denies that the actual will of providence in the world

can be known. This refusal to see providence at work in the
actual world of "determinate reality" is that very agnosticism
which Hegel believes to have been abolished by Christianity. No
matter how difficult it may be to discern the work of divine
providence in world history without slipping into personalistic
particularism, such is the task to which all Christians who
would really know God are called.

The "serious" approach to the understanding of world history is thus neither particular nor abstract, but political.
The "individuals" of history -- meaning the bodies which are
internally self-differentiated unities -- are nations and states.
The Christian who wishes to fulfill the challenge of faith within
his own historical life is called to transcend his own particular
concerns and develop a political vision and understanding of
God's work in the world. The language in which he does that
will be the language of political relationships. Christianity
provides the possibility for understanding history, but not the
tools with which to carry out that task. The Christian as a
person engaged with history is called to go beyond faith on the
basis of faith. Faith alone will not suffice to show him the
concrete plan of providence.

Hegel's suspicion of particularism in the understanding of
providence is evident throughout his discussion of reason in
history. In his remarks on the course of development which
nations pursue, he notes that those which are undergoing "an
internal degeneration" will always manifest "a tendency towards
particularism."[36] When the citizenry begin to take more interest
in their personal lives than in the welfare of the state, then
the progress of reason toward greater universal consciousness
is already in jeopardy. In such a situation, reason as self-
understanding has already been abandoned. In Hegel's view, the
personal level of life, with all its particular concerns, simply
cannot be understood. It is "at the mercy of chance," in contrast with the rational, political order, which "is as it ought
to be."[37] That is why a particularistic or personal approach
to divine providence is doomed to "trading in trivialities."

Hegel's criticism of particularism in the understanding of
providence is not based upon the assumption that personal concerns are inevitably eudaemonistic. Although he makes it clear

in his remarks that happiness "is possible only in private life,"[38] he does not claim that private life is always committed to happiness. When religious piety does become so involved with its own particular nature that it strives only after happiness, however, it removes itself from the arena of history; for "history is not the soil in which happiness grows. The periods of happiness in it are blank pages of history."[39]

Another form of particularism that is equally opposed to the progress of reason in history is morality:

> For world history moves on a higher plane than that
> to which morality proper belongs, for the sphere of
> morality is that of private convictions, the con-
> science of individuals.... Those who, on ethical
> grounds (and hence with a noble intention), have
> resisted what the progress of the Idea of the spirit
> required, stand higher in moral worth than those
> whose crimes have been transformed by a higher order
> into instruments of realising its will. But in re-
> volutions of this kind, both parties alike stand
> within the same circle of corruptible existence, so
> that it is merely a formal kind of justice, abandoned
> by the living spirit and by God....[40]

For the Christian who is searching in Hegel's philosophy of history for practical help in how to engage with history, this is one of the most startling claims he will encounter. Morality, says Hegel, concerns matters of "private conviction" and "the conscience of individuals." As such, it stands on a lower plane than the march of history. The contrast between the man who stands on his moral convictions and the man who apparently has none is very great, when the two men are judged in terms of their nobility of character. But their respective significance for history, observes Hegel, is often the reverse of their moral worth. The man whose career may have involved many "crimes" can be a greater leader, if "a higher order" transforms his crimes into "instruments of realising its will." Thus, to supply an example, the violence and crimes of Henry VIII against the church are of greater historical significance, in Hegel's view, than the martyrdom of Thomas More, which has never had any discernible political effect.

The startling aspect of this argument, however, is not that Hegel takes such a position in his philosophy of history. The difficulty for the individual Christian is that he also identifies the will of God with the "criminal" rather than the martyr. Thus the greater nobility of a Thomas More over a Henry VIII is "merely a formal kind of justice." The Christian who chooses to live and die for what he discerns to be the will of God is in fact "abandoned by the living spirit and by God," whereas the criminal who stops at nothing to realize his own objectives is in fact immortalized by philosophy as the instrument of God.

Hegel does not deny that men are morally responsible for their historical actions. He even calls the human capacity for moral choice "the hallmark of the sublime and absolute destiny of man." Men cannot, he goes on, go through life with a moral innocence such as that of animals. Their fate is to be "discontent" with the state of the world, to "contrast existence as it is with their own view of how things by rights *ought* to be."[41]

Yet this sublime discontent puts men at odds with the purpose and meaning of history. Moral man pursues the ideal of what "ought to be," while reason in history is concerned only with "the actual world [which] is as it ought to be."[42] Particularism, whether pious or moral, is incompatible with the universal meaning of history. Christianity, and the God it reveals as Trinity, is the foundation for the doctrine that God is *known* not in faith or in moral behavior but in the actual world as it is.

Hegel is fully aware that his position is at odds with traditional Christian faith. In an introductory sketch of different approaches to historiography, he explicitly rejects any effort to understand history in terms of "moral lessons" which it either teaches or illustrates. Examples of virtuous behavior, he concedes, can be drawn from history for the moral instruction of children. But an "adult" understanding, if Hegel's implication may be made explicit, will be concerned not with morality but with "the destinies of nations, the convulsions of states." In a parenthetical note he adds that biblical history is useful on the level of morality, but not on the level of understanding the meaning of history:

> Moral methods are very unsophisticated [*einfach*];
> Biblical history is adequate for this [moral] kind
> of instruction. But the moral abstractions of
> historians are completely useless [for understanding
> history].[43]

Thus the Christian who wants to fulfill God's will in history is confronted by Hegel with a dilemma. If he tries to live according to the moral teachings of the Bible, as understood by traditional faith, he sets himself against the plan God has for history. If, on the other hand, he attempts to discern that plan in the manner of Hegel's Christian secular theology of historical progress, his efforts to work toward its fulfillment may in fact be "criminal." The mature Christian, aware that God's being is revealed in the entire historical process, will strive to *identify with* God rather than *relate to* Him as a divine person who stands over against him and history. He will take up the cause of reason, accepting stoically the fact that he thereby is sacrificing his own right to the pursuit of happiness and moral self-vindication. To use a Christian image which seems close to Hegel's thought on this matter, he will bear the "cross" of reason in history, without complaining because reason "cannot stop to consider the injuries sustained by single individuals, for particular ends are submerged in the universal end."[44]

But even if he can bear this "cross" without regard for the personal and moral dimensions of biblical faith, the Christian who would try to do God's will in history on the basis of Hegel's insights faces a problem which is in some ways even more perplexing -- Hegel himself denies that it is possible:

> An initial survey of *history*, however, would indicate that the actions of men are governed by their needs, passions, and interests, by the attitudes and aims to which these give rise, and by their own character and abilities; we gain the impression that, in this scene of activity, these needs, passions, interests, etc., are the sole *motive forces*. Individuals do at times pursue more general ends such as *goodness*, but the good they pursue is invariably of a limited character.... But in many cases, passions, private interests, and the satisfaction of selfish impulses are the most potent force. What makes them powerful is [that] they do not heed any of the restraints which justice and morality seek to impose upon them, and the elemental power of passion has a more immediate hold over man than that artificial and laboriously acquired discipline of order and moderation, justice and morality.[45]

The basis for this conclusion about the relation between individuals and history is not a theory or doctrine, but Hegel's own "survey" of history. In other words, although he might admire the ideal of particular self-transcendence in service of the universal, he observes that most significant historical figures have in fact been motivated not by ideals at all but by their own lust for power, wealth, and the like. Once again, those who have tried to attain goodness have lived much more "limited" lives, for the good they pursued was never the actual goal of reason at that time. Thus those who are effective in history are those whose sole intent is to satisfy their own passions; and those who strive to transcend those passions thereby lose their historical effectiveness. It is not that Hegel is giving undue importance to a few exceptions to the rule. In his view, the *rule* is that the source of power for those in power is precisely their refusal to submit to the "restraints which justice and morality seek to impose upon them." By their rejection of rationality in their own lives, they rise above its "artificial...discipline of order and moderation."

Hegel's understanding of "passion" is one of the most subtle and complex aspects of his philosophy of history. It is particularly interesting to compare his view of passion with his comments on piety. Like piety, the passions are "governed by particular interests" such as personal will and character. Unlike piety, passion also refers to "character and volition in so far as they do not have a purely private content but are the effective motive force behind actions whose significance is universal."[46] Thus it is not, after all, the particularism of piety which merits Hegel's criticism. The "limited" nature of the personal and moral concerns of faith is due not to their particularity -- which they share with the passions -- but to their lack of universal "significance."

How is it that the passions can have such universal significance? One of Hegel's better-known statements is that "*nothing great* has been accomplished in the world *without passion*."[47] In his terms, this means that there has never been any progress in the realization of the goal of universal reason without particularity somehow being involved in that progress. The nature of its involvement is presented by him under the rubric of instrumentality:

> All these expressions of individual and national
> life, in seeking and fulfilling their own ends,
> are at the same time the *means* and *instruments*
> of a *higher purpose* and wider enterprise of which
> they are themselves ignorant and which they never-
> theless unconsciously carry out.[48]

The passions are "expressions" of individual and national
goals rather than universal goals. They are committed to fulfilling their own ends. Nevertheless, they are used by reason
to achieve its "higher purpose." Throughout their tenure of
service, historical leaders remain ignorant and unconscious of
the way in which their actions are fulfilling the goals of
reason as well as their own particular purposes. Thus Caesar,
in making himself the sole ruler of Rome, also served reason by
unifying the entire Roman Empire.[49] In this way the individual's
entire existence is sacrificed and fulfilled on the "cross" of
reason in history:

> For it is not the universal Idea which enters into
> opposition, conflict, and danger; it keeps itself
> in the background, untouched and unharmed, and sends
> forth the particular interests of passion to fight
> and wear themselves out in its stead. It is what
> we may call the *cunning of reason* that it sets the
> passions to work in its service, so that the agents
> by which it gives itself existence must pay the
> penalty and suffer the loss.[50]

                    *   *   *

With the "cunning of reason," which exploits the passions
of political leaders without revealing to them its own higher
purposes, my analysis of Hegel's philosophy of history is complete. I have attempted to explain the theological foundation
and secular language which Hegel sees as vital to the understanding of history. Furthermore, I have argued that Hegel's
position is highly problematical from the point of view of the
practice of Christian life. Although it accounts for the individual within history, it fails to make a place for him as a
self-conscious and rational historical agent, i.e. as a person
whose sense of personal "meaning" is indivisible from his morality and his understanding of the purposes of God in history.
I will return to these and similar difficulties in Chapter VI.
In the meantime, however, since my purpose is not to study Hegel

alone but to compare him with Hamann, it is important to move
on to the analysis of Hamann's theology of history, which bears
striking similarities to, and significant differences from, that
of Hegel.

CHAPTER III

HAMANN'S BIBLICAL THEOLOGY OF HISTORY

In this chapter I analyze the concept of historical meaning
in Hamann's *Golgotha and Scheblimini*. It is a concept drawn
from Hamann's understanding of Christianity, and therefore bears
many points of resemblance to Hegel's philosophy of history.
Yet it is rooted and expressed in biblical language, and thus
differs profoundly from Hegel's translation of Christian ideas
into secular terms. As the chapter proceeds, I will avoid comparison between Hamann and Hegel, in order to minimize distrac-
tions from the presentation of Hamann's position. The task of
comparing and contrasting their views on history will be saved
for Chapter VI. In order, however, to illuminate the similarities and differences as much as possible, I shall structure this
analysis along the same lines as the analysis of Hegel's theology
of history in Chapter II. Thus I shall begin with an examination
of the foundations of historical interpretation, according to
Hamann; move on to the specific language he employs to carry out
that interpretation; and conclude with a discussion of the implications of this view of historical meaning for the Christian life.

To present Hamann's thought in any sort of systematic way
involves both labor and risk, as any student of his writings can
testify. His consciously anti-systematic style -- he protests
against every "hateful consistency" at the end of the *Golgotha*![1]
-- poses problems for the interpreter in almost every sentence.
That is why the attempt to synthesize statements by Hamann in
widely different sources about presumably the same subject is
fraught with even greater dangers than is the same endeavor with
Hegel or a more systematic writer. Hamann's writings reflect
his lack of concern for comprehensiveness and consistency in
virtually every respect.

To say that Hamann's thought is not systematic does not
mean, however, that it lacks meaning or integrity. One of the
purposes of this study is to show that careful study of a major
text by Hamann does yield a coherent and challenging theological
position. As such, this essay is a complement to Karlfried

Gründer's study of the concept of history in Hamann's early, unpublished notebook, entitled *Biblical Observations*, and to Lothar Schreiner's excellent commentary on the *Golgotha*.[2]

Even when limiting myself to one text, the task of presenting Hamann's thought in a manner which is both faithful to Hamann and easily intelligible to the reader is formidable. The method which would preserve Hamann's flavor most accurately is that of commentary upon the total text. This has already been done by Schreiner, and would not serve my ultimate purpose, which is to compare Hamann with Hegel. Conversely, the method which lends itself to systematic argument is quotation of and reference to remarks by Hamann not in their own context but in the context provided by this essay. That would be easily intelligible to the reader, but risks denying to him any taste of Hamann's own style and thought patterns.

Faced with this dilemma, I have elected to pursue a compromise course. Since the first five paragraphs of the second part of the *Golgotha* are a relatively clear and connected discussion of the nature of historical truth, I shall begin this chapter with them, and base my interpretation of the foundation of historical meaning in Hamann's theology upon them. The last paragraph of the first section, however, will be drawn from elsewhere in the *Golgotha*; and I shall thereafter not try to cite or analyze consecutive passages. For those readers who are interested in the context of these later passages, a complete translation of the *Golgotha* is appended.

Even this compromise, however, will not avoid a great deal of apparent digression and distraction. As much as possible, I will not delete obscure words or phrases from the passages I offer for analysis, on the grounds that such words and phrases are important for understanding the mood and manner with which Hamann presents his ideas. To eliminate every irrelevant quip or fanciful image would not significantly benefit my argument and it would certainly impoverish or distort the impression given of Hamann. As for the question of suggesting an interpretation for every word or image, my procedure will vary from case to case. In some instances I will explain what I think a given phrase means to Hamann; in others I will either omit an obscure phrase or leave it in the passage but not attempt to

elaborate upon it. For further question, I refer the reader to
Schreiner's excellent commentary, which does clear up many of
the most difficult obscurities.

Another complication in the interpretation of the *Golgotha*
is that it is itself a comment on and parody of Moses Mendelssohn's book, *Jerusalem or on Religious Power and Judaism*, which
had appeared a year earlier (in 1783). Thus virtually every
paragraph presupposes that Hamann's reader has also read the
Jerusalem. Hamann often quotes *verbatim* entire sentences from
Mendelssohn without the slightest indication that they are quotations. The number of passing allusions through single words
or phrases is astounding. Therefore, one very important aspect
of interpreting the *Golgotha* is thorough study of the *Jerusalem*,
and it will constantly be necessary for me to offer explanations
of Hamann's meaning in terms of the argument by Mendelssohn that
he is attacking and parodying.

A final introductory word is necessary on what I mean by
calling Hamann's thought "biblical." In itself, this is meant
to be a descriptive rather than a normative judgment, although
I do present a defense of Hamann later in the essay. Furthermore,
I use the designation "biblical" as an indication of Hamann's
theological intention and effort rather than my judgment on his
success. To compare his thought with the Bible itself would
require a separate study. My references to Scripture are limited,
as are those to Mendelssohn's *Jerusalem*, to whatever seems
necessary in order to understand Hamann's meaning. But I make
no effort to evaluate the way in which Hamann uses these materials. His theology is "biblical" in the sense that he wants
it to be based upon the Bible and, as I try to show, to point
toward the Bible. If a critic could convince him that anything
he says seriously contradicts the biblical witness, I believe
that Hamann would retract the offending statement. It is in
this sense that his thought is "biblical."

The Biblical Foundations of Historical Meaning

The first short paragraph in the second part of the *Golgotha*
serves as a good introduction to both Hamann's style and the
context of his remarks on historical meaning:

> Without wearing myself and you out, devoted
> reader, with the even more speculative application,
> I would, for the sake of our mutual safety in the
> upper floor, wish no such loose foundation and sandy
> ground under the new and harsh theory of Judaism.[3]

Following the structure of the *Jerusalem*, Hamann devotes
the first section of his essay to natural law theory and the
second to the question of Judaism in relation to religious
truth in general. His technique, however, involves citing aspects of Mendelssohn's argument that are unconnected in the
Jerusalem, in order to show that Mendelssohn is not as consistent as he pretends to be, and that his argument can often be
turned against itself. The device that Hamann uses for most of
these critical and ironical allusions is one that he calls "metaschematism."

The literal meaning of "metaschematism" is "transfiguration"
or "transference of a figure." As used by Hamann, it means any
use of a phrase, image or figure of speech in a context other
than the original context given to it by its author. By sup-
plying a new context to the phrase, Hamann creates a juxtaposition
of thoughts which is not only surprising but is also usually
somewhat detrimental to the author's intention in his own use
of the phrase. It is this critical aspect of metaschematism
that is normally emphasized by scholars and interpreters of
Hamann.[4]

There is, however, an affirmative aspect of metaschematism
which deserves equal attention. This ironical combination of
an affirmative use of his opponent's words with a critical slant
on that use of those words is illustrated in the paragraph before us. In answer to the suggestion that he convert to Christianity, Mendelssohn replies with an image that implies that
Judaism, in which he does believe, is the basis on which Christianity stands: if, he asks, his philosophy really does, as
charged, undermine the foundations of Judaism, why should he
seek "safety in your upper floor?"[5] That is, if his philosophical convictions make the ground floor of Judaism unsteady, then
the upper floor of Christianity is even less safe and secure.
As Hamann's ironic allusion to this statement indicates, he
agrees with Mendelssohn that Judaism is in some sense Christianity's "ground floor." Thus he metaschematically affirms

Mendelssohn's concern to ascertain the truth, as well as part of his meaning.

He also criticizes it, however. First, he indicates that Mendelssohn's effort to solve the question of the proper relation between church and state (the subject of the first sections of the *Jerusalem* and the *Golgotha*) is unsuccessful, and will serve only to "wear out" the reader with its alleged "speculative application" of natural law theory to the church-state problem.[6] In other words, the matter of the relationship between Judaism and Christianity is too urgent, in Hamann's view, to digress from it with lengthy speculations about church and state in general. Furthermore, the result of that approach has produced only a "loose foundation" under Judaism and Christianity. This is the second critical metaschematism in this paragraph. The phrase "new and harsh" is Mendelssohn's own designation of how he expects his theory of Judaism to appear to some of his readers.[7] He anticipates negative reactions to his claim that religious organizations should neither own property nor influence political matters. Hamann does not address that issue at this point. Rather, he simply uses Mendelssohn's language to indicate that he does not find the proposed theory of Judaism to be convincing to him as a Christian.

Finally, Hamann employs another of his favorite devices to show the direction of his criticism of Mendelssohn's theory. This is an allusion not to the *Jerusalem* but to the Bible. By identifying the "loose foundation" under Judaism with "sandy ground," Hamann shifts attention from Mendelssohn's image of a two-story house to Christ's image of a house built either upon rock or upon sand (Mt. 7:26). The clear implication is that Christianity depends upon Judaism, but that Judaism in turn depends upon its own foundation as given to it by God. That foundation can be either sand or rock. If sand, it will collapse. If rock, it will withstand all storms. The image of a rock has a double meaning for Hamann. It alludes to the Old Testament and to Christ. Thus Hamann writes later in the *Golgotha*: "Moses with all the prophets" constitute "the rock of Christian faith," but those who built upon this rock (the Jews) rejected the "corner-stone" (Christ) of their building.[8] A further implication is that the Jews, by denying Christ, failed to understand their own Scriptures, for Christ, no less than Moses and the Prophets, is called the "rock" from which God gave water to the Hebrews in the desert (1 Cor. 10:4). In short, Christianity is indeed the "upper floor" in the house of faith, and true Judaism is the lower floor in that same house. But the foundation for the entire house is Christ, who is present in mysterious ways in the Old Testament and is fully revealed in the New.

This has been a necessarily elaborate interpretation of a short paragraph in the *Golgotha*, but as such it is typical, and thus a good introduction to reading Hamann. His metaschematic allusions to the *Jerusalem*, as well as his constant use of biblical imagery, can be understood only by an examination of the way such words and images function in their original contexts. Furthermore, the pattern of this paragraph often re-appears: Hamann metaschematically affirms Mendelssohn's intention even as he criticizes his proposal, and then, by the use of a biblical word or image, casts the whole problematic into what he takes to be its true terms. In this sense, his use of Mendelssohn's language is not meant to ridicule but to "transfigure" or even "redeem" it, to free it from its own errors and guide it toward the truth.

Having established that the issue under consideration is the proper relation of Judaism to Christianity, Hamann indicates in the next paragraph the direction in which his analysis of that problem will move:

> Since I, too, know of no eternal truths except those which are unceasingly temporal, I have no need to soar up into the cabinet of the divine understanding, nor into the sanctuary of the divine will; neither do I need to tarry over the difference between immediate revelation through word and writing, which is comprehensible only here and now, and mediate revelation through thing (nature) and concept, which is said to be legible and comprehensible at all times and in all places, by virtue of its soul-writing.[9]

In order to understand fully this claim for the temporality of all truths, it is necessary to summarize Mendelssohn's theory of three types of truth.[10] "Eternal truths" are those absolutely necessary to the happiness of man. They consist of doctrines about God which can be understood by unaided human reason. Thus they in no way depend upon "immediate revelation," but are known through concepts and things which are, as it were, written on the human soul in a script which is "legible and comprehensible at all times and in all places." Secondly, "historical truths" concern the dealings between God and men, especially the Hebrew patriarchs. They show the purpose for which He has created His people, and thus serve to strengthen faith in God. Because they are transmitted from one generation to the next, they must be accepted on faith rather than through reason. Finally, Mendelssohn distinguishes from both eternal truths and historical truths the moral and ceremonial law which God has given to the Jews. Like historical truths, the law cannot be known by reason. Mendelssohn says that it is revealed by God "through word and writing" in a particular language. Thus it is for Jews only, and can be readily appropriated only by those who understand Hebrew. In contrast, eternal truths depend upon mediate rather than immediate revelation, and can be known universally by all rational beings, i.e. all who have access to concepts and things.

In his metaschematic summary of Mendelssohn's theory, Hamann makes several points. He does not believe in "eternal" truths, for all truths are temporal. Thus he does not need to "soar" up to God's point of view, a desire which he sees implicit in Mendelssohn's claim to know eternal truths and to justify such knowledge by his appeal, in the passage describing allegedly eternal truths, to several Old Testament texts. Furthermore, if there are no eternal truths, then the distinction between immediate and mediate revelation is seen to be irrelevant, if not spurious. When all truths are temporal, then all depend to some extent upon tradition or "immediate" revelation. This question will re-appear in subsequent paragraphs.

The metaschematic irony of this passage is to be found in Hamann's introductory "I, too." This wording implies that Mendelssohn agrees with his belief that all truths are "unceasingly temporal," but the summary of Mendelssohn's own theory has shown that such is clearly not the case. Mendelssohn's own "I, too" occurs in a paragraph in which he is stressing just the opposite, namely, that eternal truths are knowable by reason without regard to time or place.[11] In a completely different part of the *Jerusalem* he also declares that man's "eternity" is nothing more than an "infinitely prolonged temporality."[12] By conflating these two passages with his allusive "I, too," Hamann is able

to point out both their inconsistency with each other and the
fact that Mendelssohn, according to his own understanding of
"eternity," ought to agree with Hamann's claim that all truths
are temporal. If man's "eternity" is really temporal, then all
his knowledge is also temporal. Hamann may have been the first
modern thinker to assert in such an uncompromising fashion the
temporal -- and thus, by implication, the historical and empirical -- nature of all truths.

On the basis of the temporality of all knowledge, Hamann
quotes favorably a critical comment by Mendelssohn on Lessing's
theory that human history is progressive and pedagogical:

> "Always to struggle against all theories and
> hypotheses, and to speak of facts, to want to hear
> of nothing but facts, and to look for facts least
> of all precisely at that point where it is most im-
> portant." -- Yet I...hurry to the issue, and
> totally concur with Herr Mendelssohn that Judaism,
> precisely as he understands it, knows nothing of
> revealed religion, i.e. that to them nothing has
> really been made known and entrusted by God through
> word and writing, with the sole exception of the
> sensuous vehicle of the mystery, the shadow of the
> good things to come instead of the true form of
> these realities, whose real communication God had
> reserved to Himself through a higher Mediator,
> High Priest, Prophet and King than were Moses,
> Aaron, David and Solomon. -- Just as Moses, there-
> fore, did not himself know that his face had a
> shining brightness which struck fear into the
> people: so also was the entire legislation of this
> divine minister a mere veil and curtain of the old
> covenant-religion, which still to this day remains
> unlifted, swaddled and sealed.[13]

In his theoretical discussion of history and critique of
Lessing, Mendelssohn denies any progress at all except in individual lives.[14] The point of Hamann's quotation, however, is
to remind him of his own commitment to "facts" in the matter of
discerning the meaning of history. If Mendelssohn can criticize
Lessing for ignoring the "fact" that every advance in human
history is soon followed by a comparable regress, then Hamann
can, with equal justification, demand that Mendelssohn, as a
Jew, judge the difference between Judaism and Christianity on
the basis of the facts. The relationship between these two
religions is a matter of historical events rather than speculative theories.

This realization of the priority of facts brings Hamann to
"the issue," namely, the nature of revelation, which Mendelssohn
explicitly identifies with words and writings given by God in a
particular language to a particular people. He calls such revelation "immediate," in contrast with "mediated" knowledge of
God's nature through reflection upon concepts and observation of
nature. If, however, Christianity and Judaism differ by virtue
of certain historical facts, then revelation is not simply a
matter of "word and writing" -- it is an event. Hamann agrees
with Mendelssohn that Judaism is not a religion of revelation --
not because it is superior as a religion of moral and ceremonial
law, but because it has not participated in the event which fully
reveals God's nature.

The relation of Judaism to Christianity is expressed by
Hamann metaschematically. It is, first of all, "the material
vehicle of the mystery." Judaism is the earth-bound matter in
which the mystery of Christian truth is revealed. The use of
the phrase "sensuous vehicle" alludes to Mendelssohn's comments
on Hinduism, which he criticizes for over-emphasis upon sensuous
images, for these lose their status as symbols and become "empty
vehicles" of idolatry.[15] Hamann's irony implies that Judaism,
no less than Hinduism, must be understood as a form of idolatry,
a clinging to the material form of God in lieu of the spiritual
truth.

Secondly, Judaism's historical relation to Christianity is
that of a "shadow of the good things to come" (Heb. 10:1). It
is not the "true form" or "real communication" of the reality
of those good things. Neither is it simply a non-historical
legislation. It is a partial revelation, a glimpse of the mystery, a fore-shadowing of the truth to be revealed fully in a
later event. Thus Judaism looks forward to the event which will
make it into a fulfilled fact. It is, in a word, *prophecy*, in
the double sense of something that comes from God and of something that looks forward to a future event. As an illustration
of his meaning, Hamann cites four great historical figures from
the Old Testament who adumbrated the event of full revelation:
Moses was a Mediator, Aaron a High Priest, David (as Psalmist) a
Prophet, and Solomon a King. Each of them was a "shadow" of the
reality to come, of Jesus Christ -- the "higher Mediator" and
perfect High Priest, Prophet, and King.

Because the prophetic truth of Judaism could be fully understood only when it was fulfilled in Christianity, even Moses could not appreciate the brightness of his own face as he came down from Mt. Sinai with the tablets of the law (Ex. 34:29ff.). When he saw what fear the Israelites had of him, he put a veil over his face. To Hamann, following Paul in 2 Cor. 3:7-18, that veil is a symbol of the law, for the religion of the law constitutes a curtain between God and his people. Wherever the law of Moses is still read, that curtain remains, "swaddling" those who hear it as spiritual infants who do not know the glory and splendor of God. This is the knowledge which has been given in Christ (Col. 1:26f.), thus unveiling the mystery of Judaism and lifting the curtain between God and man.

The full revelation of God in Christ is an event, an historical fact, and the basic difference between Judaism and Christianity is their respective rejection or acceptance of that fact. As Hamann recapitulates this point, he goes on to the question of how historical facts can be known as such:

> The characteristic difference between Judaism and Christianity concerns, therefore, neither immediate nor mediate revelation, as understood by Jews and Naturalists, nor eternal truths and doctrines, nor ceremonial and moral laws. It concerns merely temporal truths of history, which have come to pass at one time and never recur -- *facts*, which have become true through a connection of causes and effects at one point in time and in one place, and therefore can be thought of as true only from that point in time and that place, and which must be confirmed by authority. Authority can, to be sure, humble; but it cannot instruct. It can knock reason down; but it cannot keep it down. Nevertheless, without authority the truth of history disappears with the event itself.[16]

No less than two thirds of this paragraph consists of words, phrases and sentences from the *Jerusalem*. In his distinction between "divine legislation" and "revealed religion," Mendelssohn claims to have identified "the characteristic difference between Judaism and Christianity."[17] We have already seen that Hamann rejects the notion of revelation as utterance in favor of revelation as event, thus undercutting the issue between immediate and mediated revelation, i.e. between Jewish law and natural reason. To focus on events also undermines Mendelssohn's threefold classification of truths as eternal, historical, or moral.

The only significant difference between Judaism and Christianity concerns "temporal truths of history," facts which are unrepeatable, which cannot be known by reason through reflection upon concepts or the study of nature, nor can they be learned by ceremonial re-enactment. The locus of Christian truth is not doctrine or duty but fact, the historical event of Jesus Christ.

The question is, How can such facts be known? Quoting Mendelssohn,[18] Hamann affirms that historical truths are temporal, unrepeatable, and relative to a network of cause-and-effect which has produced them at a particular time and a particular place. Because of their relativity to a particular time and place, historical events can be directly known as facts, as events which really happened, only at that time and place. Historical events are not available for observation or direct verification after they have happened. How, then, can they be known by those who come later?

Here, again, Hamann employs Mendelssohn's own statements to make his point. Facts "must be confirmed by authority" because, as Mendelssohn says, "only authority can provide [historical truths] with the requisite evidence."[19] Thus they are agreed that historical truths must be accepted on faith. But Mendelssohn is not willing to admit that true Judaism is primarily a matter of such faith. His claim that it is really only a divine legislation is the basis for his argument that Judaism is consistent with the free enquiry of reason, for it does not require doctrinal consent as does classical Christianity. In fact, while acknowledging that many Jews would disagree with him, Mendelssohn is so confident of his interpretation of Judaism that he avows a willingness to "submit reason to the yoke of faith" if that interpretation should prove mistaken. At the same time, he indicates that such a submission would for him be hypocrisy. Authority can humble men, but it can never teach them. It can throw reason to the floor, but cannot hold it there. Doubts will always reappear so long as faith and reason stand in opposition to one another. And the overcoming of doubt, for Mendelssohn, is a matter of reconciling the word of God with independent human reason.[20]

In short, the reason for Mendelssohn's denial that historical truths can be the foundation of salvation is his concern to protect the autonomy of reason from the authority of faith,

and he knows that historical facts can be verified only by
authority. In order to protect all essential truths from dependence upon such authority, the primacy of "eternal truths"
of reason over all historical truths must be rigorously maintained. These truths alone transcend all particularity, for
they are knowable by all men without regard to time and place.
In contrast, historical facts can be known only by the reports
of witnesses. If those facts are to be believed, the witnesses
must be trusted. If the witnesses are not trusted, then their
reports are not believed, and the events themselves are soon
forgotten. That is why, as Hamann quotes from still a third
passage in the *Jerusalem*, "without authority the truth of history disappears with the event itself."[21]

If this is so, then the question arises: By what authority
is Christianity validated over against Judaism?

> This characteristic difference between Judaism
> and Christianity concerns truths of history of not
> only past but also future times, which are proclaimed
> and stated beforehand through the Spirit of a provi-
> dence as universal as it is particular, and which,
> due to their nature, cannot be received in any other
> way than through faith. Jewish authority alone gives
> them the necessary authenticity. These memorabilia
> of ancestry and posterity were also confirmed by
> miracles, proven by the credibility of the witnesses
> and transmitters of the tradition, and supported by
> evidence of real fulfillments which are sufficient
> to catapult faith over all Talmudic and dialectical
> doubts and pitfalls.[22]

First we must be clear as to the nature of historical truth.
The difference between Judaism and Christianity is a matter of
the truth or falsehood of certain events. But "truths of history" are not mere data which can be known and believed by some
direct or immediate intuition. Neither is it sufficient for
them to be proclaimed from on high by an alien authority.
Hamann's agreement with Mendelssohn about the need for authority
in matters of historical truth does not mean that he is defending
"blind" faith in every alleged "fact." On the contrary, there
is a "logic," so to speak, of historical truth, by which the
evidence for historical claims can be weighed and either confirmed or rejected.

Historical truths concern both the past and the future.
Indeed, their very truth can be known only *as* the relation of
one event to another event. If an event has happened, but has

no discernible relation to any other event, then it remains a
meaningless datum. Only as relations of the past to the future
can the events of history be comprehended.

In Hamann's view, the key to understanding such historical
truths is prophecy. To be grasped in its truth, an event must
have been "proclaimed beforehand through the Spirit." Without
God's prophetic word, the events of history are mere data, surds
which defy human understanding. All efforts to interpret them
will fail, for they will be nothing more than an attempt to
explain them by a false theory or prophecy. To be authentic,
a prophecy must have been given by "the Spirit." It is the
Spirit which, through the prophecies given in past times, illuminates the meaning of present events. It is the same Spirit
which, through the prophecies of the past and present, indicates
what events we should expect in future times. To live life in
its fully historical nature, it is necessary to live in the
present as the intersection of the past with the future, an
intersection that can be understood only in terms of the Spirit's
prophetic explanations of it.

The truths of history must be "received...through faith."
This is because it is almost never the case that one person can
witness directly both the prophecy and its fulfillment. The
present is always an intersection which can be understood only
by faith that future events will conform to past prophecies.
The prophecies which matter most to the present are those which
remain unfulfilled, which point toward the future, and which
therefore must be received in faith.

Once again, however, faith is not, according to Hamann,
merely "blind" acceptance. To Mendelssohn, the Jew, he points
out that the prophecies by which the issue between Judaism and
Christianity must be judged are Jewish prophecies. The authority
which authenticates the meaning of the event of Jesus Christ is
Jewish authority. Faith in the truth of the claim that Jesus is
the Christ rests, for Hamann, on the conformity of the life, death
and resurrection of Jesus to the messianic prophecies given by
the Spirit to the Israelites many centuries before. For a Jew
to become a Christian, only a deeper understanding of those prophecies and their fulfillment in Jesus is required. Judaism is
not simply a stagnant "lower floor;" it is a stairway from its
own foundation in Christ to its true fulfillment in Christianity.

The pattern of historical meaning is thus one of past and future, prophecy and fulfillment. In the Christian fulfillment of Jewish prophecy that pattern is revealed and established in its truth. Jewish authority thereby authenticates Christianity, just as each becomes intelligible only through the other. There remains, however, the question of the means by which the believer can become personally convinced of these truths. How is the prophetic meaning of history to be "received in faith"? What encouragements are there to accept these prophecies and fulfillments as genuine truths of history from the Spirit of God?

One such encouragement is the confirmation by miraculous events which attend the giving of the prophecy or the fulfillment. Mt. Sinai smoked when Moses received the law, and Christ healed people who had been sick or lame or even dead. Hamann is not suggesting that miracles should themselves be objects of belief or that they can serve to illuminate the meaning of the historical truths they accompany. Rather, they are one means by which God confirms that these events, such as the giving of the law or the advent of Christ, really are from Him and are to be taken seriously. Because Mendelssohn agrees that miracles confirm historical events,[23] it is not an issue that he or Hamann discusses at length. But miracles do deserve notice as one of the ways in which people can be encouraged to look more deeply for the meaning of the events which God has brought about.

A second means of encouragement is the testimony of the witnesses to an event, and of those who have transmitted the report of it over the centuries. Whereas "Jewish authority" in the strict sense refers to "the Spirit of providence," Jewish tradition presents to the believer a long history of individuals who, by their testimonies to God's prophecies, enable him to become more "receptive" to them. These witnesses seem to him to have a certain "credibility." Upon reflection, it seems unlikely that they are fabricating or twisting their accounts of the events to which they testify. The grounds of this credibility may vary considerably from witness to witness, but it is the essential element in the transmission of the tradition. Without it, the authority and truth of the Spirit could never be made available to the believer.

Finally, the believer is also encouraged by "evidence of real fulfillments" which he can observe for himself. In other words, after he has understood the historical claims of faith, been impressed by the attendant miracles, come to respect the sincerity of those who have passed the claims down to him, he still can judge for himself and see to what extent the alleged fulfillments actually "match" the prophecies of them. The overcoming of "Talmudic and dialectical doubts" is accomplished not by a suspension of critical evaluation of the evidence, but by a closer examination of it. Hamann is convinced that there is solid *historical* evidence for the claims of Christianity, for they are real fulfillments of prophecies given centuries before they happened. To accept the prophecies and fulfillments of the Spirit through faith involves both submission to that Spirit and a "critical" examination -- according to the criteria given by the Spirit -- of the historical truths which are claimed.

In order to investigate what Hamann takes to be the criteria of historical truth, it is now necessary to abandon my continuous exposition of the *Golgotha*. Skipping over one paragraph, we come to this statement by Hamann about the basis on which the historical truths of Christianity can be known and judged:

> Therefore, Christianity does not believe in doctrines of philosophy, which is nothing but an alphabetical scribbling of human speculation, and subject to the fickle changes of moon and mode!... -- in no fleeting shadows of actions and ceremonies which neither remain nor endure... -- in no laws, which must be obeyed even when not believed.... No, Christianity knows and acknowledges [*weiss und kennt*] no other chains on belief than the sure prophetic word in the oldest of all documents of the human race and in the holy scriptures of authentic Judaism, without Samaritan segregation and apocryphal mishnah. That depository made even the Jews into a chosen race for His possession, instructed in divinity, anointed and called before all peoples of the earth for the salvation of mankind.[24]

The primary purpose of the *Jerusalem* is to attack all forms of religious coercion, such as required confessions of (Christian) faith for civil offices or membership in non-religious societies. The practical importance of Mendelssohn's distinction between eternal truths known by universal reason and historical or legislative truths known through particular traditions or revelations is that it enables him to affirm the necessity for basic doctrinal agreement as the foundation of social harmony, but deny that all members of society should accept the same particular religion.

Since, in his view, all the doctrines necessary for salvation or
an orderly society are available to reason, religious affiliation
should be a matter of private conscience and preference. Furthermore, having asserted that Judaism consists of faith in historical
truths and obedience to the law, but not in adherence to any doctrinal truths that could ever conflict with the eternal truths
of universal reason, Mendelssohn can praise his faith for its
lack of "chains on belief."[25] He does not mean that all belief
should be totally free of authority or that the doctrines of
reason do not require some sort of prior "belief" in reason.
Rather, he is simply trying to distinguish between truths which
are available to members of all faiths and those that can be
understood and accepted only by adherence to a particular creed.

Since Hamann rejects the existence of such universal and
eternal truths of reason, he naturally denies that Christianity
believes in these "doctrines of philosophy." Furthermore, he
adds, Mendelssohn's so-called "eternal" truths often amount to
little more than passing fads and word-games ("alphabetical
scribblings"). Nor does Christianity believe in the "fleeting
shadows" of ceremonial rituals, which Mendelssohn praises as
the heart of Judaism.[26] Finally, Christianity does not teach
that laws must be "obeyed even when not believed." Whereas
Mendelssohn argues that Christ taught men to "serve both masters"
of state and religion without becoming discouraged over the
conflict between their demands,[27] Hamann protests that Christian
faith is a unity of belief and actions. It resolutely opposes
any such empty obedience as Mendelssohn advocates.

The "chains on belief" which Christianity does accept consist in the authority of the Bible, and particularly -- for faith
in the prophecies of Christ -- the authority of the Hebrew scriptures, which are thought by Hamann to be the oldest documents of
the human race. His concern here is not so much for the antiquity of the Old Testament as for the matter of its interpretation. It is important not to follow the rabbinic tradition of
understanding God's election of the Jews in national rather than
universal terms. Thus all "Samaritan segregation" is to be
avoided. Equally dangerous is the insistence upon giving the
Talmudic traditional interpretation, the mishnah, authority with
Scripture itself. Christianity, which is the result and truth

of "authentic Judaism," accepts only the Bible itself as its "chains on belief."

It was in order to give the "depository" of biblical truth to all mankind that God called and anointed the Jews as His own special people. Their place in the providential course of history is a very special one, but only because He chose them as His instrument for the salvation of "all the peoples of the earth." One of the most important means by which He accomplished this was through giving prophecies of the coming Messiah and Savior. In an age when a Jewish spokesman like Mendelssohn could ignore those prophecies, and when few Christians believed in the truth and inspiration of the Old Testament,[28] Hamann urged a return to the authority of the "holy scriptures of authentic Judaism."

Biblical Language and Historical Meaning

On the basis of the authority of the Bible, history is understood by Hamann to be a matter of prophecy and fulfillment. Thus he describes Christianity as a "firm and childlike reliance on divine pledges and promises" from God, like the unwavering faith of Abraham.[29] Questions arise, however, as to how a Christian should understand the prophetic meaning of the Old Testament. Which prophecies explain events that have happened? Which events fulfill the various prophecies that have been given? How can events which happened in the context of a particular people, the nation of Israel, be said to show the significance of God's plan for all mankind? What is the relationship between God and the arena of history in which He acts?

These questions concern the language of historical meaning which Hamann finds in the Bible. There are many facets and nuances in his understanding of the biblical view of history. For the purposes of this essay, however, it is sufficient to focus upon three rubrics or principles which can be used to express major elements in Hamann's biblical language of historical meaning. I designate these three as the principle of types, the principle of particularity, and the principle of transcendence.

The principle of types is, like metaschematism, a *sine qua non* for understanding Hamann's allusive style.[30] While discussing the relation of Christ to Judaism, he gives a particularly coherent account of how types function:

> Moses, the greatest prophet and the national lawgiver,
> is only the smallest most transitory shadow of his
> office, which he himself confessed to be only the
> prototype of another prophet, whose raising up he
> promised to his brothers and their descendants, with
> the injunction and command to obey him.[31]

In this statement, Hamann is agreeing fully with Mendelssohn
about the greatness of Moses as the leading prophet and law-giver
of Judaism. Even so, Hamann adds, he is a mere "shadow" of his
office, just as Judaism in general is said to be a "shadow" of
the "good things to come" in Christianity. His tenure in this
office is "transitory," for his role is really to prepare the
people of God for one who will come after him. Thus the highest
truth about Moses is that he is a foreshadowing of Christ. This
is what it means to be a "type:" Moses is like the Christ to
follow. As he himself "promised to his brothers" in Dt. 18:15:
"The Lord your God will raise up for you a prophet like me from
among you, from your brethren -- him you shall heed." For Hamann,
this is a fundamental hermeneutical principle with regard to the
Old Testament: "the entire mythology of the Hebrew economy was
nothing but a type of a more transcendent history, the horoscope
of a heavenly hero."[32]

In addition to being a type of Christ, Moses represents for
Hamann a type of Mendelssohn and all Jews who reject Jesus as
the Messiah:

> But to the law-giver Moses was entry into the promised
> land flatly denied; and through a similar sin of un-
> belief in the Spirit of grace and truth, which should
> have been preserved in the hieroglyphic practices of
> symbolic ceremonies and actions of pristine signifi-
> cance, until the times of refreshing, out-pouring and
> anointing, this earthly vehicle of a temporal, figura-
> tive, dramatic, animal legislation and sacrificial
> worship degenerated into the corrupted and deadly
> creeping poison of a childish, slavish, literalistic,
> idolatrous superstition.[33]

The incident to which Hamann is here referring is one of
the most obscure in the Old Testament. As recorded in Num. 20:
2-13, the Lord instructed Moses to "sanctify" Him by calling
forth water from a rock for the thirsting Israelites. Moses
turned to the people, chastised them, and struck the rock twice
with his staff. Water gushed forth, but the Lord then told Moses
and Aaron that they had disobeyed Him and would therefore be

denied entry into the promised land. The obscurity involves
Moses' disobedience. What precisely did Moses do that displeased
the Lord so much?

Hamann calls it a "sin of unbelief in the Spirit of grace
and truth." He refers to Moses as a "law-giver." Since the
staff is a symbol of legislative and judicial authority, it is
safe to assume that Hamann agrees with a prevailing, traditional
interpretation, namely, that Moses should not have used his
staff, for the Lord told him simply to speak to the rock. By
striking it with his staff, Moses trusted his own powers as a
"law-giver" rather than only the Spirit of grace. Thus he failed
to obey and "sanctify" the Lord.

It is the same, according to Hamann, with the acts which
Jews perform in their ritual ceremonies. These acts have no
purpose or point in themselves. They are nothing but hieroglyphs
or ciphers, symbolic actions pointing toward "the times of refreshing, out-pouring and anointing." This is an allusion to
the giving of the Holy Spirit at Pentecost. Hamann is not totally condemning the ceremonies which Mendelssohn defends. His
point is that they were given by God for a purpose, and that,
like Moses, the Jews failed to follow God's instructions and
intentions in the matter. They have turned the symbolic ceremonies into laws, rather than performing them with an awareness
of their spiritual significance. Similarly, they revere Moses
as a law-giver, having forgotten that he is a type of Christ,
the prophet whom he told them to obey.

Hamann's choice of words in this passage is, as always,
highly allusive. Mendelssohn's critique of doctrines is the
most important target, for in it he praises the ceremonies and
the Hebrew words which constitute the focus of Jewish faith, on
the grounds that they do not lend themselves to doctrinal literalism and rigidity as much as pictures of animals, hieroglyphics,
and the idolatry of image-worship. Hamann's use of Mendelssohn's
own language is metaschematic: the Hebrew ceremonies were an
"earthly vehicle" but charged with temporal and figurative (typological) meaning. They involved dramatic actions, animal sacrifices and legislation, all of which can be understood only as a
pre-figuring of the drama, sacrifice, and new "legislation" which
were culminated on Calvary. By rejecting Christ, Mendelssohn is

left with a ceremonial law which has been corrupted into the very idolatry which he condemns. The freedom and pristine faith of which he boasts is ultimately a "slavish, literalistic...superstition."

"Literalism" is a key concept for understanding Hamann's typological exegesis. To read the Bible according to the letter is to follow the "written code" which kills rather than the life-giving Spirit of God (2 Cor. 3:6). It is to forget that the old laws and ceremonies have been instituted only to guide God's people toward the new out-pouring of the Spirit. It is to value them for themselves, rather than as types and "shadows" of "good things to come." To understand the Bible "spiritually" is the opposite of understanding it (or *mis*understanding it) literally.

With regard to the question of historical meaning, the implications of such a typological exegesis and the spirit-letter dichotomy which it presupposes are far-reaching. The significance of Israel and Moses, argues Hamann, is that they pre-figure or fore-shadow Christianity and Christ. If this is so, it is impossible to understand them apart from their fulfillment. They are prophecies, types of things to come after them. Typological understanding is, as it were, the method of historical under-standing employed by one who lives by faith in the biblical pro-phecies and fulfillments from God.

Just as the prophecy cannot be fully understood apart from its fulfillment, and thus Judaism is "comprehended" only by Christianity, so also the fulfillment cannot be fully grasped apart from the prophecy of God about it. Apart from Judaism, Christianity would make no sense at all. In this same passage Hamann explicitly re-affirms that the Old Testament is "the rock of Christian faith," and that Christ is the "cornerstone" of the building built upon that rock. Those who "stumble" over him show that they do not really believe in their own Word and founda-tion.[34] Christ is the foundation and purpose of Judaism no less than of Christianity. Neither can be understood apart from its historical relation to the other.

Hamann's second hermeneutical principle for the interpreta-tion of history can be called a "principle of particularity." His statement that the "Spirit of providence" is both universal and particular has already been quoted.[35] To many modern thinkers, the particularity of the biblical claim that Israel is the "chosen people" of God seems immoral and offensive. That is why Mendelssohn tries to limit the notion of particular revelation to the Mosaic legislation, leaving doctrinal truth universally available to rational men. In contrast, Hamann accepts the particularistic implications of his belief that all truths are historical truths, and in the process spells out the very point of view that makes Mendelssohn and many of their contemporaries so uncomfortable.

Whereas the principle of typology expresses the relation between Jewish and Christian history, the principle of particularity concerns the relation between Jewish history and the history of other nations:

> The entire history of Judaism was not only prophecy; rather, its spirit was occupied more than that of all other nations, to whom one perhaps cannot deny the analogy of a similar dark divination and anticipation, with the ideal of a savior and judge, a man of power.... Moses' Pentateuch, the Psalms and the Prophets are full of hints and glimpses of this appearance of...a star out of Jacob, of...the signs of the contradiction in the ambiguous form of his person, his message of peace and joy, his works and pains, his obedience unto death, even death on a cross![36]

The meaning of this passage is straightforward enough: Judaism cannot be comprehended entirely as prophecy, if "prophecy" is taken to mean an historical event which has its significance *only* as a type of a later event. Judaism, in addition to foreshadowing Christianity, also pursued in the course of its own history "the ideal of a savior and judge." The events of the Old Testament are "hints and glimpses" of the presence of Christ among them. The foreshadowing or prophetic element should not be allowed to obscure the sense in which the Spirit of providence was constantly present in the concrete events of Israelite history, using them to reveal the nature of God.

The central difference between Israel and other nations is the Messianic "divination and anticipation" which Israel had. Although Hamann does not totally deny such intuitions to other nations, he classifies them as "analogies" with those of Israel. In other words, the quest for a savior and judge, which is implicitly the ideal inspiring all historical movement, can be recognized in other nations only by analogy with that of Israel.

The particularity of such a statement should be evident: just as the significance of Judaism is to be understood through Christianity, so the significance of other (non-Christian) nations can be comprehended by analogy with the history of Israel.

The principle of particularity does not imply, however, that Hamann is indifferent to the problem of universal historical meaning. The use of analogy in itself indicates that he does not dismiss nonbiblical histories as merely secular or meaningless. In his view, the histories of other nations contain great meaning, but meaning that can be comprehended only through the Bible. At this point, the principle of particularity and the principle of types intersect, revealing what Hamann took to be the significance of the Old Testament for understanding world history:

> But if all human knowledge can be reduced to a few fundamental concepts, and if the same sounds occur quite frequently in the spoken language, as do the same pictures in different hieroglyphic tablets, but always in different connections through which they multiply their meaning: then this observation may also be applied to history, and the whole range of human events with all their changes may just as well be grasped and divided into sections, as the starry heaven is into constellations, without knowing the number of stars. -- Therefore the entire history of the Jewish people seems, according to the parable of their ceremonial law, to be a living, spirit- and heart-awakening elementary text of all historical literature, in heaven and on earth and under the earth -- a permanent, progressive leading toward the year of the Jubilee and the governmental plan of the divine regime for the whole creation from its beginning up till its exit, and the prophetic puzzle of a theocracy is mirrored in the pieces of this smashed vessel, like the sun "on the dewdrops on the grass, which tarries for no one, nor does it wait for men." For yesterday the dew from the Lord was only on Gideon's fleece, and all the ground was dry; today the dew is on all the ground, and only the fleece is dry.[37]

Hamann's first step in this paragraph is to accept, metaschematically, Mendelssohn's description of the nature of human knowledge. In defending the irreducibility of laws, Mendelssohn contrasts them with human knowledge. In his view, laws can be summarized, yet every detail remains essential. In contrast, the fewer the axioms upon which knowledge rests, the more substantial its foundation.[38] Similarly, Mendelssohn considers the possibility of development in spoken and written language to be

contingent upon the repetition of a few sounds or hieroglyphic
pictures, with which the process of classification could commence.
Thus knowledge and its increase in any area is, in his view, predicated upon a few basic elements or concepts which can be vari-
ously connected with each other to produce a great variety of
meanings.[39]

Hamann applies this "observation" to the understanding of
history. If all knowledge depends upon a few fundamental elements, then knowledge about the meaning of history must also
consist in the division of historical events into sections, i.e.
into various classes or categories which would provide a context
for their interpretation. Such historical knowledge will not
be comprehensive. Like astronomy, which Mendelssohn praises for
its ability to divide the stars into constellations "without
knowing" how many stars there are,[40] historical understanding
must also be able to classify "the whole range of human events
with all their changes" before it comprehends them completely.
Thus Hamann sees all historical understanding as incomplete and
fragmentary. He seeks not a finished system, but a few particular types by which he can classify and understand the phenomena
of world history.

In the Bible -- both the Old and New Testaments as together
constituting for Hamann "the entire history of the Jewish people"
-- Hamann finds those basic types. It is the "elementary text
of all historical literature." That means: only when the biblical portrayal and classification of historical events is
grasped will an understanding of other historical literature
become possible. It provides the fundamental concepts which
make history intelligible.

For Hamann, the universal significance of the particular
history recorded in the Bible is twofold. First, Jewish history
is a "parable" of all other histories. As discussed above, the
law was given to lead the Jews to the living Spirit. Judaism
and Moses are shadows and types of Christianity and Christ. Thus
"the entire history" presented by the Bible offers the fundamental types by which all historical events can be classified and
interpreted. Biblical narrative and imagery is not simply the
language by which we are to understand biblical history: in
Hamann's view, it is the only means we have for understanding

history in general. The principle of types provides a hermeneutical basis for the universal significance of biblical history.

The second aspect of biblical universality has a more
strictly "historical" basis. The Bible is not limited to the
history of the Jews. As the record of the creation of all men
and the prophecy of the End toward which the entire world is
moving, it has direct relevance to every human life. Hamann
believes that the Bible is "the oldest of all documents [which
concern]...the whole human race."[41] It is the revelation of
the origins of "universal" humanity in the particular act of
creation by God. It is also the revelation of God's plan "for
the whole creation from its beginning up till its exit." Thus
it is both "permanent" (literally, "written with a diamond"
[Jer. 17:1]) and "progressive," leading toward the time of the
Jubilee and the kingdom ("governmental plan") of God on earth.

The universal purpose of Jewish history is, then, that it
is a "prophetic puzzle of a theocracy" which God will institute
at the End of the world. Mendelssohn argues forcefully that the
"theocratic" period of Jewish history ended with the destruction
of the Jewish state at the time of the Exile.[42] Hamann sees in
the "smashed vessel" of that theocracy a fragmentary reflection
of the "divine regime" that will come and have Christ at its
head. The providential plan, he implies, is like the sun on the
early morning dew, which disappears immediately from its warmth.
This quotation is from the prophet Micah,[43] who adds in the next
verse that the remnant to be saved out of Israel shall be "among
the nations" and "in the midst of many peoples." Hamann's allusion to it at this point underscores his conviction that the
historical significance of Judaism is universal, for their
"election" was to play a particular role in the salvation of
all mankind. The image of the dew leads to another biblical
story which is for him a type of this idea: when Gideon laid
out a fleece to know the Lord's will, it was wet the first day,
while the ground was dry; and dry the second day, while the
ground was wet (Jud. 6:36-40). Similarly, the Jews have been
the "fleece" by which the will of God is known. They were
anointed by Him, while the world remained dry. Now, with the
coming of a new day in Christ, they are dry, while the whole

world is anointed.[44] The Spirit of God was upon the Jewish
people in a very particular way as the first step in the plan
of universal salvation.

A third principle for the understanding of history according
to Hamann can be designated as the "principle of transcendence."
Although closely related to the principle of particularity, and
in itself a traditional and easily comprehended idea, it deserves
careful attention in preparation for the discussion in Chapter
IV:[45]

> Therefore, unbelief in the most real, historical
> sense of the word is the only sin against the Spirit
> of the true religion, whose heart is in heaven and
> whose heaven is in the heart. The mystery of Chris-
> tian holiness consists not in services, sacrifices
> and vows, which God demands of men, but rather in
> promises, fulfillments and sacrifices, which God has
> done and achieved for the benefit of men; not in the
> great and huge commandment that He imposed, but in the
> highest good, which He gave as a gift; not in legis-
> lation and moral doctrines, which concern merely human
> sentiments and human actions, but in execution of
> divine decrees by means of divine deeds, works and
> institutions for the salvation of the whole world.
> Dogmatics and ecclesiastical law belong solely to the
> public educational and administrative institutions,
> and as such are subject to the arbitrariness of the
> authorities, an outward discipline that is sometimes
> coarse and sometimes refined, according to the elements
> and degrees of the dominant aesthetic. These visible,
> public, common institutions are neither religion nor
> wisdom, which come down from above, but earthly, un-
> spiritual and devilish....[46]

What concerns Hamann here is the fundamental difference
between unbelief and faith. That difference has to do with unbelief in the "real, historical sense of the word," by which
Hamann means that unbelief is rejection of historical truths
attested by "the Spirit of the true religion," i.e. Christianity.
That Christianity is an "historical" religion does not mean that
it is totally available for inspection by all would-be historians.
It is a religion "whose heart is in heaven and whose heaven is
in the heart." By implication, therefore, faith in the "historical sense" of the word is the affirmation of this "heavenly"
transcendence in the "heart" of the world. At first glance, this
seems to be a paradoxical claim that faith is an historical relationship of a trans-historical nature. Hamann goes on, however,
to explain how he understands the transcendence of God and the
historical nature of faith to be related to one another.

"The mystery of Christian holiness" is a matter of sacrifices, promises, vows, fulfillments and services. In this regard it is like all other religions: it is based upon certain acts that must be performed for it (the religion) to exist at all. The "mystery" which, in Hamann's view, distinguishes Christianity is that it consists not of acts performed by men, even in response to God's demands, but of acts performed by God Himself. Christian holiness is accomplished not by men but by God. His promises, His fulfillments, the sacrifice of His son on the Cross -- these constitute the object of Christian faith. Unbelief, in contrast, trusts in the services of men, the sacrifices performed by men for God, the vows made by men to please God.

Hamann includes both the "great commandment" to love God (Mt. 22:36-38) and obedience to the legislation and moral teachings given by God to men among those things of religion which remain merely human. In contrast, "the highest good, which He gave as a gift," and His own execution of His decrees for the salvation of the world, constitute the divine object and foundation of faith, and transcend "merely human sentiments and human actions." In Hamann's view, there is no necessary connection between the saving acts of God and the religious deeds of men.

One task in understanding history, then, is to discern which historical events are the work of God and which are merely human. This is no easy task, for the criterion which separates them is not their subject matter. Religion, even Christian religion, does not in itself qualify as an act of God. Even "dogmatics and ecclesiastical law" are merely human institutions for the education and administration of the public. Rather than an expression of God's will and being, they are "subject to the arbitrariness of the [human] authorities" placed over them. Acknowledging that human authorities can often exercise their responsibilities with a "refined...outward discipline," Hamann nonetheless insists that they all remain "earthly, unspiritual and devilish," in contrast with true "religion [and] wisdom, which come down from above."

Thus Hamann's "biblical" language of historical meaning calls for spiritual discernment of the connections between prophetic types and those events which they illuminate and by which they are fulfilled. It requires acceptance of the particularity of

God's dealings with man, especially His election of Israel, His redemption of the world through the sacrifice of one person, and His Self-revelation in the world by the Spirit of the one true religion. And it insists upon recognition of the fact that even within institutional Christianity there is no easy equation between the acts of God and the deeds of men, for God's transcendence over the world is not reduced by virtue of His involvement in it. These principles guide Hamann's interpretation of the significance of all historical events, and shape his understanding of the relation between historical meaning and faith in the lives of individual Christians.

Biblical History and the Life of Faith

The principle of the transcendence of God over human efforts to guide the course of history raises a question with regard to Hamann's biblical understanding of historical meaning: how, if God is transcendent, can there be any interaction between Him and men at all? By what means does God relate to men so that they will be able to comprehend His transcendence or holiness in order to live lives of faith? I call such means of divine-human relationship "structures" of historical meaning, for they provide the context as well as the content of a great deal of Hamann's biblical interpretation of historical events.

There is one paragraph in the *Golgotha* in which Hamann mentions the two structures upon which I would like to focus:

> As for the standard implicit in the two questions about the best form of government and the healthiest diet, rather did the heavenly politics have to condescend to the earthly "there" and temporal "at that time," without thereby being chained to the here-and-now, in order, like the sun, to run through its luminous eternal cycle from the faith of Abraham *before* the law to the faith of his children and heirs of the promise *following* the law; for the promise, but no law, was given to the flesh of the righteous Abraham as the sign of the covenant. Precisely in this true politics do we behold...a deity, where common eyes see the stone.[47]

The question of the relation between God and men is a "political" question. In his discussion of church-state relations, Mendelssohn likens the question about "the best form of government" to that of the "healthiest diet," concluding that each will

be relative to the natural and cultural context of the people
in question. He is optimistic that a nation will always choose
that form of government which is best suited to its own needs of
the moment.[48] In matters relating to God, Hamann rejects this
"implicit standard" of cultural relativism. He affirms that the
"heavenly politics" have an identity and character quite different from the "earthly" contexts in which they intervene and are
revealed. God transcends the "here-and-now."

Yet God also manifests Himself in the "here-and-now," even
if He is not "chained" by it. To do so, says Hamann, He has
"to condescend." This means that He must accommodate His own
identity and character, which are utterly and transcendently
holy, to the circumstances of the world in which He wants to
reveal Himself. Without in any way succumbing to the power of
those limited circumstances, He must present Himself to man in
terms that are humanly comprehensible and intelligible. This
notion of God's condescension to man has been shown by Gründer
to be one of the central ideas of Hamann's early works.[49] Although this paragraph is the only explicit mention of it in the
Golgotha, I find it a useful device for interpreting one aspect
or dimension of Hamann's criticisms of Mendelssohn's moral philosophy. The concept of condescension seems to me to be a structure
of historical meaning through which Hamann asserts the centrality of the "personal" element in moral and historical situations.

God's purpose in condescending to His people is to fulfill
His plan for them, beginning with Abraham and running through to
the advent of Christ. Although the law is a major part of that
plan, because it is superseded by the gospel it cannot really be
considered an enduring "structure" of historical relationship
between God and man. Hamann emphasizes that "the promise, but
no law," was given to Abraham. This promise, however, can be
understood as the "sign" of another structure by which He relates
to men: the structure of covenant. The covenant between God
and man is the "true politics" in which the presence of God in
history can be seen by the eye of faith, even though "common
eyes" see only a stone, a lifeless weight and obstacle.

Since the concept of condescension is expressed indirectly
in the *Golgotha*, I will first analyze the more explicit notion
of covenant and its implications for the meaning of history.

On the first page of his text Hamann contrasts "the divine and
eternal covenant" which God made with Abraham with Mendelssohn's
belief in "a state of nature, which he relates to society as the
dogmatists relate it to a state of grace -- partly as presupposition and partly in opposition."[50] In the *Jerusalem*, Mendelssohn argues continually from the presupposition that "natural"
rights and duties exist which are valid and acknowledged prior
to any "social contracts." Hamann sees in this a sort of reasoning reminiscent of medieval distinctions between nature and grace:
the "nature" is posited as a presupposition and counterpoint to
the theory of grace or of society which is argued, without that
concept of nature itself actually being justified. To Hamann,
this is a shaky foundation for a theory of social contracts, and
therefore he is all the more grateful for the "contract" or covenant which God has given men to live by.

Although there are many important facets of the biblical
understanding of covenant, the one that is most relevant to the
argument of this essay concerns the question of freedom. What
does the idea of "divine and eternal covenant" mean for modern
faith in human freedom? Mendelssohn's "state of nature," as a
state existing -- at least hypothetically -- prior to the institution of laws and restrictions, represents a state of maximum
freedom. For Hamann to oppose to it the idea of covenant implies
that he is challenging this notion of a primordial freedom:

> Is it wisdom and goodness to give and to leave
> to everyone his own? Certainly, in the unique case
> where there is no other right to property than the
> wisdom and goodness of the giver. But this case is
> the only one of its type....
>
> Thus Leibniz was right for that single case which
> can be discussed only in a theodicy. Our beautiful
> and sweet spirits who, intoxicated by the strong drink
> of their omniscience and love of man...are also right,
> according to the continuous and systematic conclu-
> siveness of Roman and metaphysical-catholic despotism,
> whose transcendental understanding prescribes for it-
> self its own laws of nature.[51]

According to Mendelssohn, natural law theory posits "laws
of wisdom and goodness" by which rights to property and duties
toward such rights can be determined. One of his main points
in elaborating this theory is that men have an exclusive right
over their own capacity to create and the goods which they

produce by that capacity.[52] This implies, in Hamann's view,
that "wisdom and goodness" require isolation of individuals
from one another in matters pertaining to property. This would
make sense, he insists, only for property on which no more than
one person has any claim, and thus over which no conflict could
ever arise. While Mendelssohn's purpose is to show how conflicts
of interest can be rationally adjudicated, in fact his property-
oriented individualism makes such adjudication quite impossible.

But Hamann's main concern in this passage is with a positive, metaschematic application of Mendelssohn's language. At
issue is the concept of exclusive rights to property -- either
the means of production or the products themselves. Hamann
does grant that such an exclusive right exists "in the unique
case where there is no other right." That is, of course, the
"case" of God. As the sole creator of all that is, He can give
and deny His gifts entirely as He chooses. The only discussion
of His sovereign will in such matters will be "in a theodicy."
If God alone has exclusive rights to the goods in this world,
then the question of just and unjust distribution of those rights
will involve understanding His will rather than working out
elaborate theories of rights and duties.

What, then, of the human rights with which Mendelssohn is
so concerned? In contrast with the real rights which God has,
those claims strike Hamann as little more than the boasts of
men who are "intoxicated" by their self-love and pride in knowledge. Such men are unable to think clearly, even though they
aspire to build a system of knowledge and moral law that would
be all-inclusive. Were they to succeed, their "system" would
resemble the authoritarianism of Roman Catholicism which they
so abhor, and thus result in a form of despotism even while
presenting itself as the guardian of "natural" freedom. Natural
law theory, concludes Hamann, cannot achieve both systematic
conclusiveness and its ideal of freedom. The contradiction between these two commitments drives it back to a "transcendental
understanding" which invents its own "laws of nature" to suit
itself. Hamann's point is that the entire enterprise of identifying "natural laws" must ultimately result in a stalemate between the freedom which is presupposed as absolute and the
comprehensive knowledge which is sought after. He thinks that

systematic knowledge is in some sense inevitably despotic, denying
to the objects it "knows" the freedom to exist except according
to *its* laws. Furthermore, hints Hamann, this mania to attain
comprehensive understanding will ultimately be turned against
itself, and the freedom of its own ability to think will be reduced to similar "laws," nonetheless confining because called
"transcendental."

The question here concerns the contrast between Mendelssohn's natural law theory of freedom and Hamann's defense of
the biblical notion of a covenant between God and men. Hamann's
cryptic remarks indicate that the radical individualism of Mendelssohn's position renders the very possibility of law questionable; that the logic which Mendelssohn is applying to the individual property-holder can properly be applied only to God; and
that the very ambition to achieve total understanding is dangerous
for freedom and doomed ultimately to include itself in its own
system of laws and knowledge, thus depriving itself of subjective
freedom just as it deprives the world of objective freedom.

Mendelssohn argues in the *Jerusalem* that the legitimacy of
the "social contract" derives from the voluntary acknowledgement
of rights and duties prior to that contract.[53] He thereby implies, in Hamann's view, that freedom is to be understood in
terms of this pre-contractual or pre-legal state of being, even
if it be a merely putative one. In contrast, Hamann believes
that only God can ever be free of laws or restraints; such a
concept of freedom has no place in the understanding of things
human. The "natural" state of man, therefore, is not one of
freedom from all except voluntary or noncompulsory duties, but
one of being morally bound to laws, duties and a complex web
of relationships:

> There is however a social contract; thus there
> is also a natural contract, which must be older and
> more authentic, and on whose conditions the social
> contract must be based. Thereby all natural pro-
> perty now becomes once more conventional, and man
> in the state of nature becomes dependent upon its
> laws, i.e., positively obligated to behave according
> to those very same laws which all nature and espe-
> cially man have to thank for the preservation of
> his existence and the use of all means and goods
> which contribute to it. Man, as duty-bound to
> nature, has accordingly least of all an exclusive
> right to and odious monopoly on his capacities, or

> their products, or the fruitless mule of his labor
> and the more forlorn bastard of his usurping, vio-
> lent overpowering of the creatures subjected against
> their will to his vanity.[54]

Hamann does not dispute that society is bound together by
"contract," in the sense of a network of laws and reciprocal
obligations. His concern is for the foundations of this contract.
Whereas Mendelssohn posits a "state of nature" or freedom in
which property rights exist prior to social convention,[55] Hamann
declares that the social contract must be based upon a "natural
contract." In other words, even in "the state of nature" or
freedom man is bound by contract, and it is upon this fundamental
contract that all the property rights and conventions of society
are based.

The natural contract involves laws which are binding upon
"all nature." Yet these laws are not simply a burden upon human
freedom, for man has them "to thank for the preservation of his
existence;" they are the creating and sustaining power of God.
By restricting the freedom of exclusive property-rights to God,
and by stating that man should have gratitude for "the use of
all means and goods which contribute" to his life, Hamann is
showing metaschematically that "nature" is best understood as
"creation." The laws of nature which bind man are not blind,
impersonal, mechanistic laws; they are nothing less than the
will of the Creator of the universe.

To say, therefore, that man is "duty-bound to nature" means
that he is obligated to live according to the covenant given to
him by God at the time of creation. The fundamental fact of
existence in the world and in history is neither a state of freedom nor a social contract to limit that freedom but the covenant
which God gave to Adam. This covenant does not give man any
exclusive rights to his own capacities, let alone a monopoly on
his products. Man's labor for himself is a "fruitless mule."
His proper "labor" is to carry out the assignments given to him
by God, the first of which was the naming of the animals created
for him by God (Gen. 2:18-20). Hamann closes the paragraph with
an allusion to that assignment and the contrast between the
notion of man as a servant of creation and the fact of man as
its oppressor. Under human stewardship the creatures of the
earth have become "forlorn bastards...subjected against their

will to his vanity." The state of nature, which was created as
a state of covenant between God and man, has fallen into a state
of sin. Thus even the creation waits eagerly for its salvation
from the "frustration" of its present subjection by God to sin
(Rom. 8:19-21 [NIV]).

As "duty-bound" by God's covenant, man's pursuit of "goods"
in history and society is not subject to his own choice and
decision:

> He has, therefore, neither a physical nor a moral
> capacity for any other happiness than that intended
> for him, and to which he was called. All means which
> he uses for the attainment of a happiness which is
> not given to and shared with him are heaped up abuses
> of nature and distinct injustices. All lust for well-
> being is the spark of a hellish uproar.[56]

The happiness which man can and ought to pursue is only that
happiness which God has planned for him and to which He has
called him. Hamann is not denying that man is fundamentally
bent upon seeking his own happiness. Each man seeks that which
he thinks will make him happy or will satisfy his desires in
some way. That is a simple fact of "the state of [human] nature."
But the only goal which will give a person real happiness is the
goal that God has planned for and given to that person.

In such a covenant relationship, the meaning of human history is a profoundly moral matter. Every person is confronted
in history with the choice between living for any one of a number
of his own goals or living for the goal which God has given him.
His happiness within the covenant is a happiness which he has
received from God and shares with Him and all others who are also
submitted to God. If he rejects that goal and happiness, he
abuses his own nature as a creature of God and condemns himself
to a life of perpetrating injustices. His "lust" for his own
"well-being" releases forces of evil and violence which will,
like a raging fire, consume him.

Thus one of Hamann's primary concerns is that nothing should
jeopardize the centrality of the moral dimension of historical
action. Mendelssohn argues in the *Jerusalem* that states have
the right of coercion over the actions of individuals because
that right has been ceded to the states freely by all individuals
who participate in a society bound by social contract.[57] The
difficulty which Hamann sees in such a view is that it implicitly

gives to the king or emperor a right of coercion over others
without binding him simultaneously to a higher authority. Thus
the "morality" of the social contract and its laws dissolves into
arbitrariness, moral chaos, and "the highest non-law."[58] A law
that is based upon freedom, and grants to some a higher freedom
than to others, is ultimately going to prove to be no law at all,
but simply the brute force and arbitrary will of those who claim
to possess that higher freedom and authority.

Hamann's attack upon Mendelssohn's theories of natural freedom and social contract is based upon his understanding of the
biblical notion of a covenant between God and all men. Historical
action, when under obligation to such a covenant, cannot be divorced from morality and obedience. That the same standard applies equally to all, for rulers are also covenant-bound, is
clear from a passage in which Hamann illustrates his use of
biblical types to understand and evaluate historical leadership:

> For no Solomon, to whom the God of the Jews gave
> very great wisdom and understanding and a steady heart,
> like the sand, which lies on the shore of the sea; --
> for no Nebuchadnezzar, to whom the God of the Jews has
> given the wild animals to serve Him, in spite of their
> definiteness: but only for a philosopher without sorrow
> and shame, only for a Nimrod in the state of nature
> would it be becoming to proclaim as though he had horns
> on his forehead: "To me and me alone belongs the right
> of decision, whether? and how much? to whom? when? under
> which circumstances? I am bound to benevolence."[59]

The type of a righteous king is Solomon. In 1 Kings 3:1-12,
Solomon is described as one who loved the Lord, who confessed
his ignorance to the Lord and asked only for wisdom, and who
therefore was given wisdom by God. Hamann applies to him also
the praise of the man who fears the Lord in Ps. 112:8-9: "His
heart is steady.... He has distributed freely, he has given to
the poor." In other words, a "Solomon" is one who is wise, steady
and generous in his administration of power and wealth. This is
possible because he accepts and obeys the covenant God has made
with men. Even non-Israelite rulers must accept the sovereignty
of "the God of the Jews." For example, Nebuchadnezzar, the King
of Babylon who led the Jews into captivity, did so as a servant
of God, by whom he had been given authority over many lands and
even the beasts of the field. Thus Hamann echoes the point made
in Jer. 26:5-7: the Lord gives dominion "to whomever it seems
right" to Him.

In contrast to Solomon or Nebuchadnezzar, the type of a king who ignores or rejects God's lordship is Nimrod. To identify Nimrod with "a philosopher without sorrow and shame" is a direct allusion to King Frederick the Great. Frederick was admired by Mendelssohn and other intellectual leaders for his religious toleration and deistic convictions. He shared in and considerably advanced the cause of Enlightenment philosophy, while holding court at his famous palace, "Sans Souci" (thus Hamann's "without sorrow"). He was, in Hamann's view, an arbitrary king who failed to acknowledge the power and law of God.

The biblical type of Nimrod is drawn from Gen. 10:8-10, where it is recorded that Cush, a grandson of Noah, had a son named Nimrod, who was "the first on earth to be a mighty man." Although his might was a matter of being a good hunter, Hamann seems to have in mind that Nimrod was the founder of the city of Babel, where pride eventually led men to build a tower to the heavens in their own honor. Thus Nimrod is a symbol of human power and pride on earth, without regard for God as Creator and Lord. This is the biblical type which Hamann employs to understand the significance of man "in the state of nature."

Nimrod and Frederick are both examples of a particular spirit in Hamann's view, a spirit which he represents with the image of a horned forehead (cf. Dan. 7:19-28). It is a spirit which claims for itself total independence in deciding how to allocate the goods at its disposal. It is a spirit of autonomy, of self-legislation and self-regulation, of rejection of external or positive authorities which might be imposed upon it. The proclamation which such a one makes, declaring the right of decision to be his alone, is quoted by Hamann from the proclamation which Mendelssohn justifies for every holder of rights to property.[60] It is, according to Hamann, the expression of an attitude which turns away from the covenant with God and from the needs of other men.

Indifference to the needs of others is the problem which provides Hamann with an occasion for expounding his views on morality in terms of what I call a second structure of historical meaning: condescension. Like the structure of covenant, belief in the condescension of God to human, worldly conditions exercises a strong, if only implicit, influence over Hamann's critique of

Mendelssohn's moral philosophy. As we saw at the beginning of
this section, Hamann thinks that God "condescends" or accomodates
Himself to man, the world and time, "without thereby being
chained" by them. Only in this way could His creatures have any
perception or knowledge of Him and His will, for in His holiness
He transcends all human comprehension. This notion of the divine
coming down to meet the human on its level seems to be presupposed
by Hamann's reactions to the theory of rights and duties proposed
in the *Jerusalem*.

The first clue that "condescension" might be a key to the
meaning of historical and moral truth for Hamann is his interpretation of Mendelssohn's system of "moral capacity" and "moral
necessity" as an opposition fully as absolute as that between
divinity and humanity:

> Since for the definition of his basic principles
> the theorist needs two classes, the privileged and the
> duty-bound, he instantly creates them for himself, the
> first out of a moral capacity and the second out of a
> moral necessity. Once more a seesaw of philosophical
> indefiniteness! -- The privileged are regarded only in
> relation to the state of nature, but the duty-bound
> are regarded at the same time in relation to the state
> of society.[61]

Mendelssohn nowhere speaks of "two classes." His theory
deals not with classes, but with the relation of rights ("moral
capacity") to duties ("moral necessity"). It is put forth as a
moral axiom in the *Jerusalem* that rights and duties will always
correspond to one another.[62] There can never be two conflicting
rights or duties. For every right, there is a corresponding or
converse duty, and vice versa. For example, one man's right to
command implies and requires another's duty to obey. There can
be no contradiction within the system of rights and duties.

For Hamann, however, it is not so simple. In order to examine and criticize the implications of Mendelssohn's theory, he
takes it to what he understands as its logical conclusion. If
morality is determined in terms of rights and duties, then moral
situations must be judged in terms of those rights and duties.
This means that the question of the *persons* involved will be
irrelevant. With regard to moral judgment, persons are subordinate to the rights and duties they possess. Therefore, despite
his intention of basing moral rights and duties upon the free

decisions of individual persons, Mendelssohn inadvertently de-
personalizes his moral philosophy by putting the relation of
abstract rights to abstract duties at its center.

The result is that he ends up with "two classes" after all.
One class consists of those who possess rights, while the other
is made up of those who are obligated to fulfill their duties.
Hamann's ironic terms for these two classes serve, in effect, to
"re-personalize" them -- those who hold rights he calls "the
privileged" (*die Rechthabende*); those who are obligated he refers
to as "the duty-bound" (*die Pflichtträger*). Although Mendelssohn
intends his theory to apply to persons, its abstract foundation
in the theory of rights and duties results in a rigid opposition
of the "privileged" class to the "duty-bound" class.

According to Hamann's analysis, all of Mendelssohn's efforts
to achieve precision collapse into the "philosophical indefiniteness" of this sterile opposition. As those who possess rights,
the privileged are, in Mendelssohn's own terms, free to dispose
of their rights and property as they like. Thus they can be
understood in terms of "the state of nature" or freedom. In
contrast, the duty-bound are understood only in terms of their
obligation to observe the rights of the privileged. This means
that they are presented in the *Jerusalem* only "in relation to
the state of society." The contrast between them is virtually
absolute: the one class is free, the other is bound to duty.
The one is powerful by virtue of its possessions; the other is
weak, for it "possesses" nothing except its obligation never to
encroach upon the property rights of others.

This opposition extrapolated from Mendelssohn's theory is
similar to the sort of opposition between God and man which is
the result of human sin and which makes God's condescension
necessary. The presupposition of all accommodation theories is
that there is a gulf between the divine realm and the human,
that the relation between them is neither reversible nor reciprocal. Applied to human relations, it indicates a situation
of extreme inequality. Those who "have," so to speak, "play
God" in relation to those who "have not." By casting Mendelssohn's theory in the terms of two classes, and then re-personal-
izing them, Hamann manages to demonstrate how immoral or unjust
the implications of that theory can be, for it endorses a state

of mutual alienation among men, much like the alienation of men
from God.

The centrality of personal condescension in Hamann's thinking
about moral relations is also hinted at by the solution which he
proposes to the dilemma of conflict over goods or things:

> But for every right there is a corresponding duty:
> thus for the moral capacity to use a thing for the pur-
> suit of happiness there is a corresponding incapacity;
> [it is] a need rather than a necessity. Therefore,
> there are in the state of nature no other duties than
> those of omission, no doing but a pure not-doing.
> If I have a right to use a thing for the pursuit
> of happiness, then everyone in the state of nature has
> an identical right, just as a soldier has the right to
> kill the enemy in time of war, and the enemy may kill
> him. Or are the laws of wisdom and goodness as mani-
> fold as my and every other ego? Or does even the
> metaphysical law of royal self-love and self-concern
> belong to the law of nature?[63]

Here the connection between the problem of indifference to
the needs of others and the notion of condescension becomes clear.
Hamann's comment on the correspondence between rights and duties
is so worded as to point to the "corresponding incapacity" of
those who are duty-bound to "use a thing for the pursuit of
happiness." Such persons, when viewed in the terms of Mendelssohn's analysis, are understood only in terms of the "moral
necessity" under which they stand. Hamann's objection to this
entire line of reasoning is summed up in the phrase, "a need
rather than a necessity." The relation that these people have
with the goods in question, which are possessed by others, is
not simply that of their duty to leave such goods alone; it is
also, or even more so, their own *need* for those goods. To see
conflicts of interest over specific goods only in terms of "moral
necessity" is to condone and cultivate, on the grounds of moral
theory, an indifference to the needs of others. It encourages
those who have control over goods and wealth to maintain an
attitude of possessiveness over against those who are poor and
in need. The only way for this impasse to be overcome is for
those who are supposedly "privileged" to condescend to encounter
other persons on the basis not of unassailable rights and irre-
vocable duties but on the basis of need.

Hamann's "Therefore" indicates that he sees a direct connection between his shift from necessity to need and the concept

of a "state of nature." Since that state embraces the "natural" rights of freedom which belong to the privileged, it is clear that he is describing the duties which the privileged have in relation to the needs of others in Mendelssohn's system. Those duties are, quite simply, nil. They are duties only of "omission," of "a pure not-doing," which means a complete failure to respond to the needs of others.

Having suggested that Mendelssohn's theory of rights leads to an immoral justification for doing nothing to alleviate the suffering and needs of others, Hamann now examines the implications of the claim that such rights belong to everyone equally in the "state of nature," even if that state is only an hypothesis. In order for freedom in any state of nature to be real, there must, Hamann assumes, be equality. Thus property rights are "identical" prior to social contracts. This means that in a state of total freedom all persons have the same rights to the same goods. Without a "natural contract" or covenant from God, there is no way of assigning rights to one person as opposed to another. Rights will be determined by might. In a state of nature such as Mendelssohn proposes, there will not be a perfect harmony of corresponding rights and duties. On the contrary, there will be a "state" very much like the state of war. Every man coming into conflict with another man over any goods will have the "right" to kill his opponent, and no moral protest can be uttered against those who do so. The situation is governed not by moral laws of wisdom and goodness but by the "manifold" demands of "every other ego." It is a state of moral anarchy.

In his last question, Hamann indicates that the issue of natural freedom cannot be dealt with apart from the fact of egoism. His reference to "self-love and self-concern" as a "metaphysical law" makes clear that he sees no way for them to be overcome by such moral laws as Mendelssohn proposes. In short, given the sinfulness of "fallen" human nature, it is useless to speculate about the theoretical relation between rights and duties. The problem which man -- as a sinner -- faces is the problem of being indifferent to the real needs of others due to his own egoism, which leads him to set himself up as his own ("royal") king. This egoism cannot succeed in its effort to disguise itself behind the so-called "law of nature." The

only way to overcome it is for those who are "privileged" to
condescend to the needs of those who are not, just as God in His
holiness condescends to meet man in his neediness.

There is a third passage in which Hamann discusses Mendelssohn's moral philosophy in such a way as to indicate that the
concept of condescension is in the background. In this text he
stresses the personal and contextual application which is the
test of every theoretical law:

> But the law of justice is so constructed that,
> by its own testimony, it depends upon conditions and
> upon a relation of the predicate to the subject. To
> be sure, a law loses some of its categorical perfection
> through conditions; and the relation of the predicate
> to the subject seems to be an attribute abstracted from
> the logical truth. Meanwhile, I don't want to stand on
> niceties with the patchwork of philosophical justice,
> since I never can figure out which subject and predi-
> cate in this whole law are really in question. Is it
> that all conditions under which a right occurs are
> given to the privileged? Then the duty-bound man is
> perfectly robbed of his consciousness and conscience
> and of all moral capacity. But a part of imperfect
> rights, namely, the conditions which were not given,
> still depends upon the consciousness and conscience of
> the duty-bound: for, where the privileged are concerned,
> duties and conscience appear to be totally dispensable
> concepts, unknown quantities and *qualitates occultae*.
> Who may condemn his own conscientiousness? Who will
> press him to weigh such a critical decision?[64]

Here Hamann returns to the question of the proper relation
between moral theories and moral subjects or persons. Despite
his effort to construct a law of justice that expresses the
unity of wisdom and goodness without any qualifications or contradictions, Mendelssohn must admit that such abstract purity is
impossible. In his own words, the law of justice "depends upon
conditions and upon a relation of the predicate to the subject."[65]
The meaning of this statement is that "justice" is determined
in many cases by the decision of "the subject," who is the person
holding the right to the goods in question, about how to dispose
of those goods, which are "the predicate." In short, does he
want to keep his goods, sell them, or even give them away? In
all those situations which Mendelssohn designates as "imperfect"
or voluntary, a person can transfer his rights if he personally
wills to do so.

Such "conditions," however, deprive a law of "its categorical perfection." The irony of this comment is twofold. In the
first place, it is obvious that matters involving "imperfect"
rights do not have total "perfection" in Mendelssohn's sense.
That is, a moral issue cannot be both voluntary and compulsory
simultaneously. Here Hamann is parodying the natural law theory
which Mendelssohn recites with such solemnity and yet which
strikes him as either self-evident or trivial. In the second
place, the phrase "categorical perfection" makes fun of Mendelssohn's attitude toward theory. It is clear that he wants to
arrive at a clear and complete statement of the "logical truth."
It is equally clear that he can never do that, for the simple
reason that his abstract theories fail to embrace the concrete
and complex nature of all moral issues. As Hamann puts it, in
the *Jerusalem* the actual "relation of the predicate to the subject seems to be an attribute abstracted from the logical truth."
In other words, Mendelssohn is approaching moral issues backwards,
trying to move from theories to specific instances rather than
from real situations to general implications. With such an approach his theory is bound to lack the "perfection" for which
he is striving.

Hamann expresses impatience and confusion with Mendelssohn's
fundamental distinction between so-called "perfect" and "imperfect" rights and duties. It is, he charges, nothing but a
"patchwork" of "niceties," so constructed as to hide from the
important question of "which subject [person] and predicate
[goods] in this whole law are really in question." It is an
artful dodging of the real issue in the name of "philosophical
justice." For Mendelssohn, the importance of the distinction
derives from the fact that only "perfect" or compulsory duties
may be enforced by the state. "Imperfect" or voluntary duties
are conditional, i.e. relative to the will of the "subject" involved. Thus they are not subject to enforcement.[66] In Hamann's
view, this whole distinction actually performs quite another
function within the context of Mendelssohn's philosophy.

To put the matter in its simplest terms, Hamann discerns
in Mendelssohn's theory of perfect and imperfect rights and
duties the subversion of personal morality. The duty-bound
person, i.e. the person in need of a particular thing, is

deprived of his personal "consciousness and conscience" (*Wissen und Gewissen*). This means that he has lost all "moral capacity" to do his duty! Hamann ironically refers to this loss as having been "perfectly robbed," implying that a "perfect" right for one man corresponds not to a perfect duty for another but to the destruction of the very possibility of the other doing his duty. If "all conditions under which a right occurs are given to the privileged" alone, then the duty-bound man has no part in moral judgments. Therefore, Hamann is saying, it is impossible for him to exercise his duty. The pre-condition for doing one's duty is the capacity to participate in the moral judgment, to understand it in one's consciousness or knowledge, and to accept it subjectively in one's conscience.

Mendelssohn's theory subverts personal morality with regard to "imperfect" as well as "perfect" duties. In remarking that "imperfect rights" are, unlike perfect rights and duties, subject to the "consciousness and conscience of the duty-bound," Hamann is pointing up the contrast between matters of "perfection" and "imperfection." The former involve the protection of existing rights, and all decision-making power is denied to those who are "have-nots." The latter involve the distribution of any unwanted surpluses, and here the "conditions" are dependent not upon the will and consciousness of the privileged, but upon the powers of persuasion or cajolery of the needy. As far as the privileged are concerned, the concepts of duty and conscience can be dispensed with, for nothing in Mendelssohn's theories requires them to share their surpluses or respond in any way to the needs of others. Thus any sort of moral demand which might intrude upon the *status quo* is precluded by Mendelssohn's distinction between perfect and imperfect rights and duties: the privileged have to exercise their own "moral" wills only in the protection of their perfect rights; they are free to ignore all demands upon their imperfect rights or surpluses. Conversely, the duty-bound are free to exercise their "moral" will only with regard to the imperfect rights (surpluses) of others; they may never participate in the distribution of goods which are not already theirs.

Thus once again Hamann's treatment of Mendelssohn's moral philosophy seems to be inspired by the structure of condescension, according to which the righteousness of God can be seen not in

the way He jealously guards His own power and holiness, but in
the way He accommodates Himself to the needs of men. The concept
of condescension provides Hamann with a means for interpreting
the rights and wrongs of moral issues within history. It is a
model drawn from his understanding of the nature of God, a model
which he implicitly holds up for imitation by men. As I shall
show in Chapter V,[67] God's condescension to man is also the basis
on which man's "condescension" to other men becomes possible.

*   *   *

The concept of condescension adds a personal dimension to
the understanding of historical meaning, just as the concept of
covenant adds a moral dimension. Together they illustrate that
Hamann's theology of history provides the individual Christian
with a "biblical" vocabulary for both understanding and partici-
pating in history, if he is willing and able to accept the
authority of the biblical witness as the foundation for all historical meaning. The task of comparing and contrasting this
interpretation of history with that of Hegel will be saved for
the summary and conclusion in Chapter VI. In the next chapter,
I analyze Hegel's article on Hamann, in order to investigate
the reasons for his failure to grasp the conceptual content of
this biblical theology of history.

CHAPTER IV

HEGEL'S CRITIQUE OF HAMANN

In this chapter I present an analysis of Hegel's understanding of Hamann. I begin with a discussion of the extent to which Hamann remains an enigma for Hegel, especially with regard to his theology of history. The "historical" dimension of Hegel's analysis is limited to his effort to relate Hamann to his own times; he discerns no substance or "content" in his writings. I maintain that the reasons for Hegel's failure to understand Hamann are to be found in their differing attitudes toward and use of language. In his effort to comprehend his subject's cryptic style, Hegel resorts to an *ad hominem* method of explanation. He is convinced that Hamann's personality and religious genius are so self-involved that they never achieve self-expression in a language comprehensible to others. Hamann is, in his view, simply unwilling and unable to communicate. In conclusion, I outline what sort of language Hegel expects from Hamann, in order to indicate the perspective from which he is making his criticisms.

It is not known when Hegel was first exposed to Hamann's writings.[1] During his Nüremburg period (1808-1816) he was acquainted with Friedrich Roth, who later edited the earliest collection of Hamann's works. But the first certain evidence that Hegel was reading Hamann is a letter of June 11, 1826, to his old friend and fellow-philosopher, F. I. Niethammer, in which he expresses his appreciation to Roth for the recent publication of his seven-volume edition, *Hamanns Schriften*.[2] In that same letter, Hegel remarked that he was eager to receive the projected eighth volume, which was to include commentaries and indices, so that he could write an article on Hamann for a journal he helped to edit, the *Jahrbücher für wissenschaftliche Kritik*. Roth never did complete that eighth volume (it was added to the edition more than fifteen years later by G. A. Wiener), but fortunately Hegel was undaunted and went ahead with the project anyway. His study of Hamann, which is more than seventy-five pages long, was originally published as two articles in the 1828 series of the *Jahrbücher*.

Hamann as Enigma

To begin an analysis of Hegel's critique with an examination of his grasp of Hamann's theology of history is neither arbitrary nor an imposition of an irrelevant issue on him. Hegel's generation was well aware of the decisive influence Hamann had had on Herder and others who helped to propagate the "Romantic" fascination with history. Indeed, in his enthusiastic response to Hegel's letter announcing the projected essay on Hamann, Niethammer cited Hamann's doctrine of history as the very question he hoped Hegel would answer:

> I find his [Hamann's] standpoint such that a funda-
> mental judgment on it ought to dissolve the popularly
> held misconception of how philosophy and history are
> related to one another. I don't think this task will
> be easy. It would be difficult to deny that, when
> comparing his age with our own, Hamann stands over
> his contemporaries as a visionary. Yet our age -- if
> one is to allow this name of honor to the motley crew
> -- understands him even less than his own did. Evi-
> dently the time has fully come, and with it one who
> can open our eyes. From my heart I bid him welcome.[3]

There is a curious tension in this statement by Niethammer. On the one hand, he is hopeful that a penetrating analysis and "judgment" of Hamann's thought will resolve the question "of how philosophy and history are related to one another." Niethammer believes that Hamann's thought surpasses that of his contemporaries in this area so much that he deserves to be called a "visionary" (*ein Seher*). On the other hand, he does not think that the task of interpreting Hamann will be easy. Despite the fact that Hamann's thought has proven prophetic of the age of Hegel and Niethammer, their generation understands him "even less than his own did." The key to the meaning of history may lie in the depths of Hamann's writings, but so far no one has been able to find that key and make it intelligible for "the motley crew" of "our age." Niethammer expresses confidence that Hegel will prove equal to that task.

Hegel, too, was fully aware of the difficulty of the task he had undertaken. Interpretation of Hamann had been dominated, he felt, by a tendency to quote him in an uncritical fashion. His disciples, such as Herder and Jacobi, popularized his thought as though it had oracular authority; and the primary journal of the German Enlightenment, the *Allgemeine Deutsche Bibliothek*, treated him as fascinating but too esoteric for public consumption. In both cases, an unfortunate "halo" of obscurity was created around the famous "Magus from the North." Hegel's resolve was to dispel that halo, to penetrate through it in order to determine "who Hamann was, what his wisdom and knowledge were."[4]

Despite Goethe's positive evaluation of his success,[5] Hegel does not seem to have achieved a clear understanding of Hamann's "wisdom and knowledge." Even after Niethammer's encouragement, Hegel's article shows little awareness of the concept of history presented in the *Golgotha* or in Hamann's earlier writings. Although he specifically cites the *Golgotha* as "without doubt the most significant thing he wrote,"[6] Hegel does not seem to consider this significance worthy of serious study. His fascination with Hamann yields to impatience, and he finally dismisses even the *Golgotha* as little more than "subjective particularities" and "smug inspirations" which could hardly have been "enjoyable or interesting to his friends, and still less to the public."[7]

Thus it is not Hamann's constructive theology of history which makes him fascinating to Hegel. The source of Hegel's interest and qualified affirmation is to be found in Hamann's unrelenting protest against the abstractions of Wolffian natural law theory. In his introductory remarks on the *Golgotha* as a critique of Mendelssohn's *Jerusalem*, Hegel remarks that "it is wonderful to see how in Hamann the concrete Idea ferments and turns itself against the divisions of reflection."[8] Examples of such divisions, which Hamann rejects and Hegel would prefer to "transform" into higher unities, are the state and church, "perfect" and "imperfect" duties, and actions and sentiments. Hegel's opinion is expressed in his statement that "the penetrating genius of Hamann is to be recognized in the fact that he rightly considered those Wolffian determinations (*Bestimmungen*) as only a pompous display." But this praise is immediately qualified by the comment that "it has no true effect to...reject out of hand (*überhaupt*) these categories; such a process must appear as empty declamation."[9] Hegel understands Hamann to be rejecting all "subordinate categories" as if they had no proper place in philosophical reflection. To over-value those categories is indeed only a "pompous display;" but to ignore them, as Hamann seems to him to do, is "empty declamation."

There are two passages from the *Golgotha* which Hegel quotes and comments upon, and which illustrate the thrust of his interpretaion and criticism. One served as the text for my discussion in Chapter III of the principle of transcendence.[10] I will therefore quote it here in an abbreviated form:

> ...unbelief...is the only sin against the Spirit of the true religion, whose heart is in heaven.... Christian holiness consists not in services, sacrifices, and vows, which God demands of men, but rather in promises, fulfillments and sacrifices, which God has done and achieved for the benefit of men.... Dogmatics and ecclesiastical law...are subject to the arbitrariness of the authorities, an outward discipline that is sometimes coarse and sometimes refined, according to the elements and degrees of the dominant aesthetic. These visible, public, common institutions are neither religion nor wisdom, which come down from above, but earthly, unspiritual and devilish....[11]

The extent to which Hamann's thought remains an enigma for Hegel is clear from the latter's comment on that passage:

> One sees that, for Hamann, Christianity has only such a simple presence that neither morals, the commandment of love as commandment, nor dogmatics, the doctrines and belief in doctrines, nor church are essential dèterminations [*Bestimmungen*] of it; he sees everything relating to them as *human*, *earthly*, so much so that it could even, according to how the circumstances are found, be devilish. Here Hamann was utterly mistaken, for the living reality of the divine Spirit does not hold itself [back] in this concentration, but rather develops itself into a world and a creation. And it does this only by bringing forth distinctions, whose limitations must certainly be recognized, but no less the right and necessity of their life as finite spirit.[12]

For Hegel, Hamann's statement amounts to a denial of truth to the doctrines, determinations and institutions of this created world. He reasons that such a denial of truth to all things human and earthly must ultimately be a denial of all distinctions among the many ways in which God is present in the world. Hegel admits that distinctions within the world imply limitations, but the limited nature of finite existence does not destroy its right to exist. In Hegel's view, Hamann denies precisely that right. He will not accept any distinctions or determinations with regard to the truth of God. He conceives of God as so transcendent that Christianity can be nothing more than an awareness of Him as "a simple presence." The Spirit, as Hegel interprets Hamann, remains withdrawn in a state of simple "concentration."

According to my interpretation in Chapter III, however, this passage is a statement by Hamann of the transcendence which God maintains even as He acts in the world for the benefit of mankind. The issue for Hamann is not whether there are distinctions of importance within the historical world; it is how those distinctions are to be perceived and interpreted. Hegel's secular approach to historical meaning leads him to identify God's being with all human history, and therefore to understand only distinctions within the limits of human existence. Hamann, with his belief in a God who transcends history and yet condescends to enter into it in ways which are very specific and can be "determined" by use of a hermeneutical method based upon the Bible, sees a more important and fundamental distinction to be made between human and divine agency. God's presence in history is not, in his view, merely "simple"; but neither is it merely human. The complexity of God's presence in history is expressed for Hamann by the principles and structures which I have tried to explicate in Chapter III.

The other passage from the *Golgotha* which Hegel quotes and comments upon is also one which I have discussed, and which illustrates both a principle and a structure of Hamann's understanding of history. It is the text dealing with Solomon, Nebuchadnezzar and Nimrod as types of different attitudes which historical leaders might have toward the covenant which God has given to man.[13] Hegel's opening comment on this passage is curious, given his earlier statement about the "significance" of the *Golgotha*:

> Still another of the same mystifications can be quoted from the *Golgotha und Scheblimini*, a writing whose content would well have earned a reputation as pure farce.[14]

In his interpretation of this passage, Hegel shows that he again fails to understand Hamann's position. He has no difficulty appreciating Hamann's theology of opposition between the "universal" will of God and the "particular" wills of individual men, and the need for submission by men to God's covenant. What Hegel fails to grasp is that this concept of covenant provides Hamann with a way of thinking about the meaning of his own historical period. Hamann calls on Frederick the Great to submit to God's covenant, like Solomon and Nebuchadnezzar, instead of

boasting like Nimrod. Hegel understands this call as Hamann's
refusal to submit himself to Frederick in the way that he claims
to be submitted to God. His "oppressed" position as an underpaid
civil servant made him incapable, in Hegel's view, of thinking
through the political implications of his theological insight.
Thus the entire passage degenerates into a "farce" or meaningless
harangue against the monarchial principle as exemplified by
Solomon, Nebuchadnezzar and Nimrod.[15]

Given Hegel's identification of God with the historical
process, and his conviction that reason works through "world-
historical individuals" who are men of political power rather
than deep faith or morality, it is fair to conclude that King
Frederick represents for Hegel in a very real way the purposes
of reason and therefore also the presence of God in the historical moment in which he lived and ruled. In contrast, Hamann is
a man of inwardness, concentration, and powerlessness. If political power really is the criterion of God's presence in history,
then Hamann's insubordination to Frederick can be interpreted,
as it is by Hegel, as a sign of his religious hypocrisy and insubordination to God. His theological ramblings can then be
dismissed as nothing more than "the perception of a German subordinate in the tax office" run by Frenchmen, and the expression
of his "abstract hatred for the Enlightenment."[16] In short,
Hamann's efforts to interpret history theologically are understood by Hegel as nothing more than expressions of his personal
inability to come to terms with history.

Hegel does recognize that such a withdrawn attitude is a
form of "subjective freedom" over against the turmoil of world
history. As he remarks in his lectures on the philosophy of
history:

> The religiosity and ethicality of a restricted sphere
> of life (for example, that of a shepherd or peasant),
> in their concentrated inwardness and limitation to a
> few simple situations of life, have infinite worth;
> they are just as valuable as those which accompany a
> high degree of knowledge and a life with a wide range
> of relationships and actions. This inner centre, this
> simple source of the rights of subjective freedom...
> remains untouched and [protected] from the noisy clamour
> of world history, and not only from external and tem-
> porary changes, but also from those produced by the
> absolute necessity of the concept of freedom itself.[17]

The "limited" concerns of personal faith and morality are exemplified, for Hegel, by the lives of shepherds and peasants. He does
not deny that their "concentrated inwardness" is just as worthwhile as the broad knowledge of those who have a "wide range of
relationships" and are capable of greater diversity in their
behavior. He is simply convinced that the two cannot go together:
freedom which is based upon the "inner centre" is merely subjective; it can neither be influenced nor jeopardized by the "noisy
clamour" of those who are advancing the cause of objective freedom in world history. The person who understands his freedom
in the subjective terms of religion and morality is, in Hegel's
view, sealed off from both the world's transitory changes and
from its real progress in his own time toward greater objective
freedom.

In his concern with faith and morality and his extraordinary
subjective freedom, Hamann seems to Hegel to be such a person.
But in his "wide range of relationships" and profound influence
upon such notable thinkers as Herder and Jacobi, he is anything
but "a shepherd or peasant." The challenge Hegel faces in his
article on Hamann is that of reconciling this apparent contradiction. How is it that Hamann could possess such extreme subjective freedom and yet also participate in the historical movement of thinking spirit in his time?

Hegel's answer to this question constitutes the historical
analysis which, in marked contrast with his failure to grasp
Hamann's own understanding of history, provides the article with
its "Hegelian" flavor and brilliance. He describes the latter
half of the eighteenth century, when he and Goethe were mere
students but Hamann and Kant were venerable sages, as a turning-
point:

> a time in which the *thinking* spirit in Germany, which
> had at first been independent only within the schools
> of philosophy, began rather to launch into reality,
> and to lay a claim to whatever therein was firmly and
> truly valid, and [thus] to vindicate the whole field
> of reality.[18]

In other words, the task of reason's progress toward freedom in
Hamann's time was to assert the autonomy it had already achieved
in philosophical matters in all of reality. To do this was to
declare itself to be the rightful judge of what was "firmly and

truly valid" in reality. It also involved "vindicating" reality,
which, as we have seen, means for Hegel the demonstration of the
axiom that the real (historical) world is as it ought to be.[19]

The move "into reality" from "the schools of philosophy"
refers to the contrast between the formalism of Wolffian Ration-
alism and the attention to such concrete, historical realities
as the church, the state, and matters of law which characterizes
the thinking of Hegel and his contemporaries. Hegel observes
that this discussion had originated among the upper classes in
France, where it had been opposed by the middle classes. In
Germany, however, this "Enlightenment" of the real world by
independent thought was adopted by the middle classes, who became its "most active and effective collaborators."[20] Furthermore, in Germany the middle-class Enlightenment soon divided
into two opposing groups which challenged and tested each other,
while in France there developed such a monopoly on the intellectual and spiritual energy that "thinking spirit" came to appear like common sense. Although Hegel does not say so, he seems
to imply that this division and tension in Germany was a source
of valuable creative energy.

The two groups into which Hegel sees German Enlightenment
thinkers falling are presented by him in geographical terms.
Berlin was the center of the movement, and represents the dry,
utilitarian, shallow "understanding" side of the Enlightenment.
Its leaders were such thinkers as Nicolai, Mendelssohn, and the
general forum of the *Allgemeine Deutsche Bibliothek*. On the
"periphery" of Berlin, scattered throughout Germany, was the
side of genius, passion, talent and profound "reason." Its
representatives were thinkers and writers such as Kant, Herder,
Goethe, Schiller, Fichte, Schelling, Jacobi, and even, despite
his residence in Berlin, Lessing, who remained indifferent to
the "impulse" of that city.[21]

It is among these "peripheral" thinkers that Hegel places
Hamann. Whereas the participants in the Berlin Enlightenment
were devoted to monotonous efforts to understand the realm of
finite phenomena, Hamann and those elsewhere in Germany were
striving for a great variety of poetic and philosophical expression of their consciousness of the infinite. In contrast with
the intellectual greyness of Berlin, they seemed like "a wreath

of original individualities," among whom Hamann seemed by far
the most original of all -- for "he persisted in a concentration
of his deep particularity, which showed itself to be incapable
of all forms of universality."[22] In short, whereas Berlin illustrates for Hegel the understanding's one-sided pursuit of universality, Hamann's alleged rejection of all concern with universality in favor of concentrated particularity exemplifies
the opposite extreme.

Another way to state the same contrast is to draw a distinction between the concern for "objectivity" of the Berlin
thinkers and the intense subjectivity of Hamann. It is in this
subjectivity that Hegel sees Hamann's power and freedom as a
Christian thinker:

> Hamann stands over against the Berlin Enlightenment
> first and foremost through the profundity of his
> Christian orthodoxy, but in such a way that his man-
> ner of thought is not the rigidity of the petrified
> orthodox theology of his time; his spirit retains the
> highest freedom, in which nothing remains merely posi-
> tive, but rather is subjectivized into the spiritual
> present and its own possession.[23]

By virtue of his Christian faith, Hamann achieves a depth which
was inaccessible to the thinkers of the "Understanding" in Berlin. His is not an orthodoxy of doctrinal rigidity. It is,
says Hegel, a deep, subjective faith which holds itself free
from all bondage to the "positive" or authoritarian side of religion, for it accepts only what it can appropriate as its "own
possession" in "the spiritual present."

Thus Hegel's first avenue of approach to the enigma of
Hamann is an historical method of analysis. He sees his subject
as an extreme example of the concern with the subjective side
of reason which was prevalent among the creative geniuses of
his generation in Germany. In order to try to explain the unique-
ness of Hamann's "originality," even in contrast with others who
were far from the spirit of Berlin, Hegel turns to Hamann's own
reflections on his childhood and the development of his personality. His remarks on these matters reveal a great deal about
Hegel's opinion of two of Hamann's salient characteristics:
religious piety and creative genius.

Hamann as a Religious Genius

The *ad hominem* character of Hegel's critique of Hamann is actually not as personal as it at first appears. The structure of his article is *ad hominem* analysis, in the sense that Hegel begins with a lengthy discussion of Hamann's early autobiographical (and never published in his lifetime) *Thoughts on the Course of My Life*, ends with a description of Hamann's last year -- a year not of writing but of visiting Jacobi and other friends in Münster -- and interprets all his writings within the framework of personal factors established by these two discussions. But Hegel's rationale for this procedure is not simply a hostile attitude toward Hamann, or a prejudice against him as an individual. As we have seen in his lectures on the philosophy of history, Hegel is convinced that religious piety is in itself a matter of individual withdrawal from engagement with universal thought and political realities into personal life. This systematic basis for his *ad hominem* treatment of Hamann's thought is illustrated and developed in Hegel's remarks on the biographical background of Hamann's "religious genius."

Although the word "concentration" has appeared several times in Hegel's comments on Hamann, it should not be understood in the sense of an ability to "concentrate" upon something. Indeed, the personality characteristic which Hegel sees as predominant from Hamann's youth on is his inability to focus or discipline himself in any area of his life. This lack of discipline began in his home in Königsberg, where Hamann was born on August 27, 1730, the elder of two sons of the town barber. His life at home was secure in a material sense, for a town barber in that period was also the town surgeon and manager of the town bath -- in short, a respected member of the professional class. But Hamann's intellectual training lacked focus. As he grew up, his home was one of both piety and openness to a great variety of students, which led him to indulge his whimsical nature rather than learn to study diligently. Hamann complains that his schooling was inadequate in history, geography, and writing, but Hegel insists that the responsibility be at least shared by the "characteristic temperament [*Temperatur*] and mood of his spirit."[24]

The crucial ability which Hamann never, in Hegel's view, developed was the capacity to organize and examine his own thoughts. Hamann himself complains about his tendency to "dabble" here and there as a student. First he delved into the study of heresies, then poetry and French literature, finally law. None of these pursuits went very far, Hamann later lamented, because his motive in them was "to please the imagination" rather than to acquire an understanding of the subject matter. Hegel thinks that Hamann's brief and unsuccessful university career was characterized by "arrogance," for he tried to justify his lack of discipline on the grounds that "it was better to be a martyr than a day-laborer and hireling of the Muses." Only years later did Hamann admit, while discussing his earlier attitudes, "how much nonsense is expressed in round and sonorous words!"[25] In short, Hegel thinks that Hamann added to his lack of intellectual focus by his predilection for allusive or even poetic language, in hopes thereby of veiling the lack of substance in his thoughts.

In Hegel's view, Hamann's career as a translator in a government tax office failed to help him learn self-discipline. Because his responsibilities were minimal, he was free to read a great part of every day. He used this time, however, to wander through books of the greatest variety. His study had neither rhyme nor reason. His memory of what he read was, in his own words, short-lived:

> For a long time I have enjoyed a writer only so long as I have his book in my hand. As soon as I put it down, everything flows together in my soul, as if my memory were blotting-paper.[26]

As with his reading, observes Hegel, so with Hamann's remarkable capacity for friendship: it consisted of variety without discipline or purpose. He maintained relationships with a wide circle of friends, most of whom were so different from him that he must have felt alienated from them with regard to important matters and convictions. The only explanation Hegel can find for this bizarre pattern of behavior is that Hamann was bored with his work and therefore read books and sought out friends not out of genuine interest in them but to escape the boredom of his own life.[27]

Hamann was not always so diffuse in his approach to others;
it is in the collapse of his deep friendship with a fellow student, Johann Christoph Berens, that Hegel discerns the "development" of his "whole individuality as well as his style and manner
of description."[28] Whereas most commentators identify the decisive change in Hamann's life as his conversion experience in
the spring of 1758, Hegel takes it to be the failure of Hamann
to integrate that experience into the relationships which had
previously constituted his life and work. The importance Hegel
attaches to Hamann's conflict with Berens, and his relative lack
of interest in or respect for Hamann's own account of his conversion, are a concrete example of his feeling that Hamann's piety
was, at this point in his life, mere "pretention."[29]

Berens came from a family in Riga which was prominent in
what one scholar has designated as the "rising Enlightenment
business interests."[30] After Hamann had left the university and
was engaged as a private tutor in the northern Baltic states,
Berens convinced him to move to Riga and work for his family,
not so much as a businessman but as a cultured representative
in various situations. The assignment given to Hamann was to
contact the Russian ambassador in London on behalf of the Berens
family. Although the details of the project remain a mystery,
it is clear that rapidly changing political circumstances made
it impossible for Hamann to complete his mission. Nevertheless,
once in London he stayed there, falling deeper and deeper into
a state of lonely depression and moral as well as material desti-
tution. Then, in March of 1758, Hamann had an experience of
repentance and conversion to what he describes as faith in Jesus
Christ as his personal Lord, Savior and "friend." This is not
the place to go into the fascinating psychological and theological questions which Hamann's "conversion" raises.[31] What
interests Hegel is not so much the conversion itself but the
way in which Hamann related to his former friends when he returned to Germany later that year.

Initially Hamann resumed his place in Riga with the Berens
family. By the end of 1758, he was engaged to marry Berens'
sister. In January, 1759, however, Berens cancelled the engagement and Hamann returned to his father's home in Königsberg.
From his analysis of the correspondence which followed between

Hamann and Berens, often *via* their mutual friends, J. G. Lindner and Kant, Hegel concludes that the break occurred because Hamann's new faith was repugnant to Berens. Hamann had shown his London diary to his friend, who found that record of pious self-recriminations disgusting. In Berens' view, says Hegel, Hamann had simply exploited the Bible in order to justify his return to Riga and thus avoid starvation.[32]

To some extent, Hegel seems to share that opinion. He accuses Hamann at this time of invoking "divine grace" to "isolate" himself from his friends.[33] His comments on the lack of focus in Hamann's life echo Berens' frustration over Hamann's refusal to find employment, despite his substantial debt to his friend and employer. Hamann maintained that the proper work of a Christian is prayer and reading the Bible; when pressed as to what he *did* with his time, he answered that he "lutherized"![34] He refused to be forced into a position of responsibility either personally or professionally. When Berens expressed concern over the debt, Hamann willed to him his corpse as security!

The theme which emerges here is similar to the Pauline distinction between living under the law and living under the freedom of grace. Hamann understood his personal life in just these theological terms, and Hegel mentions that he came to accept his rejection by Berens on the model of the sufferings of Christ. To Hamann, his own rejection was a rejection of Christ also. He came to see himself during this period as a prophet to the "hypocrites," and was disappointed when Berens, and Kant, whose help in the struggle to win Hamann back to normality Berens had enlisted, failed to accept that description of their spiritual role in the drama.[35] The appeal to grace constitutes in Hegel's view little more than a refusal to commit himself to anything definite. Hamann had succeeded in "absolving himself inwardly" from his sins, but he failed to arrive at anything more than "the pantheism of false religiosity, that everything is God's will."[36]

Hegel has great difficulty understanding how Hamann could carry on so faithfully his life-long friendships with Kant, Lindner, Herder and Mendelssohn, even while disagreeing violently with everything they wrote. Hamann's belief that friendship is "a gift from God" which has "nothing to do with doctrines, lessons, turning around and conversion" is, in Hegel's view, tantamount to saying that friendship is based entirely upon "accident and subjective inclination." He applauds the fact that Hamann stopped trying to convert his friends, but he continues to be bewildered by a man who could write a scathing review of a good friend's book and then not publish it for fear of hurting that friend's feelings.[37]

In Hegel's judgment on Hamann's piety, the origins of his interpretation and criticism of Hamann's theology of history are visible:

> Hamann's religious turning had taken on the shape of
> an abstract inwardness, whose hardnecked simplicity
> did not recognize objective determinations, duties
> and theoretical or practical principles as absolutely
> [schlechthin] essential, and did not even have an
> ultimate interest in them.[38]

Just as Hegel understands Hamann to be denying any meaningful distinctions within history, so he also thinks that he has no interest in the "objective determinations" which normally constitute the basis for friendship. Hamann refuses to accept the duties and principles by which men normally govern their social relations, not because he is advocating an alternative set of values, but because he has no interest in such "objective" or "essential" determinations at all. His understanding of others is only a "hardnecked simplicity," much as his view of history appears to Hegel to be only a sense of a "simple presence." Although the potential for such an unfortunate development is discerned by Hegel in Hamann's character as a youth, it is his "religious turning" which is at the heart of this "abstract inwardness." In Hamann, Hegel sees a man who has turned away from the challenge of objective relationships to find peace and solace in the indifference of his own, isolated, inner life.

The marvel is that Hamann retains any interest at all for Hegel and his contemporaries. Eighteenth-century Germany was not lacking in Pietists who turned away from the world to dwell upon the state of their own souls. Why did Hamann hold such a fascination for the secular thinkers who followed him? This question is, of course, the question about Hamann's "wisdom and knowledge" which had initially impelled Hegel to begin the study. He clearly sees in Hamann much more than just another Pietist, and yet he seems to find it difficult to sort out and identify the crucial elements in his personality and his work.

The difference which Hegel sees between Hamann and such Pietistic groups as the "Stillen im Lande" in Frankfurt, where Pietists could share and encourage one another in what Hegel sarcastically refers to as their "self-complacent sinfulness," is to be found in "the principle of worldly righteousness." Rather than turn away from the world to the pseudo-transcendence of private religiosity, Hamann managed to retain his worldliness. He even rejected the efforts of the "Stillen im Lande" to claim him as one of their own. When they gave him the honorific title of "Magus of the North," he responded by putting a picture of a horned Pan on the title page of his next publication. Thus he kept his distance from the other-worldliness of Pietist circles, not only groups in far-off Frankfurt but also in his native Königsberg.[39]

One reason for Hamann's rejection of other-worldliness is, according to Hegel, the "root of friendship" and natural "vivacity" which were characteristic of his spirit.[40] Hamann himself speaks of his "sickness of passion" which endangers all those who are healthy and are exposed to him (this ironic reference is to Kant). Hegel sees in Hamann's capacity for passion in friendship and all of life an anchor in the world -- although he does not express agreement with Hamann's claim that this same passion gives him "a strength in thinking and feeling which a healthy man does not possess."[41]

A second reason given by Hegel for Hamann's "worldly righteousness" is, surprisingly, the "strong positive element" of his religious conversion. Hegel attributes Hamann's growth beyond mere self-righteousness and arrogance to his intensely personal appropriation of the teachings of Christianity. This is the "highest freedom" which, as we saw above, Hegel credits to Hamann. It is the ability to subjectivize everything "positive," by which Hegel means the revelation which Christianity teaches as given by God to man rather than in any way created through or with the human spirit. Although Hegel is often thought of as disapproving of any form of authority or "positivity" in religion, he shows here an appreciation for different forms of piety, ranging from the "quiet, unprejudiced piety of a righteous

Christian" to the "narrow-minded, pietistic, mawkish or fanatical piety" of such groups as the "Stillen im Lande."[42] Although he does not think that Hamann attained to the former, Hegel praises him for avoiding the latter. He resisted the temptation to let his submission to "positive" faith remain a merely objective or "external" thing for him, an externality which Hegel sees exemplified in the Host of Roman Catholicism, the literal word-faith of Protestant Orthodoxy, and the belief of many traditional Christians in an historical datum of memory. Contrasting Hamann with these approaches to faith, Hegel praises him for his free and original appropriation of faith for his own purposes:

> the positive is for him only a starting-point and [something] essential for shaping, expressing and symbolizing [his meaning] for an animated application. Hamann knows that this animating principle is essentially his own individual spirit, and that the Enlighteners, who were not ashamed to boast of the authority of the letter, which they only *explained*, played a false game, in that the *meaning* which exegesis gives is at the same time comprehended, subjective meaning....
> Thus Hamann's Christianity is an energy of living individual presence; in the determination of the positive element he remains the most free, independent spirit, and therefore at least formally open to the most remote and heterogeneous appearances, as the examples of his reading have shown.[43]

This passage provides a key to Hegel's interpretation of Hamann's faith. In the comparison of their theologies of history, we have found a major difference in their attitudes toward the "otherness" of biblical authority, the transcendence of God, and the particularity of God's immanent dealings with His people. For Hegel, all of these elements can be included under the rubric of "the positive element." When that element is carried too far, the result is otherworldly Pietism. In Hamann's case, however, the positive element did not serve to alienate him from himself; instead, he exploited it for himself.

It would be easy to read into Hegel's statement more than is actually there with regard to positivity. He is not saying that Hamann considered the "animating principle" of the positive element in his thought to be *only* his own individual spirit. Rather, that principle is "essentially his own individual spirit," in the sense that he understood that nothing could be believed

unless it was first "comprehended" (by reason) as having "subjective meaning." It was this subjective side of truth which
was overlooked by the leaders of the Berlin Enlightenment. They
"played a false game" of merely literal explanation; Hamann,
however, knew he had to appropriate the texts subjectively in
his spirit.

Thus the positive element was for him "only a starting-point"
and means of giving form and symbolic expression to his meaning.
According to Hegel, Hamann would not allow that positive element
to be tied down to any external thing, whether the Host or a
literal word or an historical datum. He remained utterly individual and free in his spirit in his pursuit of the various
shapes and symbols of his Christianity. He "determined" the
positive element as he wished, and therefore was able to remain
"at least formally open" to the great variety of ideas, books
and persons with which he had contact. The freedom of his piety
with regard to the positivity of Christianity allowed him to follow his friendships and worldly passion wherever they might lead.

A third reason for Hamann's "worldly righteousness" is perhaps most responsible for his great fascination to Hegel and
subsequent generations: his genius. This genius is, as Hegel
portrays it, the natural product of Hamann's passionate and free
form of faith. His "piety" is said to carry "in itself the worldly element of an eminent creative genius."[44] This genius is the
ability to take the "positive" starting-point and transform it
into his own application by means of symbolic expression. In
the passage quoted below, Hamann speaks of his love for symbols
and of his passion for the simple joys of eating and drinking
with his friends. Creative involvement with symbols is not an
external expression of Hamann's faith. It is, in his own words,
the core of his faith. For Hegel, this statement by Hamann expresses the deepest truth of his piety:

> "All my Christianity is a taste for *signs* and for
> the elements of water, bread and wine. Here is a
> wealth of hunger and thirst...the *teleion* [goal]
> lies beyond." What Hamann calls his taste for signs
> is that all of his own inner and outer states, such
> as history and dogma, which are *objectively* present
> to him, are valid only insofar as they are appre-
> hended by the spirit, are made spiritual; so that
> this divine meaning is not simply thoughts or pic-
> tures of an ecstatic fantasy, but is alone the truth

of the matter [*das Wahre*], and thus does have actual
reality.[45]

By his own testimony, Hamann remains an apostle of the "beyond" which all the elements of his faith only symbolize. According to Hegel, however, his spiritual depth leads him to appropriate that "beyond" as objectively present to him and true only insofar as it becomes "actual reality." Thus he is the most subjective of those explorers of reason who lived on the periphery of Berlin. He alone goes to the extreme of denying all pursuit of universality. But because of his extraordinary creative genius, his subjective spirituality results not only in private prayers but also in a wealth of symbolic works. Because Hamann struggles to give his insights symbolic expression, Hegel believes that he transcends the limitations of Pietism and establishes himself as a religious genius.

The Language of Religious Genius

Hegel's comments on Hamann's literary style are among the best known in his essay. They are also the statements which reveal most clearly the way in which Hegel's own philosophy impeded his ability to grasp the meaning and purpose of Hamann's writings.

Although Hegel affirms Hamann's thought as essentially "spiritual," he also criticizes it for carrying "subjective freedom" too far. Indeed, in his discussion of Hamann's "dialectic," Hegel describes the "principle" of his subject as "the religious," which, in Hegel's view, "claims its superiority over the so-called worldly duties." By asserting the "superiority of its accidental personality," the "religious" dialectic soon degenerates into sophistry.[46] In other words, the religious principle is so self-oriented that it eventually loses touch entirely with the reality of other selves.

As a "religious genius," Hamann could be expected, in Hegel's schema, to have a style that would reflect this sense of the "superiority of its accidental personality" over the objective requirements of social communication. As Hegel puts it in one of the article's most famous passages:

> The French have a saying: *Le stile c'est l'homme même*
> [the style is the man himself]; Hamann's writings do not
> so much *have* a characteristic style as they *are* style

through and through. In everything that came from Hamann's pen his personality is so very obtrusive and
domineering that the reader's attention is everywhere
drawn more to it than to whatever might be conceived
as the content. In those productions which are presented as writings and should treat a subject matter,
the incomprehensible eccentricity of the author is
immediately conspicuous. They are really a fairly
tiresome enigma, and one sees that their final word
is the individuality of their author.[47]

Just as the "religious dialectic" is dominated by the particular
and accidental personality of the individual, so is the corresponding religious style. Hamann's writings purport to deal with
various subjects, but their content is always immediately obscured by Hamann's eccentric personality. Since "style" refers
to the individual aspects of an author's use of language and
treatment of subjects, Hegel can quip that Hamann's works do
not *have* a style -- "they *are* style"! All concern with subject
matter in them is overwhelmed by the constant interference of
irrelevant and particular references, allusions and images. Thus
these writings are a reflection of Hamann's subjective states
rather than treatises which actually deal with real subjects in
a substantial way.

Hegel sees in Hamann's earliest published piece, the *Socratic
Memorabilia* (1759), such a purely "personal" piece, one which has
only "the appearance of an objective content." Written and published shortly after the collapse of his friendship with Berens,
the book portrays Socrates, a hero of the Enlightenment, as representing the proper attitude of philosophy toward faith. In
Hegel's opinion, Hamann does not offer an insightful portrait
of Socrates, but does succeed in using Socrates to express his
own complaints to and about Berens and Kant. Thus "Socrates"
is a self-portrait by Hamann, and the book, which pretends to
discuss the relation of philosophy to faith, is a continuation
of the letters that Hamann had previously been sending to his
friends. Under the guise of discussing such noble matters as
religious truth, Hamann smuggles in his own personal concerns,
thereby trying to claim "the right and the power" of religious
truth for the "particular and accidental nature" of his subjective faith and experience.[48]

In the end, Hegel accuses Hamann of bad faith as a writer.
It is not simply that his works are too particular and stilted

to be of interest to others, although that is a serious charge against them.[49] The major problem is that Hamann does not genuinely want to communicate with his readers. He seems to Hegel to be hostile, for he arouses the hope of profound meaning and then offers only "trivial particularities." "He baroques...he means to mystify." His allusions are so obscure that often he himself cannot recall later what he meant by them![50] Hegel points out that Goethe was excited by Hamann as a young man, but soon saw that he displays only genius without taste, and that the ambiguities of his style would never reward the labors required to decipher their meaning. Hegel also concurs with Mendelssohn's judgment that Hamann could have become one of Germany's best writers, but, "seduced by the desire to be original, became one of the most reprehensible."[51]

The clearest evidence of Hamann's hostility toward his audience, in Hegel's estimation, is his use of humor. Although a good friend of the great Königsberg humorist, Hippel, Hamann's own humor never went beyond "lightning, desultory expression... without richness and variety of sentiment, and without any impulse or effort toward form."[52] It was just one more manifestation of his inability to deal with objective subject matter. Whenever he encountered a conceptual difficulty, Hamann would turn to humor, and "unfortunately to a humor with a too contrary spirit. His humor is consistent with his subjective nature, and leaps about too much in self-complacency, turning into subjective particularities and trivial contents."[53]

The purpose of all this obscurity, particularity and ambiguity by Hamann is, according to Hegel, nothing less than self-concealment. Although communication is for mutual self-revelation, Hamann talked and wrote in a way that was calculated to maintain his mysteriousness for his audience. Even in the final year of his life, when he was among a circle of close friends and disciples whom he could trust (in Münster, 1787-88), Hamann was unable, Hegel reports, to stop withholding "the naked, concentrated intensity of his mind and faith" from full and open communication. He could share with his admirers only his unclarity, for "his whole position is unclarity itself."[54]

Yet Hamann did have his admirers; and many of them, such as Jacobi and Herder, were thinkers and writers of considerable merit. In his effort to come to terms with this fact, Hegel

shows that the problem of "spiritual form" or language was really
at the heart of Hamann's failure to communicate to his peers:

> Hamann was for many not only an interesting and
> intervening phenomenon, but a handle and fulcrum
> at a time when they needed one against despair
> over the times. We who come later must marvel at
> him as an Original for his time, but we can lament
> that he did not find already worked out in it a
> spiritual form with which his genius could have
> fused, and produced truthful figures [*Gestalten*]
> for the joy and satisfaction of his contemporaries
> and posterity; or that fate did not preserve the
> serene and well-intended meaning by moving him to
> work it out himself in such objective figures.[55]

Recalling Hegel's conviction that "truth" in any age is to
be found in the manifestation of spirit in that time, his comment
here that Hamann served as a refuge for those who were in despair
over their times can be understood as a highly ambivalent remark.
Hegel acknowledges Hamann's value and importance for others, but
not that his thought had objective truth or value. He was "an
Original," in the sense that his ideas cannot be traced to the
world in which he lived. As we have seen, Hegel considers the
source of his originality to be his extraordinary personality,
and its result to be unclarity.

The reason which Hegel suggests for Hamann's failure to
present his ideas in a coherent manner is that he failed to find
or to work out for himself a "spiritual form" (*geistige Form*)
which could express his genius. Such a form is necessary if a
writer is to produce words, symbols, allusions and figures of
speech which have meaning and are thus truthful and satisfying
to his contemporaries and posterity. Hegel's word, *Gestalten*,
refers here to the entire range of means of expression. With
regard to a writer, it can also be called "language." Hegel's
lament over Hamann is that he fails to find or develop a language which could give "objective" expression to his thoughts.

The question of objective language is crucial to understanding Hegel's interpretation of Hamann. All of his accusations of
excessive subjectivity and extreme singularity refer to Hamann's
actual achievements as a writer, to his style and language rather
than to his awareness of truth. Hegel admires Hamann as a Christian who realizes that the only basis for genuine reconciliation
between God and man is the objectively trinitarian nature of God.

No matter how intensely he may have subjectivized this and every
other truth he accepted, he never denied the objective side of
their truth. Thus there was a tension within him between the
subjective and objective aspects of truth, and it was this tension that he failed to develop and express in thought and language: "his faith had to endure the contrast in itself, to the
point of becoming utterly concentrated, formless vitality."[56]

The charge that Hamann's religious genius remained a "formless vitality" of internal tensions, failing to express itself
in language, raises the question of how Hegel understood Hamann's
many statements on the subject of language. This question is
all the more important in view of the fact that Hamann believes
that his entire criticism of transcendental philosophy is in
terms of "the sacrament of language," as he puts it in his "Metacritique of the Purism of Reason" (1784),[57] a short, satirical
response to Kant's *Critique of Pure Reason* (1781). At the beginning of his discussion of the "Metacritique," Hegel both
acknowledges and "distances himself"[58] from this approach:
"Hamann places himself in the middle of the problem of reason
and states its solution; but he grasps this in the form of language."[59] Hegel's "but" indicates that he does not agree that
the problem of reason is to be resolved by attention to the
question of language. Furthermore, his different conception of
the role of language in religious consciousness is, as I will
try to show, the source of his misunderstanding of many aspects
of Hamann's thought.

Hegel's method of analysis of the "Metacritique" is that
of copious direct and indirect quotation with very little expli-
cation. He cites Hamann's opening observation about the "puri-
fications" (*Reinigungen*) through which modern philosophy has put
itself. First it purified itself of any dependence upon tradition or faith; then it freed itself from the influences of experience and inferences from experience. Now, suggests Hamann
ironically, the time has come for "the third, highest, and as
it were empirical purism" of philosophical reason -- namely from
dependence upon language! Hegel includes Hamann's immediate
warning, however, to the effect that language is "the only, first
and last instrument and criterion of reason," and he notes Hamann's emphasis upon the ambiguity of language. Without comment,

he quotes several passages from the "Metacritique" about language as the basis for the capacity to think and, at the same time, "the middle point of reason's misunderstanding of itself."[60]

This is not the place for an analysis of Hamann's critique of Kant. What is relevant to this study is Hegel's systematic misunderstanding of Hamann's language, to the point where he could conclude that Hamann had no "spiritual form" or language at all. In order to understand the issue between them, it is necessary to identify first the area of Hegel's misunderstanding and then the basis for that misunderstanding. Why did Hamann's language about history and about language itself appear to Hegel to be no language at all?

A clue to the answer to this question can be found in Hegel's discussion of Hamann's image of a "tree of Diana." Hamann borrows the image of a tree metaschematically from Kant, who suggests that sensibility and understanding constitute "two stems of human knowledge...which perhaps spring from a common, but to us unknown, root."[61] To Hamann, this distinction by Kant of sense knowledge from intellectual knowledge is a "separation of that which nature has brought together." By thus alluding to the teaching of Jesus on divorce (Mt. 19:6), Hamann suggests that knowledge is only one "tree," even though it may indeed have two "roots"; and that to divide those two roots is, like divorce, a sin against God. Hegel's comment on Hamann's next remark shows the way in which he fails to grasp the meaning of this highly allusive language:

> Perhaps, continues Hamann, there is "still a chemical tree of Diana, not only for the knowledge of sensibility and understanding, but also for the reciprocal explanation and extension of their areas and their limits." In fact, it can have to do with a *developed* knowledge, what Hamann calls the tree of Diana, only in the sense of science, for this very tree must at the same time be the touchstone of the principles which should be claimed as the root of thinking reason. The statement and determination of this root can be left neither to the will and arbitrariness nor to inspiration; only its explication constitutes its content and its proof.[62]

Here Hegel assumes that Hamann intends the symbol of the tree to refer to "*developed* knowledge," that is, a knowledge which has developed out of the distinction and reciprocal re-

lationship between the sensibility and the understanding. This
is consistent with his own view of the dialectical, progressive
and cumulative manifestation of reason in history as the self-
conscious knowledge of thinking spirit. Hegel is convinced
that Hamann has nothing substantial to say about knowledge, and
that his insights and allusions are little more than "arbitrariness" and "inspiration." He insists that only in its development
can thought be made rational and demonstrable. Hamann fails to
work out those principles by which the "root" of knowledge itself could be identified and assessed.

But Hegel overlooks two very important aspects of Hamann's
statement. Most obviously, he ignores the two-sidedness of
Hamann's challenge to philosophical knowledge. On the one hand,
Hamann anticipates Hegel himself by calling for "the reciprocal
explanation and extension" of sensibility and understanding in
their relationship with each other. On the other hand, he expresses a most "unhegelian" concern: that sensibility and understanding also reciprocally explain the "limits" on their respective areas of knowledge. For Hamann -- and this is the point
of his constant harping upon the ambiguity of language -- there
are severe limits to the capacity of human knowledge. A major
aspect of philosophical thinking must be, therefore, the determination of those limits. His admiration for Socrates is based
upon his belief that "Socratic ignorance" is such an awareness
of the limits of rational, philosophical knowledge. In Hamann's
view, the only way in which the "extension" of knowledge (Hegel's
"development") can be reliably executed is by a prior acceptance
of the limits beyond which knowledge cannot penetrate. Such
thinking is clearly uncongenial to Hegel. Convinced that Christianity has removed all "religious" obstacles to full knowledge
of God and God's world, he advocates the uninhibited pursuit of
knowledge in all fields.

The second aspect of Hamann's statement which Hegel overlooks is even more decisive, for it indicates the systematic
nature of Hegel's misunderstanding of his subject. When Hamann
speaks of "a chemical tree of Diana," he is alluding to the tree
of knowledge which provided the occasion for Adam's fall into
sin (Gen. 2:17, 3:1ff.).[63] Thus the notion of limits on human
knowledge involves a moral and religious dimension in addition

to the cognitive problems inherent in any extension or development. The reason man is not capable of unlimited knowledge is that he is a sinner. Indeed, if the biblical story is to be taken seriously, it is the very desire to go beyond the limits of knowledge which led Adam and Eve to sin in the first place. God had placed the tree in the Garden of Eden as the only "limit" to the freedom, power, and knowledge of man. But man, as represented by Adam, would not accept that limit. His desire to have unlimited knowledge constitutes disobedience toward God. The "tree of Diana" seems to point toward an element in Hamann's thought that is both alien and unintelligible to Hegel.

There is supporting evidence for this interpretation in the "Metacritique."[64] Hamann accuses the "metaphysics" of "pure reason" of being "that ancient mother of chaos and night in all the sciences of morality, religion and law" who has "obscured, confused and desolated" the limits of knowledge so severely that only a new creation could restore "a pure natural language." This means that philosophical reason is guilty, in Hamann's view, of over-stepping its limits by the abuse of language. It functions as though it had "a pure natural language" at its disposal. In fact, however, it is like "the wicked snake in the bosom of ordinary popular language," which does not wait for the eschatological new creation but simply invents "parables" to claim unity for all the dichotomies which are the subject of philosophy. Again, the serpent is a symbol of the sin by which humanity lost real unity (with God); the serpent's tactic now is to create false impressions of unity wherever he can. The "thesis and antithesis" method of philosophy aids him in this endeavor.

My purpose here is not to pursue a thorough analysis of the "Metacritique," but to indicate that the "enigma" of Hamann's meaning is considerably lessened when one takes his biblical allusions seriously and interprets his statements in terms of the biblical texts to which he makes reference. Hegel systematically refuses to do this. In his discussions of the *Golgotha* and the "Metacritique," as well as countless other texts and letters by Hamann, Hegel consistently either ignores the biblical language and imagery or interprets it in terms of his own secular understanding of the problem under discussion. Whether it be the acts of a transcendent God in human history or the

biblical overtones of the image of a tree of knowledge, Hegel
reads Hamann as though the Bible were irrelevant to his meaning.

Indeed, it is so inconceivable to Hegel that the Bible might
be the key to Hamann's meaning that he summarily dismisses all
biblical language as ornamental. In discussing Hamann's style
as mere "farce" and "mystification," Hegel declares that it is
"not improved by the use of biblical expressions."[65] Hamann's
discussions almost always, he complains, degenerate into images
of filth, which, "like most of his other expressions, are borrowed from the Bible."[66] Instead of exploring these ever-recur-
ring biblical images, Hegel dismisses them as incapable of con-
veying serious thought or meaning. Although he sees that Hamann
has an ability, in Lindner's words, "to turn earth into gold and
straw huts into fairy palaces" in his interpretations of biblical
passages,[67] Hegel does not ask if that ability might not come
from Hamann's attitude toward biblical language and the role it
plays in his thinking.

In the next chapter I offer my own interpretation of the
relationship between Hamann's thought and language and his attitude toward the Bible. For the present, it is sufficient to
emphasize that the subjective freedom of Hamann's genius was
marred, in Hegel's view, by his failure to move beyond the "religious" principle of remaining concentrated in and upon his own
"accidental personality." Thus his style is pure eccentricity,
and his purpose in writing is more self-concealment than self-
revelation. According to Hegel's judgment, Hamann never develops
the "spiritual form" or variety of "figures" which are necessary
to constitute a genuine language of communication; he fails to
express himself as more than a "concentrated, formless vitality."
For Hegel, Hamann's demand for articulation of the limits of
knowledge, based upon his interpretation of the biblical portrayal
of the "tree of knowledge," is incomprehensible. He dismisses
all biblical allusions by Hamann as merely ornamental efforts to
"improve" his own mystifying style. In short, in order for Hamann's genius to realize its full potential, it would have to
develop beyond its "religious" or personality-bound roots into
an adequate language of self-expression, a language which, in
Hegel's view, cannot be that of the Bible.

Hegel's Concept of Religious Language

Although it is not possible, within the context of this study, to offer a thorough examination of Hegel's understanding of religious language, a brief discussion of it is necessary in order to comprehend the dilemma he faces in trying to fathom the meaning of Hamann's writings. I have already shown that Hegel perceives Hamann as a "genius" in terms of his subjective freedom and capacity for symbolization, but as too "religious" or self-involved to harness that genius and give shape to those symbols so that they might constitute a genuine language. In a sense, the very freedom which makes him a genius is also his own worst enemy. This paradox emerges from such statements by Hegel as: "singularity can bring forth neither works of art nor any sort of scientific works."[68] Likewise, although in Hegel's view Hamann's mind is highly complex and symbolical, he remains unaware of the true nature of that which he symbolically portrays, for "the need to become conscious of the content in thought...was totally alien...to his spirit."[69] In order to comprehend these judgments by Hegel, it is necessary to investigate what he expects of Hamann. What concept of religious language leads him to believe that Hamann could find a form of self-expression for his genius? Why, in Hegel's view, could biblical language not serve this purpose?

In his closing remark on the "Metacritique," Hegel gives an indication of how Hamann's religious genius could be expressed in thought:

> One sees that the Idea, the *coincidence*, which constitutes the content of philosophy and has already been described above in relation to his theology and also his character, and which he should have made parabolically representational in language, directs Hamann's spirit in a very firm manner; but that he only offers a "clenched fist" and leaves for the reader the further task, which alone serves the interests of science, of "unfolding it into an open hand." Hamann did not make the effort on his part which, so to speak, God made, in a higher sense of course, to *develop* in reality the closed kernel of truth which He is (ancient philosophers said that God is a round ball) into a system of nature, into a system of the state, of legality and ethics, into a system of world history; into an open hand with fingers outstretched in order to catch the spirit of man and draw it to itself, a spirit which even so is not a merely abstruse intelligence, a dull, concentrated weaving within itself, not only feeling

> and practicing, but is rather a developed system of an
> intelligent organization, whose formal apex is thought,
> i.e. the capacity, according to its nature, to go out
> initially over the surface of the divine unfolding, or
> rather to go into it by means of thinking *about* it,
> and then in that very place to think the divine unfold-
> ing: an effort which is the determination of thinking
> spirit in and for itself and is its express duty since
> *He* Himself took off His form as a closed ball and
> turned Himself into the *revealed* God.[70]

Hegel affirms that Hamann's spirit is "directed" by the Idea,
which, as we saw in Chapter II, is the philosophical term for God.
The content of the Idea is, for Hegel as for Hamann, the "coincidence" of opposite poles of unified realities. The working out
of such unities in thought is "the content of philosophy" -- and
may be called the process of *Aufhebung*. "Coincidence" is also
the substance of Hamann's theology, for he accepts the objective
truth of the Trinity even while he maintains a radically subjective relationship with God. The resulting tension produces that
"formless vitality" of internal contrasts or contradictions without the achievement of explicit unity. It is the same sort of
concentrated intensity without focus which Hegel holds responsible for Hamann's inability to discipline himself in life or in
creative work.

At the end of the "Metacritique" Hamann announces that it
is up to the reader to unfold the "clenched fist" of insights
into the nature of language which he has presented. Hegel finds
this statement and the attitude it represents offensive. Hamann
should, in his view, work out the tensions of those "coincidences"
in the language of parable and representation (*an der Sprache
gleichnisweise vorstellig*). Only such an "unfolding" of the
kernel or core of truth can advance science (*Wissenschaft*), by
which Hegel means human knowledge in general. Turning Hamann's
professed Christianity against him, Hegel chides him for not
imitating the God he claims to worship by making the effort to
develop his awareness of truth into a systematic representation
of reality.

The extent to which Hegel understands the relation between
God and the world to be an identity is very clear in the rest
of this passage. Although God may have been described as a
round ball by ancient philosophers, Christianity has revealed
His unfolded or developed Being in the rational orders of nature,

the state, ethics and world history. If Hamann imitated this
God, he would open his hand himself, and stretch his fingers out
to "catch the spirit of man." He would articulate that spirit
in its "formal apex" of thought, rather than leave it in the
dull, concentrated form of "a merely abstruse intelligence."

What, then, is "thought" for Hegel? It is nothing less
than the human capacity to penetrate the Being and truth of God
by thinking it, to explore and survey and even participate in
God's unfolding of Himself in and as reality. This task is the
duty of thought, in response to God's self-revelation in the
world. The effort to think God is in fact the determination of
thinking spirit, i.e. that which makes thought what it is and
ought to be -- a self-related reality. In thinking God, thought
exists "in and for itself," for it knows its object to be itself, and thus it has internalized the otherness of that object
in its own self-relatedness. We have encountered this sort of
dialectical "internal self-differentiation" in Hegel's concept
of the state. In order to understand it in terms of his views
on thought and language, it is now necessary to deviate from the
method of concentrating upon selected texts, in order to investigate Hegel's understanding of religious language. This can be
found in a text which dates from the same period as the other
texts before us, the *Lectures on the Philosophy of Religion*,
which Hegel delivered in Berlin throughout the 1820's.

Hegel's analysis of religious language occurs within a
broad discussion of "the concept of religion."[71] According to
the schema he works out there, this concept begins with the idea
of God, proceeds to the idea of the believer's "religious relationship" with God, and culminates in the union or reciprocal
"transformation" of both ideas in the act of worship (*der Cultus*).

It is in the section on the religious relationship (*das
religiöse Verhältnis*) that Hegel examines the various forms of
religious consciousness. The most elementary form is the "immediate" knowledge that God exists. Although Hegel calls this
the form of "feeling," he does not mean that the believer actually
"feels" the presence of God, but rather that he has a sense of
God's existence but has never reflected upon this sense or in what
it might consist. Thus Hegel is quick to add that the consciousness of God in feeling is really thought in spite of itself. This

assertion is based upon a syllogism which Hegel presupposes: thinking is an activity of that which is universal; God is "the totally universal object, not any sort of particularity but the universal personality;" therefore, even "immediate" knowledge of God, as the universal, must be a form of thinking.[72]

The importance of this syllogism is clear in Hegel's development of the idea of "thinking" about God. Because even a primitive sense of "unity" with God is a form of thought, there must enter into consciousness the awareness of the difference between the believer and God. Although Hegel never demonstrates why, it is axiomatic for him that thought is always ultimately self-conscious of itself as over against its object, different from its object, and in some sense free of that object. In words that echo Descartes, Hegel affirms that "I can probably doubt everything, but I cannot doubt my own existence, for I am the one doubting, I am the doubt itself."[73] Thus the thinking believer will inevitably doubt God, and his relationship with God, but not himself as thinker. Such doubt is logically self-contradictory and therefore, in Hegel's view, inconceivable and impossible.

Having established that religious "feeling" is a form of thought and that all thought must doubt the objects which it knows, Hegel goes on to describe the dynamic of religious feeling as a constant tension between the subject which thinks or knows and the object which is an "other" to it. Because that "other" is God, the particular subject reveres it and is correspondingly alienated from itself. It can never lose the overwhelming sense of its relationship with God, and the "feeling" of being in such a relationship leads to the feelings of fear, repentance, gratitude and the like. The fluctuation of feelings and the corresponding intensification of the tension will drive the believer to even more reflection on his relationship with God.[74]

The mention of a tension within consciousness between subjectivity and objectivity recalls Hegel's comments on Hamann. Lest there be any doubt about his interpretation of Hamann's consciousness as essentially one of religious feeling, I will list the comments which Hegel makes on the dangers of remaining at this level of consciousness. He describes feeling as made up of many different, even contradictory, elements, and as having only an "accidental" content. Feeling is said to isolate an individual and make communication impossible for him. Feeling

cannot extricate itself from the animal, sensuous level of expression. In order to have consciousness of an object, feeling
must receive some knowledge of that object from the outside;
thus it inevitably involves a "positive" element. Finally, the
popularity of feeling as a mode of consciousness is to be explained by the fact that it is limited to the realm of particularity, vanity and self-complacency. The justification that
feeling is an aspect of will, in distinction to thought, is
false. The will, asserts Hegel, is "rational" and therefore
justifiable only insofar as it is an activity of thought.[75]

The tension between the subject-believer and object-God in
religious feeling can take several forms. As a simple feeling
of relationship it remains in a state of subjectivity. When,
however, it becomes absorbed in its object, its form of consciousness becomes the intuition (*Anschauung*) of God, and subjectivity
yields to the objectivity of art.[76] The unity of subjective
feelings and objective, artistic images is accomplished in a
preliminary way in the form of consciousness which Hegel calls
"representation" (*Vorstellung*). It is this sort of representational language which he sought and failed to find in Hamann.

Representation is not merely feelings about images or images
of feelings. As the *Aufhebung* of feelings and images, it is a
form of thought which attempts to rise above the identification
of God or the Idea with any sensuous images, and know Him as
universal. In so doing, it develops three kinds of representational language about God: natural, historical and spiritual.
These three forms of representation are different ways of uniting
the universal activity of thought, which was first manifest in
the form of feeling, and the element of sensuous intuition, which
first appeared as image under the rubric of art. In all of its
forms, representation is a form of expression in which an opposition between thought and sensuousness exists. Indeed, when Hegel
says that religious consciousness takes the form of representational language, he is referring primarily to this aspect of
alienation of subject from object and thought from image.

Thus the language of natural representation expressly uses
images which are not meant to be taken literally. In Christianity, Christ is spoken of as the "Son" of God who is "begotten"
of the "Father." Similarly, believers attribute such feelings
as wrath, repentance and vengeance to God, which are not meant

to be taken in their "own or literal sense" (*eigentlichen Sinn*).[77]
Elsewhere in the lectures Hegel describes such natural representation of God as "childlike" (*kindlich*) in comparison with actual
descriptions of God, for example, the doctrine of the Trinity of
God (meaning God not as Father, Son, and Holy Spirit but God as
unity-in-diversity).[78] The consciousness which is expressed in
natural representation might properly be called "mythical": it
tries to describe God using images drawn from natural relationships but is well aware that these images cannot be literally
understood.

It is the same with historical representation. The life of
Christ is represented as an historical narrative that is also an
illustration of a divine or moral truth. Thus the language expresses the tension between the thought of Christ's divinity and
the images drawn from his life to illustrate it. Within the con-
fines of historical representation, there can be no resolution
of this tension.[79]

Finally, Hegel identifies spiritual representation as the
language in which religious consciousness can express its truth
as one that is "related to itself and in the form of independence." This language is no longer sensuous or historical. God,
for example, is not described but defined as "all-wise," "good,"
etc. Because these terms for God can be accepted literally,
Hegel calls them "spiritual." They are not yet analyzed in
terms of their relation to one another, and the tension between
the knowing subject and the object (God) remains. It will be
the task of philosophy to overcome these inadequacies. But the
distinctions between subject and predicate, between God and His
attributes, and thus between the thought of God and the images
used to express that thought, are finally represented as distinctions within the one reality of God rather than between two
separate realities.[80] For example, if the religious consciousness wants to express the connection between God and another
reality such as the world, it must always fall back upon images
which have the form of contingency. Thus natural representations
will express the religious truth of the doctrine of creation by
saying that God fashioned the world the way a potter makes a
pot; historical representation will simply say that God created
the world at the beginning of time; and spiritual representation
will say that God is always the Creator of all that is.

Hegel's claim that spiritual representation is "in the form of independence" can be explained in terms of the illustration I have offered of language for creation. In both the natural and the historical versions, the language is drawn from and dependent upon the biblical account. In the spiritual account, however, God's creativity is simply affirmed. It could be known from any one of a number of sources. Thus it is "spiritual" not only in its self-relatedness but also in its freedom from the "letter" of the words of the Bible. Hegel claims this freedom at the begging of the *Lectures*, citing Paul's statement that "the letter kills, but the Spirit gives life" (2 Cor. 3:6) in support of his position.[81] But his appeal to Paul's authority is paradoxical at this juncture, for his point is that Christian thought, when genuinely spiritual, is freed from the language and authority of Scripture. Thus he invites biblical exegetes to see if the Bible supports philosophy's affirmation of the trinitarian concept of the fully revealed and knowable God. If, however, exegesis cannot do this, then, says Hegel, the Bible is to be abandoned for "another source."[82]

In his study of Hamann, however, Hegel encounters a thinker who seems to him to be free of all positive authorities such as the Bible, and yet who continues to use only natural and historical images in his literary style. Those images reflect the tension between Hamann's subjective concentration in "feeling" and his objective intensity of "intuition." But they in no way help to resolve it by spiritual representation. When Hegel charges that Hamann fails to find a language for the expression of his religious genius, he means that his religious thought atrophies on the threshold of spiritual representation. He never engages in the reflection which could move him beyond "natural" and "historical" description to "spiritual" definitions of God. Since those descriptions are subjectivized by his own spirit, they cease to be alien or "positive" for Hamann's personal, subjective consciousness. But as descriptions that use images which cannot be taken literally, they fail to express the actual nature and truth of God.

Having decided that Hamann is "free" of all external or positive authorities, in the sense that he internalizes them all, and believing that biblical language is invoked only as such a positive authority, Hegel does not take Hamann's biblical

allusions seriously. Thus he fails to understand the complexity
of Hamann's thought on history, of his personal character and
piety, and of his views of language. In this sense, it is with
regard to language, its relation to positivity on the one hand
and to reason on the other, that the foundation of Hamann's
theology and his enigma for Hegel can be explained.

* * *

In this chapter I have tried to show that the root issue
between Hegel and Hamann is the question of the most adequate
language for the expression of Christian truth. Hegel's failure
to comprehend Hamann's theology of history as presented in the
Golgotha leads him to conclude that the substance of what Hamann
has to say cannot, in fact, be comprehended, for it is simply an
expression of his own particular personality and eccentricity.
Although he does relate Hamann to the movement of thinking spirit
in his time, Hegel's analysis ultimately rests upon an *ad hominem*
explanation in terms of personal character and personal experience. He perceives Hamann as utterly subjective, as uninter-
ested in articulating the objective truth of his insights or
communicating those insights to others. Despite his genius for
symbolic expression, Hamann fails to find or create symbols which
could constitute a meaningful language. In making this judgment,
Hegel assumes that Hamann's biblical allusions and imagery are
merely ornamental. According to his analysis, Hamann's religious
genius is such that he subjectivizes all the "positive" symbols
and doctrines of the Bible and Christianity. The subjective
freedom of his spirit goes beyond the language of the Bible,
but fails to leave behind sensuous and historical representations
for spiritual representation. This means that his language retains the positivity or "otherness" in speaking of God that his
spirit has transcended. The possibility that Hamann considers
the positivity and "otherness" of biblical language to be fully
adequate for speaking about God never seems to occur to Hegel.

CHAPTER V

THE TONGUES OF MEN: A DEFENSE OF HAMANN

In this chapter I defend Hamann against Hegel's charge that
he is a writer without a genuine language.[1] Given Hegel's failure to understand the biblical language that Hamann uses to
interpret history, the question arises: What justification can
be offered for Hamann's style, particularly for his constant
and cryptic allusions to the Bible? For what "reason," if any,
does he resist the move toward more abstract or intellectual
conceptualization which Hegel demands of him? There are three
parts to the answer which I propose on the basis of the *Golgotha*:
Hamann's belief in the "positivity" of language, that is, that
language is given to man rather than created by him; his ground-
ing of that belief on the historical revelation recorded in the
Bible; and his conviction that the positive revelation of the
nature and use of language demonstrates the priority of faith
over reason.

The Positivity of Language

On the second page of the *Golgotha*, Hamann makes clear how
central the question of the nature of language is to his criticisms of Mendelssohn's theories:

> Without composing out of state, religion, and
> freedom of conscience three moral beings or persons,
> whose immoral dissension and feuding must appear all
> the more astonishing if the moral order refers to
> laws which cannot contradict one another, state, re-
> ligion, and freedom of conscience [*Gewissensfreiheit*]
> are first and foremost three words, which at first
> glance say everything, or rather nothing. Therefore
> these words are to other words as the indefiniteness
> of man is to the definiteness of animals.
> "Very well! let the quarrel be settled by an
> explanation of words." Yet the words to be explained
> stand immediately in the forecourt of the theory. It
> appears to me (*in parenthesi*) to be as clearly the
> case with the moral capacity as with a moral being.
> The capacity is called moral if it is compatible with
> the laws of wisdom and goodness: therefore wisdom
> coupled with goodness should also be called morality.
> But this coupling is actually called justice: thus a
> capacity which is compatible with the laws of wisdom
> and goodness should by rights be called just.[2]

137

Hamann's technique in this passage is to use Mendelssohn's argument metaschematically, in the sense of affirming one part of it over against another part. The point which he affirms is that moral laws "cannot contradict one another," a principle posited by Mendelssohn at the beginning of his discussion of natural law theory.[3] In order for rights and duties to correspond rather than clash with each other, the laws of wisdom and goodness must not dictate contradictory moral actions for identical situations. Hamann agrees with Mendelssohn in his basic understanding of the nature of moral law.

The application of this law, however, is another matter. In the first place, Hamann sees the personalizing of institutions as a threat to this legal logic of non-contradiction. The natural law theory adopted by Mendelssohn is intended as a foundation for his theory of church-state relations and freedom of (religious) conscience. Elsewhere in his argument, he explicitly defines both the state and religion as "moral persons."[4] Since it is presupposed throughout the *Jerusalem* that cases of moral conflict arise between persons over their respective rights and duties, the designation of state and religion as "persons" means that there will be conflicts between them, too. If this is the case, then they can hardly be related to one another only through moral laws which are never contradictory. In short, either these institutions are to be defined as persons, or in terms of laws. They cannot be defined as both simultaneously, for persons have conflicts whereas laws do not.

Hamann's second point goes beyond Mendelssohn's self-contradiction on the nature of institutions to a more constructive criticism. He observes that state, religion and freedom of conscience cannot be designated as laws or persons unless they first exist as words. Without words, there can be no definition and no theory. Words, however, are very human things. Parodying Mendelssohn's speculation that animal-worship originated in the relative "definiteness" (*Bestimmtheit*) of animals in comparison with the "indefiniteness" of man,[5] Hamann uses this description of man with reference to words: "at first glance [they] say everything, or rather nothing." In short, there are certain ambiguities in such words as "state" and "religion" which must be examined before they can be explained in terms of either consistent laws or conflicting persons.

The exclamation which Hamann quotes at the beginning of the next paragraph is his own ironical rendering of an imaginary response to his point about words: if the conflict between state and church is not to be settled as a conflict between persons, let it be settled as a conflict between words. Hamann's "yet" shows that he does not consider this response to be adequate. The words, he says, stand in "the forecourt of the theory." This means that the theory uses the words before it examines them. If, then, the theory using these words gets into conflict with itself, it is too late to examine the words in order to solve the theoretical conflict. Indeed, that very conflict would not arise if it were not for the unexamined way in which the words are being used. The examination of words will not constitute a solution to the problem; it will undermine the assumptions which gave rise to the problem in the first place. This is what it means to affirm that the words are prior to the theory, and therefore should govern it rather than be exploited by it.

This interpretation is supported by the example which Hamann gives of Mendelssohn's misuse of words in his theory. In the *Jerusalem*, the word "moral" is applied to anything "compatible with the laws of wisdom and goodness." This identification is followed by the definition of "justice" as "wisdom coupled with goodness."[6] Hamann sees in the juxtaposition of these two definitions an arbitrary use of words. If anything compatible with the laws of wisdom and goodness is called "moral," then should not the union of wisdom with goodness be called "morality?" Conversely, if this union really constitutes "justice," should not actions compatible with it be called "just?" Mendelssohn's natural law theory appears to posit a great many definitions, but when closely studied, Hamann is saying, they turn out to be little more than principles which use language in arbitrary and contradictory ways. In order to sort out the issues involved in the moral law, the first task is to put aside all theories and establish a vocabulary with which the task can be approached. Without such a self-critical approach to the choice of language, the result will be only more confusion.

If words are "given" prior to their use in theories, and the theories must adapt to them rather than freely exploit them for their own purposes, then language has, in relation to theoretical reflection, a certain "positivity," a position of at

least potentially "alien" authority.[7] Hamann's theological explanation for the positivity of language is the subject of the
next section. At this point, my concern is simply to examine
two of his criticisms of those who, in his view, fail to use
language properly. In both cases that failure is based upon an
implicit refusal to acknowledge the positivity of the words they
employ.

One of Hamann's criticisms of using language in theories
without prior attention to the complex and ambiguous meanings
of words is that this practice will often lead to the creation
of pseudo-dichotomies. Thus (in a passage which could serve as
a model of Hamann's style) he declares:

> Circulated through the serpent's deception of
> language, under just as various as manifold verbal
> forms, in the whole of Jerusalem [there is] the
> eternal *petitio* of one and the same hypocritical
> *principii* of outward perfection of rights and ac-
> tions, of inner imperfection of duties and senti-
> ments -- Indeed, everything does depend upon both
> those questions, which I must repetitiously touch
> upon.

> I. "According to the law of reason, are there
> rights to persons and things which can be
> connected with doctrines, and can be earned
> by assent to them?"

> As worms pass through children, laws, which are
> the golden hemorrhoids and nymph Egerie of many a
> philosophical government, also pass through the craven
> men-of-letters. If a connection between the physical
> and the moral cannot be denied, and the different
> modifications of writing and kinds of marking also
> must have had different effects on the progress and
> improvement of concepts, opinions, and knowledge,
> then I don't know why it should be so difficult to
> imagine a connection between moral capacities and
> doctrines. According to the law of reason, i.e. of
> the unchangeable connection and essential bond be-
> tween concepts which presuppose or exclude one another,
> doctrines are as closely connected with a moral capa-
> city in general as with the special right of decision
> in cases of conflict. Doctrinal agreement has an ef-
> fect on our sentiments, which in turn influence our
> moral judgment and corresponding behavior.[8]

Although the word "Jerusalem" is not underscored (by spacing
of the letters) in the Nadler text, it clearly refers not only
to the religion of Israel but also to Mendelssohn's book. There
Hamann finds a principle of claims (*petitio* or *Bitten*) based

upon the opposition of "perfect" or compulsory rights and duties to those which are "imperfect" or voluntary. In his analysis, Mendelssohn describes the former as "external" and therefore subject to force, in contrast to the latter, which are merely "internal" and may be rejected by the one petitioned.[9] He also argues that the state has a "perfect" right to compel outward behavior or actions in accordance with what it determines to be "perfect" duties, while the church has only an "imperfect" right to persuade "inner" convictions or sentiments (*Gesinnungen*) as voluntary duties.[10] In Hamann's view, this is a false evaluation of actions in relation to sentiments, a criticism which he expresses here by the ironic use of the nouns "perfection" and "imperfection" in place of Mendelssohn's use of the less blatant adjectives. More to the point is his initial statement that these "manifold verbal forms" originate in "the serpent's deception of language." As we saw in the "Metacritique," human sinfulness is understood by him as a pollution not just of moral character and will but also of language. Thus Mendelssohn's errors are due to his use of words, and the way he abuses them in fashioning his claims and principles.

The question which Hamann quotes from Mendelssohn is the occasion for the writing of the *Jerusalem* -- as a protest against ever letting rights be made contingent upon sentiments or doctrinal assent. This question provides Hamann with an occasion also -- to attack the appeal to "laws" made by Mendelssohn and others of his generation who speak in terms of "the law of reason" and laws of wisdom and goodness. He likens these "laws" to the "golden hemorrhoids" of a philosopher-king, a not untypically crude jab at King Frederick's philosophical pretensions and, in Hamann's view, the arbitrariness of his government. For such men laws are only irritants, to be passed by or expelled from their own "body" as "worms pass through children." Hamann's use of the word "craven" (*seuchtigen*) shows that he understands this way of dealing with laws to be corrupt. It also alludes to 1 Tim. 6:4 in Luther's translation, which speaks of "craven" men who love "controversy and disputes about words." The biblical allusion to battles over mere words leads into Hamann's metaschematic use of Mendelssohn's phrase, "men-of-letters" (*Buchstabenmenschen*). This term of approbation is used in the

Jerusalem to criticize the extent to which relationships have become "literary," i.e. conducted through writings rather than in person, since the invention of writing.[11] In Hamann's context, however, it becomes a term of derision for all those who deal in a "craven" or literalistic manner with either words ("letters") or laws. They proclaim words and propound laws, but submit to the truth of neither. Such is the deceptiveness which Hamann sees lurking in Mendelssohn's theoretical language.

The question comes down to how Mendelssohn can justify all the dichotomies he presupposes and without which his theories collapse or lose their relevance. Hamann makes this point not with reference to the outward/inner or perfect/imperfect distinctions, but in regard to Mendelssohn's basic separation of rights and doctrines. On the one hand, the argument against picture-writing and hieroglyphics in the *Jerusalem* (on the grounds that they encourage idolatry)[12] presupposes a "connection between the physical and the moral." Thus "modifications of writing" have had a marked effect on "concepts, opinions, and knowledge," which are the stuff of doctrine. On the other hand, Mendelssohn argues throughout the *Jerusalem* against connecting moral rights and doctrines; the question quoted by Hamann is forcefully and negatively answered by Mendelssohn in the next paragraph.[13] He cannot, contends Hamann, have it both ways. If something as physical as writing can have an effect on human thinking and doctrine, then doctrine must be able to have an effect on something as physical as moral actions. The last sentence in this paragraph sums up Hamann's reasoning: doctrines have an effect on sentiments or opinions, "which in turn influence our moral judgment and corresponding behavior."

In support of his protest against Mendelssohn's pseudo-dichotomies, Hamann quotes a logical principle laid down in the *Jerusalem* against him: "reason" is said to be "the unchangeable connection and essential bond between concepts which presuppose or exclude one another."[14] This is an apt expression of the principle of "the coincidence of opposites," which we have seen is central to Hamann's thinking. For Mendelssohn, however, the "bond" between concepts which "exclude" one another seems to have been forgotten along the way. His argument is built upon one dichotomy after another, each posited as an artificial

absolute opposition which fails to express any "connection and
essential bond." Examples discussed by Hamann are numerous. In
addition to rights and doctrines, he criticizes the division of
actions from sentiments and state from church. This last dichotomy he likens to the judgment of Solomon, in which the lying
mother was willing to have the living child cut in half in order
to defend her pretended "right" of motherhood (1 Ki. 3:16-28);
and to the event of death, which creates a "body without spirit"
on the one hand (the state as corpse) and a spirit without a
body on the other (the church as ghost).[15] The abuse of language leads to false dichotomies which are full of deception to
the point of being vehicles of death.

Hamann's appeal to the principle of "the coincidence of
opposites" in order to criticize thought which sets up pseudo-
dichotomies should not be interpreted to mean that he is a fore-
runner of Hegel and the theory of *Aufhebung*. In Hamann's view,
the solution to false dichotomies is not to "transform" them
into new unities but to reject and foreswear the initial step
of dichotomization, which is a falsification of the truth. To
accept the dichotomy as real and true, if only within the context of its own conceptual "stage," is what I call "dialectical"
thinking. Dialectics reflects upon the opposition in the dichotomies it has set up; it may also try to overcome that opposition. In either case, it accepts the opposing terms of the
dichotomy as an essential truth of the reality it is attempting
to understand.

Hamann uses the word "dialectical" only once in the *Golgotha*,
when referring to those historical truths which are "supported
by evidence of real fulfillments which are sufficient to catapult
faith over all Talmudic and dialectical doubts and pitfalls."[16]
Here "dialectical doubts" are portrayed as a way of thinking
which ignores or tries to refute empirical evidence. This understanding of "dialectical" as implying an indifference to the
given data seems to be borrowed from Kant, who criticizes all
efforts to turn away from "reliable information" or empirical
data and treat thought as self-constituting ("an *organon*") rather
than as simply self-critical (" merely a *canon*").[17] This turn
of thought, says Kant, occurs when general logic becomes "dialectic." Hamann affirms this negative understanding of dialectics as a method by which thought attempts to avoid dealing with
the realities given to it.

In the case of pseudo-dichotomies, the "given" realities
which concern Hamann are words. "Dialectical doubt" involves a
misuse of language. It fails to deal with the empirical usage
and meaning of the words it exploits to construct its theories.
A thorough investigation of Hamann's thought on this matter would
have to include a detailed exegesis of the "Metacritique," where
Hamann actually speaks of language as "the first and last organon
and criterion of reason, with no other credentials than tradition
and usage." Several paragraphs later he adds that "the whole
ability to think is based upon language," which is "the central
point of reason's misunderstanding of itself."[18] The problem
with dialectical thinking is that it does not give adequate attention to the words it uses in its efforts to reason. Hamann
endorses the principle of the "coincidence of opposites" as a
rejection of pseudo-dichotomies. Such terms as "church" and
"state" are not to be rejoined in a "higher" unity, but should
be returned to their original and genuine complexity and ambiguity of meaning. The most forceful statement in the *Golgotha*
against dialectics is the following paragraph:

> In a valley of vision full of vague and vacil-
> lating concepts, it is not good to boast of a greater
> Enlightenment! -- of a better development! -- of a
> more accurate distinction! -- all by means of a more
> sophisticated use of language and common sense! --
> over against the times and the system of a Hobbes.
> I have already denounced the relationship with what
> one calls a right and the other calls might. Com-
> pulsory duties, whose perfection consists in the
> fact that they can be extorted by force, seem to
> border just as closely on the obligatory nature of
> fear. Furthermore, when just as much is won through
> the expression of benevolence as is lost through sac-
> rifice: then cases of conflict between benevolence
> and self-interest, or between duties to oneself and
> to one's neighbor, are just as much fruits of a mis-
> erable sophistry as of a simulated conflict between
> the rights of the deity and of mankind, the conflict
> on which the theorist blames all evil which has been
> practiced since time immemorial under the philosophi-
> cal and political cloak of truth and justice. Love
> of man is a congenital weakness, and benevolence lit-
> tle more than a foppery into which and right away out
> again one is always trying to talk oneself, which pes-
> ters the reader with school jargon and lives like a
> lord, indulging itself on the side by guzzling the con-
> tents of concepts and making fun of the partisan public
> with the empty skins. Soon the whole Penelope's web
> comes down to cleverness at making every other untorn
> unity appear as two, which then instantly fall back

> into one another, so that through the same hocus-
> pocus under both aspects the standpoint and per-
> spective are every now and then distorted, and the
> speculative man-of-letters becomes dizzy from twirl-
> ing -- meanwhile the ephah of theory [is] hovering
> between heaven and earth in the land of Shinar, and
> *Jerusalem* shall not still be inhabited in its place,
> in Jerusalem, but will come to the same end as Babel.[19]

Hamann opens this paragraph with an allusion to Isaiah's
prophecy against Jerusalem as "the valley of vision" which is
thrown into "tumult and trampling and confusion" by the Lord
(Is. 22:1-5). In the "vague and vacillating concepts" of Mendelssohn's *Jerusalem*, Hamann sees a similar confusion. While
criticizing Hobbes' effort to base right upon might and duty
upon fear, Mendelssohn claims that progress beyond Hobbes has
been made possible by better definitions and distinctions within language and common sense.[20] To Hamann, this is simply an
empty "boast" (cf. 1 Cr. 5:6). He has already shown that Mendelssohn argues only for the inviolable rights of those who already possess goods and property.[21] Since property rights are
the source of power or "might" in the world, Mendelssohn is not,
in fact, distinguishing between might and right any more than
Hobbes does. His boast is hollow with regard to duties also,
for, by making them "perfect" or compulsory, he bases them upon
fear, once again agreeing with Hobbes. Thus his claim that "language" and "common sense" have achieved a "better development"
for distinguishing rights and duties from might and fear is
rejected by Hamann.

Having denounced Mendelssohn's boast about language, Hamann
goes on to attack his abuse of language as a "miserable sophistry." This is the term which Mendelssohn uses for the Christian
belief that the Fall resulted in a relationship of conflict between God and man, so that now the believer has one set of duties
toward God and another toward men. He blames this belief for
all the violence, persecution and evils which have been perpe-
trated in the name of religion.[22] Hamann implies that he agrees
that it is an error to oppose duties toward men and duties toward
God by his phrase "just as much fruits of a miserable sophistry."
However, he places the blame for such sophistry not upon religion
but upon "the philosophical and political cloak of truth and
justice." The deception, he seems to be saying, has not been the

work of those who were seeking reconciliation with God, but of
those whose real concern was to acquire political power under
the guise of seeking the noble ideals of truth and justice. Thus
their sophistry has produced such fruit as the theory that acts
of benevolence and sacrifice can be performed out of self-interest
rather than for the good of one's neighbor (which is precisely
what Mendelssohn argues).[23]

The problem to which Hamann is pointing here is that of the
relation between a thinker and the words in which he thinks. Mendelssohn's claim to have surpassed Hobbes' failure to distinguish
between might and right is based upon his own self-deception,
which is in turn due to his failure to examine the meaning of his
words. His theories are sophistries which unwittingly identify
not only right with might and duty with fear, but also self-interest with benevolence. He speaks of sacrifice and neighborly
love, but he fails to show why or even how they are desirable
and possible. "Love of man" and "benevolence" are a good case
in point. In Mendelssohn's own words, they are only "a congenital weakness" and "little more than a foppery" without faith in
God, divine providence and a future life. On any other basis
they are no more than illusions into which men try to trick one
another, so that those who are clever can make fun of their fool-
ish victims.[24] Hamann uses this language metaschematically to
make the point that talk and debating cannot be justified by the
inclusion of such words as "God," "providence," and "afterlife."
When these words are used simply to bolster a theory of humani-
tarianism, they are only "school jargon." Thus Mendelssohn is
inadvertently warning against his own clever tricks. He lives
"like a lord" over the simple folk, exploiting words for his own
self-indulgence, "guzzling" the inner conceptual meaning and
using the "empty skins" to make fun of "the partisan public."
While he uses words such as "right," "benevolence" and even
"God," he has turned them into empty words by ignoring the positive meanings they have in ordinary language. Thus his poor
reader is pestered rather than enlightened, and is left strug-
gling with his own "partisan" or falsely dichotomous understanding.

According to Hamann, Mendelssohn himself by no means remains
within the limits established by his initial dichotomizing definitions. Having emptied his key terms of their real, complex

meanings as given in language, he uses them the way Penelope wove
and un-wove her web to keep the suitors from forcing her to a
decision.[25] He plays with empty words "dialectically" in order
to avoid dealing with the empirical reality they symbolize and
the difficult issues they raise. He divorces words from their
full range of meaning, abstracting them from their own ambiguity
and forcing them into artificial, abstract oppositions with other
words. To overcome these oppositions, he then "instantly" declares them to be one again. In short, he plays a game of division and reunion with words which cannot in truth be divided from
one another.

Hamann compares this way of using language to a "hocuspocus
under both aspects." This is an allusion to the Roman Catholic
theology of transubstantiation. According to that doctrine, the
bread of the sacrament of the Eucharist becomes the body of Christ
by virtue of consecration, thus fulfilling the words of Jesus
when he instituted the sacrament: "This is my body" (Mt. 26:26).
The opponents of that doctrine came to speak of it as "hocuspocus," from the Latin, *Hoc est corpus meum*.[26] By his allusion
to it at this point, Hamann is saying that Mendelssohn's theoretical language is like the Catholic theology of transubstantiation, for it divides and then tries to re-unite what should never
be divided. This theme is developed further in the "Metacritique," where Hamann speaks of linguistic "transubstantiation"
and "the sacrament of language."[27]

As an example of Mendelssohn's dialectical "cleverness,"
Hamann cites his distinction between the temporal and the eternal,
which is immediately followed by the claim that eternity is nothing but an "infinitely prolonged temporality," and a warning
against distinguishing so sharply between this life and the next
that the "outlook and perspective" of simple folk will be distorted.[28] Hamann thinks that Mendelssohn should take his own
warning to heart. With all the "hocuspocus" of his word-games
and reasoning, he shows himself to be a "speculative man-of-
letters" who has become "dizzy" from his own intellectual "twirling."

Finally, the theories of the *Jerusalem* are like an ephah
(a Hebrew bushel) in which "wickedness" sits, and which hovers
in the land of Shinar while a base is being prepared for it

(Zech. 5:5-11). This biblical allusion concludes the analysis
of Hamann's critique of the false use of language. Because Mendelssohn uses empty words, his theories "hover" between heaven
and earth. That is, he neither bases his thought upon divine
revelation nor forthrightly represents it as simply his own fragmentary and inadequate human suggestions. It has evil lurking
within it, and once it finds its own base, then the door may
once more open to let that evil out into the land. That land
is Shinar, where Nimrod built the city of Babel! Hamann sees
in this evil and the theory which contains it a false presupposition of autonomy from God. In this context, pseudo-autonomy is
to be understood particularly with reference to language. The
Jerusalem, with all its dichotomies and dialectics, will *not*
"still be inhabited" as God had promised to the Holy City (Zech.
12:6); rather, it will meet the "same end as Babel," where God
confused the tongues of men as a check on their self-will, their
pride and their unlimited ambitions (Gen. 11:1-9).

It is at this point that Hamann explicitly states that the
dichotomies of state and church, inner and outer happiness, and
temporal and external existence are those which he has in mind.
In each case, we may conclude, there is a complex and ambiguous
unity which is artificially divided into an abstract dichotomy,
and then this false dichotomy is overcome by what amounts to,
in Hamann's view, nothing more than verbal dialectics. Thus his
criticism of an understanding that merely dichotomizes, a criticism which seems similar in spirit to Hegel's thought, leads on
to this total rejection of any claim to being able methodically
or "dialectically" to reconcile opposites. In short, Hamann
takes a position which implies rejection of Hegel's notion of
Aufhebung or "transformation." He does not deny that complex
and internally-differentiated unities exist, any more than he
questions the existence of "opposites" which "coincide" or in
some other way manifest their relationship if not their identity.
What Hamann rejects is the claim of "dialectical" thinking to
manipulate original unities into dichotomies and reconstituted
unities, when it should deal concretely and directly with words
in their determinate contexts. To commit oneself to such a
method of thinking, he implies, is to move away from concrete
thinking to a level of abstraction which has lost its base "in

the land," but has not been connected to an inspiration or revelation from heaven. Such a theoretical method, he prophesies,
will one day be opened up and found to contain unimagined "Wickedness." For it is false on two counts: it "uses language as
an empty puppet-show;" and it employs its sophistries to win the
confidence of the people "at the expense and to the peril of
unrecognized living truths."[29] It is to these living truths,
and particularly to the truths of revelation which explain what
the "positivity of language" means in a constructive sense for
Hamann, that we now turn.

Language and Historical Revelation

The foundation of Hamann's understanding of language is his
belief that all things human are gifts given by God to man in
history. After life itself, the first and foremost of God's
gifts at the time of creation was the capacity for language:

> For he spoke, and it came to be! -- "and what-
> ever the man called every living creature, that was
> its name." According to this image and likeness of
> definiteness, every word of a man was supposed to be
> and remain the event itself. On this similarity of
> the impression and the inscription to the model of
> our race and the master of our youth; on this right
> of nature, to make use of the word as the most real,
> noble and powerful means of revelation and communica-
> tion of our innermost declaration of intention; on
> these is the validity of all contracts based, and
> this mighty fortress of the truth in the inward being
> is superior to all French practice, tax-machinery,
> pedantry and bartering tactics. Therefore, the mis-
> use of language and its natural testimony is the
> grossest perjury, and it turns the transgressor of
> this first law of reason and its justice into the
> most wicked enemy of mankind, traitor, and adversary
> of German uprightness and sincerity, on which our
> dignity and happiness are based.[30]

Language is not, for Hamann, in any way an epiphenomenon or
addendum to Creation. It is the very means by which God created
the universe at the beginning of time. The first event in the
history of existence was a language-event, for God *spoke* into
existence the light, the firmament which He called "Heaven,"
the dry land which He called "Earth," and so on (Gen. 1:1-26).
The words of Ps. 33:9: "For He spoke, and it came to be!" show
that the foundation of all existence is language -- the words
of God.

By language God also created man (Gen. 1:26). He placed
man in a garden created for him, and spoke to him, saying that
all but one of the trees in the garden were accessible to him.
He created animals to be companions to man, and gave him the
capacity and responsibility for naming those animals. The first
human act recorded in the Bible is not worship, not striving,
not even sin; it is a language-act, the act of uttering the
names of the animals. Hamann quotes part of Gen. 2:19 directly
in juxtaposition to the quote about God's speaking (from Ps. 33:
9) in order to emphasize the momentous nature of this event:
"and whatever the man called every living creature, that was
its name." God uses language to create the world. Man uses
language to respond to the world which God is creating and giving to him. "Naming" is thus an expression of gratitude to God.

Given the problems which language now poses -- the difficulty men have saying what they mean or finding the right word
to fit the reality -- Hamann wants to emphasize that language
was not always so problematical. The names which Adam gave to
the animals were their real names. His words fit reality. Again
Hamann refers ironically to Mendelssohn's discussion of the
"definiteness" of animals which made their image so adaptable
to idolatry.[31] His point is that the definiteness of animals
is not just an occasion for sin. It is a gift from God, and
the standard of definiteness given in animals should be adopted
by man for his own speech. "Every word of a man" should correspond to that which it names so closely that it, in effect,
is "the event itself" (*die Sache selbst*). The first act of the
first man was a language-act, and the model for all human use of
language ever since is revealed in that act. The relationship
between words and reality is to be one of exact and definite
correspondence, just like the relationship between spoken prophecies and the events which fulfill them. There is no necessary
gap between language and the objects or events to which it refers. Rather, word-events are the medium by which human consciousness is related to reality. For a gap to enter into this
mediation is to be cut off from reality.

The theological basis for Hamann's claim that language
constitutes the substance of human being in the world is none
other than the doctrine of the *Imago Dei*. The first indication

that he has this in mind is the phrase "image and likeness."
Although it refers here to animals, the phrase itself is drawn
from Gen. 1:26, where it is used by God to describe His intention
of creating man in His "image" and "likeness" and giving him
dominion over the earth. To emphasize that the "image" of God
in man is to be found in man's capacity for language, and that
therefore it is through language that he is to exercise his
dominion over other creatures, Hamann goes on to say that it is
"this similarity" -- to express or articulate events -- which
likens man to God, who is the "model of our race and the master
of our youth." To say that man is created in the image of God
is to say that he is given a capacity to use language to name
and rule the world.

A second aspect of the *Imago Dei* is that it implies that
human language and human behavior need not be in opposition,
any more than God's acts contradict His words. This point is
implied by Hamann's use of the phrase "and inscription." In
Mk. 12:13-17, Jesus is "tested" by the Pharisees about the law-
fulness of Jews, who have no king but God, paying taxes to Caesar.
He responds to their challenge by observing that if a coin bears
the picture "and inscription" of Caesar, then "render" it unto
Caesar. By implication, therefore, if a person is created in
the image and likeness of God, he should give himself to God.
And if the human capacity for language is the special locus of
that likeness, then it especially should be consecrated to God.
This allusion to Mk. 12 also points metaschematically to Mendelssohn's claim that Christ teaches "an obvious contradiction"
between duties to God and duties to Caesar, and that men should
therefore "bear both burdens" as best they can.[32] Hamann rejects
this interpretation, for it sets up a double standard of "religious" and "civil" behavior. If God is Lord of all life, He
will not be satisfied by merely ceremonial religious actions and
mechanical conformity to civil laws; He wants every word and
deed to serve Him in their fundamental unity.

As the foundation of man's historical being and of his
relations with God and other men, language is also Hamann's solution to the apparent contradiction between freedom and contracts.[33] Mendelssohn tries to resolve that tension by proposing
a state of nature in which men freely acknowledge their natural

rights and duties, and freely draw up contracts to make some of those rights and duties compulsory while leaving others on a voluntary basis. In contrast, Hamann thinks that language is the foundation of freedom and contracts equally. It is the "right of nature" by which all communication is made possible; and it is the basis for "the validity of all contracts." Thus language mediates between rights and duties, and the "correspondence" between them which Mendelssohn had merely hypothesized[34] can be firmly established by a close examination of usage. Rights and duties exist only when and as they are spoken rights and duties, and the key to understanding them lies not in abstract speculation but in careful hearing of what is spoken. The condition for all communication and contracts is the "right" to "make use of the word." Only in the correspondence of words to intentions can the validity of contracts be found. Language is a "mighty fortress" (like God in Luther's hymn) of "the truth in the inward being" (Ps. 51:6), in sharp contrast with the duplicity and deceit of Frederick's imported (French) bureaucrats.

Finally, because language is the means by which God creates man and man relates to reality, to misuse it is no mild misdemeanor. Language involves its own "natural testimony," and the effort to use it in any other way -- i.e. autonomously, as though it did not have this positivity -- is "the grossest perjury." Mendelssohn protests against religious oaths on the grounds that they lead to perjury,[35] but Hamann turns that protest back against him, for his misuse of language is a far greater perjury. This implies not that oaths are wrong, but that they are superfluous, for the right to speak is a God-given right, and therefore all use of language is, so to speak, "under oath." To misuse words is to transgress the "first law of reason and its justice," which means, for Hamann, to perjure oneself in the strict sense -- to lie before God. It is to become an enemy of mankind, the representative of an alien power rather than a rightful heir and ruler of one's own ("German") territory. Language is not only the means of creation; it is also the foundation of all morality.

This reference to oaths and the morality of language points toward the covenantal structure of man's linguistic relationship to others. Indeed, covenant and condescension are just as much

structures of language as of the revealed meaning of history.
In the following paragraph Hamann discusses the relation between
covenant and society, on the one hand, and reason and language
on the other:

> Since, therefore, if everybody wants to establish
> his unphilosophical ego as the royal referee in cases
> of conflict, neither a state of nature nor a state of
> society is possible; rather, in both states the deci-
> sion about natural or appointed laws must devolve upon
> One universal Lord and Heir. So it is scarcely worth
> it to poke about at greater length in the speculative
> and theoretical rubbish of the right to use property
> for self-interest, the right to decide issues of bene-
> volence, and the totality of logical conditions neces-
> sary for the perfection of the rights of compulsion;
> rather, all social contracts are based, according to
> the law of nature, on the moral capacity to say "Yes"
> or "No," and on the moral necessity to make good that
> spoken word. The moral capacity to say "Yes" or "No"
> is grounded in the natural use of human reason and lan-
> guage. The moral necessity to fulfill one's given word
> [is grounded] in the fact that our inner declaration
> of intention cannot be expressed, revealed or recog-
> nized other than orally or in writing or by our actions;
> and our words, as the natural signs of our sentiments
> and no less of our deeds, must stand. Therefore rea-
> son and language are the internal and external bond of
> all social life, and through a divorce or separation
> of that which nature by its appointment has joined
> together belief and trust are abolished; lies and de-
> ceit, shame and vice, are confirmed and stamped as
> means of happiness. Fundamentum est justitiae FIDES
> -- dictorum *constantia* et *veritas*. -- Est enim *primum*,
> quod cernitur in universi generis humani societate,
> eiusque autem vinculum est RATIO et ORATIO....[36]

One purpose of the *Jerusalem* is to establish the right of
individual decision with regard to the distribution of private
property. In opposing the coercive practices of the dominant
(Christian) religious institutions, Mendelssohn is appealing to
a theory of moral individualism that Hamann considers as imprac-
ticable as it is immoral. In his view, if every individual has
the right of decision in cases of conflict over his property,
then neither the freedom of Mendelssohn's "state of nature" nor
the order of his "state of society" is possible; both dissolve
in anarchy. The only alternative to anarchy is the acceptance
of God's rule and authority equally over all. The only right
of decision belongs to God, to the "One universal Lord' who, as
the incarnate Son of God, is also "Heir" to all goods and all
property. In short, the issue which concerns Hamann in this

paragraph is once again that of the covenant which God offers to
man and which man should accept and obey.

If God's covenant is the foundation for all decisions about
property, then it is no longer worthwhile to attempt to clear up
the problems by means of speculation and theories about the rights
and limits of self-interest, benevolence, and the conditions under which force may be used to compel compliance with established
norms of duty. Such theoretical reflection is only "rubbish"
in comparison with the directives which God has given as part
of His covenant. As the Creator of nature, He has established
the only "law of nature." And as the incarnate Word who lived
among men, He taught that it is not good to take oaths, which
are the normal way of sealing a contract. Rather, "all social
contracts are based...on the moral capacity to say 'Yes' or 'No.'"
In the words of Jesus: "Simply let your 'Yes' be 'Yes,' and your
'No,' 'No'" (Mt. 5:37 [NIV]; cf. Jam. 5:12). This teaching in
the Sermon on the Mount is the basis on which Hamann rests his
position on the role of language in morality. Jesus taught that
men should say what they mean. Hamann applies that teaching to
Mendelssohn's distinction between moral capacities (rights) and
moral necessities (duties), ironically declaring it to be "the
law of nature." Thus he says that the moral capacity on which
all social contracts (and implicitly all social relations) are
based is the capacity to speak the truth, to avoid misusing language; and the moral necessity which follows from that is the
duty to conform behavior to the spoken word. Consistent with
the *Imago Dei*, Hamann understands this "covenant of language"
in terms of the model of prophecy and fulfillment. The covenant
is to use language as God ordains. And the examples God gives
of the right use of language are His own promises and prophecies
which He never fails to keep and fulfill.

Having appealed to the authority of the teaching of Jesus
on morality and language, Hamann next tries to explain in greater
depth the nature of their connection. He is not, in his view,
appealing to an authority which is either above or opposed to
reason. Indeed, the very capacity to say "Yes" or "No," i.e.
to make and express decision, is "grounded in the natural use
of human reason and language." This means that all rights
("moral capacities") need and presuppose language. Likewise,

there can be no fulfillment of duties ("moral necessities") without language. For Hamann, duties are related to the "inner
declaration of intention." This is another allusion to the Sermon on the Mount, where Jesus teaches that the mere desire to
commit a sin is tantamount to sinning in fact (e.g., Mt. 5:28
on adultery). On this basis, Hamann rejects the distinction
between will and action which is so crucial to Mendelssohn's
moral philosophy and the separation of church and state. He
does not deny that actions can express intentions as much as
speech or writing can. But he hastens to add that the "natural
signs" by which actions, no less than sentiments, will be understood, are words. As the basic units of language, words are
the common mediator and bond between intentions and actions.
Only in language is the consciousness of desires or deeds possible. The morality of language shows how fruitless it is to
try to distinguish sharply between these different aspects of
word-behavior. That is why, turning once again to the Sermon
on the Mount on which this concept of language-morality is based,
it is just as serious to say to someone "You fool!" as to kill
him (Mt. 5:22). The words of a man must stand; if they are
false, all his intentions and actions are also false.

If language is the mediating bond between intentions and
actions, where does reason fit? As Hamann puts it, words can
become "empty skins" which have had their conceptual content
guzzled out of them.[37] Here he is even more explicit: there
is one "bond of all social life," of which language constitutes
the "external" aspect and reason the "internal" aspect. As
with the metaphor of wineskins, reason is the inside of language, and language is the outside or expression of reason.
Together they are the foundation of all society and morality.
If divorced or separated, however, the possibility for belief
and trust of citizens in their society is destroyed. Reason
and language are bound as by marriage, and Hamann alludes to
Jesus' teaching against divorce (Mt. 19:6) as a metaschematic
rebuttal of Mendelssohn's appeal to the same text in defense of
his view that all Jews, including Jesus, are "wedded" to the
law.[38] Hamann's point is that the divorce to be avoided at all
costs is not from the law but from a right relationship with
language. To support this point, he invokes Cicero, one of the

Enlightenment's favorite philosophers.[39] When the bond of reason and language (*ratio et oratio*) is dissolved, the first and
fundamental basis for universal human society is broken. Therefore, Cicero proclaims that faith or trust (*fides*) is the foundation of justice, and that the object of this trust is none other
than "the constancy and truth of what is said" (*dictorum constantia et veritas*). The morality of language is the expression of
truth in reason. The unity of language and reason is the basis
for all contracts among men and all covenants between God and
man.

The concept of covenant is one of the moral "structures"
by which I have interpreted Hamann's understanding of history
and language. The other such structure is condescension, which,
although once again only implicit in Hamann's discussion of moral
laws, can be discerned in his remarks on the problem of definition
of words:

> As a duty-bound reader I voluntarily resign
> myself to the fact that I can dispute no privileged
> scribe's power to use an obsolete Leibnizian defi-
> nition of a word as an aid to the discussion of the
> first letters of his natural law, all the less since
> the laws of wisdom and goodness which never contra-
> dict each other have a covert falling out with the
> knowledge and will of the theorist, and need to be
> brought together anew through justice.
> But as a privileged man-of-letters I would wish
> for myself devoted readers of better consciousness
> and conscience, to whom I might submit only the ques-
> tion: "How should justice, which gives to each his
> own, be able to stop being what it is, to renounce
> its own being, to rob from wisdom and goodness their
> own, and to give over its own unchangeable oneness
> for two, which are as different from each other as
> it is from them both."[40]

In these two paragraphs Hamann ironically portrays a writer
as the possessor of rights in Mendelssohn's sense. In the first
paragraph Hamann himself is a "duty-bound reader," and Mendelssohn is the "privileged scribe." As one who is under obligation,
Hamann must, according to Mendelssohn's analysis, accept the
decision of the one who has rights over the goods in question.
The irony of his statement that he will "voluntarily resign"
himself to Mendelssohn's "power" lies in the fact that the power
in question is the right to decide upon the meaning of words,
and the meaning of words is not something which can be decided

by individual *fiat*. Thus this metaschematism represents another
way of saying that words precede and place conditions on theories:
to apply the theory of pre-contractual rights and duties to language results in a patent absurdity.

Hamann's second point is that Mendelssohn's choice of definition is done in a manner that is literalistic rather than according to the Spirit and truth. Rather than a living meaning,
he prefers one that is "obsolete," having been proposed by Leibniz
a century before. This is because his purpose is to discuss
"the first letters" of the natural law. By the substitution of
"letters" for Mendelssohn's word "principles,"[41] Hamann indicates
the artificiality which such theoretical definitions have for
him. They use words according to a literalistic understanding
rather than in their full "spiritual" complexity and ambiguity.
The text to which Hamann is alluding is once again Paul's statement that "the letter kills, but the Spirit gives life" (2 Cor.
3:6).

That such definitions are disconnected from present, living
meanings of words is, in Hamann's view, only a symptom of the
root problem: the relationship between the content of the
theories proposed and the theorist -- the person -- who proposes them. The theories are about laws of wisdom and goodness
which "never contradict each other."[42] Yet, as Hamann had shown
a few pages earlier,[43] there is a great deal of confusion and
contradiction in Mendelssohn's portrayal of those laws, especially in the relation of justice to morality. Here he suggests a
more constructive analysis of the issue: the conflict in question is not among the laws of wisdom and goodness nor between
morality and justice. The real conflict is between all these
moral laws and principles on the one hand and Mendelssohn's
own "knowledge and will" on the other hand. The role of "justice" is not identical with that of morality. For all the confusion in Mendelssohn's presentation, it is clear that "justice"
is proposed as the means by which the conflict between abstract
moral theory and personal moral will can be overcome.

Having said this, Hamann returns in the next paragraph to
his own view of the matter. A word about what he means by a
conflict between the "theorist" and the moral laws may be helpful at this point. The discussion of natural law theory in the

Jerusalem begins with the definition of rights and duties in
relation both to goods and to each other.[44] Rights compatible
with the laws of wisdom and goodness are said to be "moral."
Only with the introduction of "justice," as "wisdom coupled with
goodness," do extenuating or extra-legal factors enter in. It
is here that Mendelssohn discusses the conditions under which
rights and duties are "perfect" or "imperfect" for those who
possess them. Imperfect rights, he says, depend upon the "consciousness and conscience of the person who has to fulfill them,"
whereas perfect duties do not. Thus it is under the rubric of
"justice" that Mendelssohn actually addresses the problem of
how all his many laws, which cannot contradict each other, actually relate to people. The conflict which causes all the confusion is not within the legal system, but between it and the
people who should obey it.

The next paragraph offers confirmation that this is Hamann's
interpretation, for it metaschematically parodies the effort by
Mendelssohn to reconcile the law with the people under it by
means of an abstract word such as "justice." Here Hamann ironically puts himself in the "privileged" place of a "man-of-letters"
who can use words as he likes, with the qualification that he
submits his proposed usage to the "consciousness and conscience"
of his readers. It is the question itself, however, which reveals his understanding of the moral law problem as a problem
not within the law but between it and the people who are alienated from it. This question is taken by Schreiner to be a
quotation by Hamann from another source which has not yet been
identified (although the phrase, "to each his own," is from
Cicero, and was popular among natural law thinkers).[45] It seems
to me, however, that Hamann himself may have been the author of
this question, and that the key to interpreting it is to be
found not in its allusion to Cicero but in the biblical imagery
of God's condescension in Christ.

The grounds for such an interpretation are threefold: the
wording, the content and the context of the question. With regard to the wording, there is only one clue, but it is striking:
the use of the word "rob" for the relation between justice on
the one hand and wisdom and goodness on the other. "How should
justice," asks Hamann, "rob from wisdom and goodness their own?"

The word "robbery" also occurs in a New Testament text which is
one of the most profound and complex biblical statements about
God's condescension, Phil. 2:5-8. There it is said that Christ
"thought it not robbery to be equal with God" (AV; *nicht einen
Raub* in Luther's translation). Here Hamann is asking how it is
possible for justice to "rob" wisdom and goodness of their own
being. In itself, the usage could be mere coincidence, or only
arbitrarily allusive imagery. But the content of this question,
and the context in which it is placed, seem to point to a conscious connection by Hamann with the Pauline text.

The content of Phil. 2:5-8 is as follows:

> Have this mind among yourselves, which is yours in
> Christ Jesus, who, though he was in the form of God,
> did not count equality with God a thing to be grasped,
> but emptied himself, taking the form of a servant,
> being born in the likeness of men. And being found
> in human form he humbled himself and became obedient
> unto death, even death on a cross.

Compare now the content of Hamann's question: How can justice, he asks, which has the power, according to Mendelssohn,
to give "to each his own," give up that sovereign power? How
can justice renounce its own being? How can it displace wisdom
and goodness? Finally, how can it give up its own unity for
two others, which are different from it as well as from each
other?

In terms of content alone, these two passages show several
remarkable parallels. Just as Christ is equal with God, justice
"gives to each its own," which is Hamann's way of saying that
"Justice" *is* God.[46] That is, we are dealing with the mystery
of the sovereignty and unity of God, and the question raised by
the biblical allusion is whether His sovereignty and unity are
best grasped as Christ or as "justice." That question turns on
the capacity of Christ or "justice" to renounce his/its own
"equality" with God, and to allow the sovereign unity to yield
to disunity and diversity.

When these parallels are looked at once again in the context of Hamann's concern with the conflict between the laws of
wisdom and justice, which are from God, and the will and knowledge of those who are under those laws, the connections are even
more striking. To be equal with God was no "robbery" for Christ/
justice, but to renounce that equality will in some sense "rob

from wisdom and goodness their own." In short, the condescension of God in Christ will not only deprive God of His undisturbed unity; it will also deprive the law of its subjects. To say that God became incarnate in Christ in order to deliver men from the law is familiar Pauline theology. But to say that justice renounced its own being in order to deliver men from the laws of wisdom and goodness (of which it is the harmony and expression) is nonsense. In short, Hamann's juxtaposition is intended to demonstrate that the task of reconciliation between the moral law and individual men cannot be achieved by an abstraction such as "justice," but only by the person of God Himself, who condescends by His incarnation to come "in the likeness of men."

This comparison is developed further by Hamann in the phrase, "gave over its own unchangeable oneness for two." If that which "gives to each its own" is only "justice," then this phrase means that it must somehow give up its unity for wisdom and goodness, which "are as different from each other as it is from them both." Such a transaction is difficult to imagine for such abstractions as justice, wisdom and goodness. But if the subject Hamann really has in mind is God, then this is another allusion to the mystery of His self-accommodation to man. God gives up His own absolute unity in order to send His Son to save the world and His Spirit to sanctify those He calls out of the world. The second and third persons of the Trinity are "as different from each other" as they are from the Father. The three persons of God provide an answer to the problems raised by Mendelssohn's moral theories: by their personal condescension to man they succeed where the theoretical and legal abstractions of the *Jerusalem* fail.

The condescension of God in Christ is the third and final point of connection between language and historical revelation in the *Golgotha*. The foundation for that connection is the belief that man is created with a capacity for language because he is made in the image of the God who speaks. God intends man to use language properly; to misuse it is to lie before God and thus to perjure oneself. The basis for Christian moral relations is linguistic honesty, which is a covenant to say what one means and do what one says. Without this honesty, there can be no morality and no social relations or contracts of any kind. Finally, the difficulty with such a morality is that the will and knowledge of the individual person are in conflict with the very ideal of justice, and with the moral law which is meant to produce justice. This problem, however, has been overcome -- not by a better theory of justice, but by the historical act of God's condescension in the person of Jesus of Nazareth. By this saving act God entered history and gave to man a "new covenant" for the restoration of the true "image" and of the capacity for morality in language.

In the "structures" of covenant and condescension, the fully reciprocal relation of history and language as Hamann understands them is manifest. The meaning of history can be grasped only by means of the biblical language which speaks of a world created by the transcendent God, fallen due to the sin of man, and redeemed by the sacrifice of God's Son on the Cross. This is the language which reveals the meaning of history. Conversely, this language is also fully historical. It was given to Adam in the moment of creation. It was corrupted by the Fall no less than all other things human were corrupted. And it is redeemed by the Word of God, Jesus Christ. Thus language is every bit as "positive" as history. Words confront men with their own "otherness" just as historical events do. The only authority by which true words can be distinguished from false or empty words, or true understanding from false understanding of events, is the "textbook" which God's Spirit has given to man -- the Bible. The Bible is the key that unlocks the mysteries of history and language. As the "chains on belief" for all Christians, it affirms the transcendence of God over the world and the "positivity" of all the gifts He has given to man, not the least of which is faith itself.

Language and Faith

On the basis of the theological positivity of language, Hamann criticizes all thinking which does not let itself be guided and governed by the revelation of God. Thus he rejects the dichotomies and dialectics of philosophy in favor of such notions as covenant and condescension, which are drawn from the biblical witness and thus not available to human reason unaided by revelation. In order to understand and appropriate them, faith is necessary. Since language is the external expression

of reason, it is possible to say that Hamann offers a re-state-
ment of the classical Christian conviction that faith must precede reason. The Bible, however, does not explicitly discuss
the relationship between faith and reason/language. Hamann's
method for offering what he takes to be a "biblical" doctrine
of that relationship is to interpret reason by means of the
"type" of the law. In his view, the biblical portrayal of the
law illuminates the meaning of reason. This is all the more so
because "law" and "reason" have coalesced as methods of thinking
in modern times. Although they differ in terms of their respective orientations toward past and future, they are allied in
their way of responding to the historical fact of sin:

> Next to the infinite mis-relation of man to God,
> "public educational institutions dealing with the re-
> lation of man to God" are noisy unrhymed sentences of
> dry words which infect the inner sap, the more a specu-
> lative creature gets to suck in of them. In order,
> first of all, to lift up the infinite mis-relation and
> clear it out of the way, before there can be any talk
> of relations which are said to serve as the basis for
> connecting public institutions, either man must become
> a partaker of a divine nature, or else the godhead must
> take on flesh and blood. The Jews through their living
> legislation, and the Naturalists through their divine
> reason, have seized upon a palladium for equalization:
> consequently, no other mediating concept remains for
> Christians and Nicodemuses than to believe with all
> their heart, with all their soul, with all their mind.
> For God so loved the world -- This is the victory which
> has overcome the world, our faith.[47]

The "infinite mis-relation of man to God" is sin, a willful
rebellion in which man refuses to obey the terms of God's covenants with him. If there were no such fact as sin, then perhaps
"public institutions dealing with the relation of man to God"
could be set up by man without undue difficulty. This is, in
fact, Mendelssohn's definition of "church," which he contrasts
with public institutions dealing with man's relation to man, or
the "state."[48] But it is not, in Hamann's view, so simple.
Metaschematically juxtaposing this quotation with Mendelssohn's
remarks on the "miserable sophistry" of an alleged conflict between duties toward God and duties toward man, Hamann turns Mendelssohn's warning about "unrhymed sentences of dry words" which
"infect the inner sap" against him.[49] The dangerously infectious
dry words are not those which describe the sin by which man is

separated from and thrown into conflict with God. They are those
words which "speculative creatures" like Mendelssohn "suck in"
and use for justifying institutions which ignore the fact of sin
and are therefore doomed to failure.

Hamann states the problem clearly in the next sentence: the
"infinite mis-relation" of sin must be overcome before there can
be any progress which would provide a foundation for the sort of
public institutions Mendelssohn desires. How can this be accomplished? In Hamann's view, the logic of the situation requires
that either man become divine "or else" God must become human.
In order for there to be a full atonement or reconciliation, one
of the estranged parties must bridge the gap between them. Without such a bridge, there is no basis on which to discuss "connecting public institutions."

There is, of course, a third logical possibility: that of
compromise. In lieu of a radical divinization of man or an
equally radical condescension of God to flesh and blood, it is
possible to imagine and strive toward a solution whereby both
sides might move toward the other simultaneously. Thus the Jews
have "their living legislation" from God, just as Naturalists
revere and employ reason as "divine." Hamann does not dispute
the divine origins of either the law or reason. His objection
is directed rather at the use to which these divine gifts have
been put by their human recipients. In both cases, the gifts
from God become substitutes for God, in the sense that the law
and reason are treated as a "palladium for equalization" (*Palladium zur Gleichung*). This phrase includes several allusions.
The Greek "palladium" was the image of the goddess Pallas which
was kept in the citadel of Troy to keep the city safe from harm.
Hamann's choice of this word implies that the Jews and Naturalists
have used the law and reason as idols. Secondly, Troy was destroyed, despite its palladium. The Jews and Naturalists should
take note and be warned of the dangers involved in trusting in
idols. Finally, a palladium is, according to Hamann, a human
manipulation of a divine gift "for equalization" of men with
God. That is, by means of their idolatrous use of the law and
reason, the Jews and Naturalists attempt to lift themselves up
to the level of the godhead. They attempt to partake of the
divine nature by their own efforts. This is the worst possible
sin and abuse of the gifts they have received.

As a result of this idolization, "law" and "reason" cannot serve as words or concepts for the expression of a right relation with God. The problem of sin is not overcome by them, and therefore some "other mediating concept" is still required. The only one, Hamann concludes, is faith. Since keeping the law and using one's reason have proven to be spiritually dangerous, Christians "and Nicodemuses" must "believe with all their heart, with all their soul, with all their mind" (Mt. 22:37). "Nicodemuses" are those who confess the Christ as their Lord only in secret, as Nicodemus came to Jesus "by night" (Jn. 3:2).[50] "Christians" are presumably those who confess their faith openly. Both share God's ultimate gift, which alone is adequate to overcome the gap created by sin. This gift is none other than God's own Son, whom He gave because He "so loved the world" (Jn. 3:16). On the basis of the gift of atonement -- of God become flesh and blood and offered up for mankind -- it is possible to claim "the victory which has overcome the world, our faith" (1 Jn. 5:4). It is faith rather than the law or reason which is the mediating concept by which man can know his own reconciliation with God. Faith solves the problem of sin, a problem which the law and reason only intensify.

Although similar in their way of trying to avoid the radical nature of sin, the law and reason differ in their strategies for doing so. Hamann identifies this difference in terms of their respective temporal orientations, and then goes on to argue that, in modern times, law and reason have come to be almost indistinguishable:

> To be sure, it is a cause for grief not to know what one is oneself, and almost ludicrous to be just the opposite from what one wants and intends to be. Thus the Jew was without any other god than that over which the archangel Michel contended three thousand years ago; the Greek has expected for two thousand years a science and a queen, who is still said to be coming, and of whom one will one day be able to say: this is Jezebel![51]

In this paragraph, Hamann approaches the problem of the relation of the law to reason in terms of the identities of their respective devotees -- Jews and Greeks. Ironically alluding to Paul's lament in Rom. 7:15 ("I do not understand my own actions. For I do not do what I want, but I do the very thing I hate"),

Hamann charges that even worse than the grief of self-ignorance
is the "ludicrous" situation of being "just the opposite from
what one wants and intends to be." "Thus," he goes on, the Jews
and the Greeks have always thought that they worshipped different
gods. The Jew remained loyal to "the body of Moses" over which
the archangel Michel contended with the devil (Jude 9), i.e. the
law. And the Greek never gave up his hope for "a science" or
adequate knowledge which he could worship as "a queen."[52] This
queen, however, if she ever came, would be like Jezebel risen
up from the grave. Jezebel, the wife of King Ahab, was the enemy
of the servants and prophets of the Lord (2 Ki. 9:7). Her deeds
were so wicked that the Lord had her corpse eaten by dogs. She
was denied the burial customarily given to royalty "so that no
one can say, This is Jezebel" (2 Ki. 9:37). The juxtaposition
of this allusion with that to the corpse of Moses is striking.
Hamann seems to be saying that whereas the Jew worships a corpse
-- the law -- the Greek lives in expectation of a dead "science"
of reason which he, too, will be able to worship as an idol.
Thus both are corpse-worshippers, and the difference between
them is reduced to the temporal direction in which they expect
to find their respective corpses: the past or the future.

After the reference to Jezebel, Hamann returns in that same
paragraph to "the Jew," whom he accuses of collaborating with
the Romans to do away with God's anointed (Christ) and then re-
placing the religion of blood-sacrifices in the temple with a
religion of "schools." Conversely, Frederick pretends to be a
"philosopher à la Grecque," but his manner of governing includes
going after every purse with his "circumcision knife" and admin-
istering his kingdom through a bevy of unscrupulous French
"priests and Levites." Thus, as Schreiner observes, the roles
of Jew and Greek seem to have been "exchanged."[53] The Jew, by
clinging to the corpse of Moses' law, has rendered his faith
merely academic. And the Greek, by looking forward to the corpse
of a queen and science yet to come, has succumbed to the rituals
of his own greed and priestly complacency. The Jew has become
a Greek, and the Greek a Jew, not in the oneness of Christ who
is "the power of God and the wisdom of God" for them both (1 Cor.
1:24), but in the disobedience and arrogance of their preference
for a manageable corpse over the living truth of the Spirit of
the crucified and resurrected Lord.

There are two other examples proposed in the *Golgotha* of
Greek Jews and Jewish Greeks. One is, of course, Mendelssohn
himself, to whom Hamann constantly refers by alluding either to
his Jewish faith, his rationalistic convictions, or to their
combination in him. One phrase which recurs in different forms
several times in the *Golgotha* is "rabbi of divine reason." Mendelssohn is a Jew by origin and training, and thus a "rabbi."
But he is a Greek by conviction, for the object of his faith is
"divine reason" rather than the God of the Old Testament. Putting both of these together, Hamann coins the phrase "rabbi of
divine reason"[54] to indicate that Mendelssohn is really a Greek
Jew. As for a Jewish Greek, his most interesting example is
not King Frederick but the English philosopher, David Hume:

> It befalls even a David Hume that he judaizes
> and prophesies, like Saul the son of Kish. When
> Philo, the Pharisee, finally confesses to the hypo-
> crite Cleanthes a fit of astonishment and melancholy
> from the greatness and obscurity of the unknown ob-
> ject, and his contempt of human reason, that it can
> give no solution more satisfactory with regard to so
> extraordinary and pompous a question as that of his
> own existence: then indeed is the entire devotion
> of the natural religion lost in the Jewish anachronism
> of a longing desire and expectation that Heaven would
> be pleased, if not to abolish the disgrace of so great
> an ignorance, at least to alleviate it through another
> Gospel than the Cross, and through a Paraclete who is
> said to be coming (*adventitious Instructor*).[55]

Hamann's interpretation of Hume in this paragraph is based
on Philo's closing speech in the *Dialogues Concerning Natural
Religion*.[56] It is a speech in which, Hamann implies, Hume
"judaizes and prophesies, like Saul." Just as Saul, after being
anointed by the prophet Samuel, was seized by the Spirit of God
and prophesied with a band of prophets in confirmation of his
anointing (1 Sam. 10:1-13), so also Hume, despite his religious
scepticism, is capable of prophesying like a Jewish prophet of
old. The most famous example of this interpretation of Hume
by Hamann concerns Hume's claim that Christianity, which began
with miracles, still "cannot be believed by any reasonable person without one."[57] With metaschematic irony Hamann explicitly
affirms this sceptical statement, just as in the *Golgotha* he
interprets the words of Philo as a true "prophecy" by Hume himself.[58]

Hamann presents the opposition between Philo and Cleanthes as that between a Pharisee and a hypocrite. Although he does not elaborate on the "hypocrisy" of Cleanthes, it is presumably connected with the latter's confidence in his own powers of rational argumentation. As we have seen, Hamann is sceptical about all efforts to arrive at comprehensive and unambiguous statements of truth in philosophical language, and Cleanthes' argument from design for the existence of God is just such an effort. Thus his "hypocrisy" concerns the morality of language. Cleanthes, like Mendelssohn after him, misuses language as he goes about his theoretical projects.

In contrast, Philo is a "Pharisee" who expresses scepticism about the ability of human reason to solve the problem of the existence of God. Hamann gives a suggestive metaschematic twist to Philo's question. Whereas Philo speaks of his "astonishment" at the "greatness of the object" (God), his "melancholy" over its "obscurity," and his "contempt of human reason" for being able to produce "no solution more satisfactory with regard to so extraordinary and magnificent a question," Hamann's substitution of "pompous" for "magnificent," and his qualification of the question as really about "his own existence," turns the entire question back against Philo/Hume. Rather than a humble statement of agnosticism with regard to the existence of God, it is now presented as a "confession" of frustration with himself for being unable to solve the riddle of his own existence. In short, the question of God's existence is used by Philo/Hume as a way of avoiding the question of his own existence and obligations, much as the Pharisees taught that a gift given to God cancels the need to honor one's parents with a gift (Mt. 15: 5).

Although primarily concerned about his own existence, Philo uses reason to present his question as though it were about the existence of God. In either case, however, the result is the same -- ignorance. Despite his previous claim that the only real worship is knowledge of God,[59] Philo must fall back from this stated ideal -- "the entire devotion of the natural religion" in Hamann's phrase -- upon a position which he himself describes as "a longing desire and expectation that Heaven would be pleased to dissipate, at least alleviate, this profound

ignorance by affording some more particular revelation to mankind." Furthermore, Philo continues, when the imperfections of
reason are understood, then the philosophical sceptic will receive the aid of revealed truth more avidly than even "the
haughty dogmatist."[60] Thus the sceptic, but not the dogmatist,
is said by Philo to receive the "adventitious instructor" of a
"more particular revelation." Hamann, seeing that this "longing
desire" is for "another Gospel than the Cross," sums up his
judgment of it by calling it a "Jewish anachronism."

Mendelssohn is a Jew who thinks like a Greek, and Hume is
a Greek who thinks like a Jew. The worshippers of the law have
become devotees of reason, and reason involves the same spiritual
dilemmas as the law. Thus the Greek now looks forward to a new
revelation, and the Jew abandons the revelation he has received
for "universal" reason. The Jew is now the philosophical opti-
mist, whereas the Greek claims that philosophical scepticism is
a prerequisite to faith. According to Hamann, however, it is
faith which must be the prerequisite of both the law and reason.
The language by which the law and reason are given by God and
received by man presupposes a basic attitude of belief, not
doubt. Without this fundamental trust, there can be no reason
or obedience at all:

> Belief and doubt affect man's capacity to know;
> as fear and hope affect his instinctual appetite.
> Truth and untruth are tools of the understanding:
> (true or untrue) representations of good and evil
> are tools of the will. All our knowledge is im-
> perfect, and all human grounds of reason consist
> either in belief in truth and doubt in untruth or
> in belief in untruth and doubt in truth. "This
> (partly negative, partly positive) belief is prior
> to all systems. It has produced them first, in order
> to justify itself," says the venerable friend of Herr
> Moses Mendelssohn. But if the understanding believes
> in lies and finds that tasty, and doubts truths and
> finds them sickening like bad food, then the light in
> us is darkness and the salt has lost its savor --
> Religion is a pure church parade -- philosophy, an
> empty display of words, superannuated opinions with-
> out meaning, obsolete rights without power! There-
> fore scepticism with regard to the truth and gulli-
> bility about self-deception are just as inseparable
> symptoms as chills and warmth in a fever. The one who
> believes himself to be farthest removed from this sick-
> ness of the soul and fervently wishes to be able to
> cure it in all his fellow-men himself confesses to
> have so often performed this cure on himself and tried

it on others that he has become aware of how difficult
it is and how small the chances of success are. -- Woe
to the unfortunate wretch who dares to find fault with
these inoffensive, purified words![61]

This is the last long paragraph in the *Golgotha*, and it sums
up Hamann's view of the relation between faith and knowledge and
the mediating role which language plays between them. He begins
with the observation that belief (*Glaube*) and doubt are prior
to all knowledge, and affect the content of knowledge, just as
emotions such as fear and hope affect a man's appetites. According to this analogy, knowledge is a natural "instinctual appetite" (*Begehrungstrieb*), but not one that operates independently
of the person's basic perception of himself in the world. If
a man is afraid, he loses his appetite; if hopeful, it increases.
In the same way, belief in God is a pre-condition for knowledge
of God, and doubt in God's existence will find itself "confirmed"
by its own ignorance of God.

One of the basic dichotomies asserted by Mendelssohn in
defense of his claim[62] that social pressure should never be
brought to bear upon doctrinal assent is that between the will
and the understanding. In his initial attack upon all interference by the state in matters of belief, he argues that "Fear
and hope affect man's instinctual appetite," in contrast to
"the grounds of reason" which "affect his capacity to know."
According to Mendelssohn's anthropology, the will is rooted in
instinctual appetite, while reason transcends it. Thus he continues: "Representations of good and evil are instruments of
the will, [whereas those] of truth and untruth [are instruments]
of the understanding."[63] The German here is ambiguous as to
whether such representations are tools for governing the will
and understanding respectively, or tools by which they express
themselves. Either way, however, a basic dichotomy between will
and understanding, between morality and reason, is affirmed.
Concern for good and evil can generate fear and hope, but should
not be used to influence the rational efforts of the understanding to arrive at truth. This distinction is repeated later in
the *Jerusalem* when Mendelssohn is defending Judaism as a religion of moral teaching without doctrinal requirements. "Belief
and doubt," which he identifies with (intellectual) agreement
and disagreement (*Beifall und Widerspruch hingegen*), are said

to be governed not by "fears and hopes but by our knowledge of truth and untruth."[64]

By his metaschematic use of Mendelssohn's phrases Hamann registers his disagreement about the relation of will to understanding. He agrees that "fear and hope affect man's instinctual appetite," and that "Truth and untruth are instruments of the understanding." Whereas Mendelssohn says, however, that "belief and doubt...are governed...by our knowledge of truth and untruth," Hamann turns that statement around to read: "Belief and doubt affect man's capacity to know." Having reversed the order of priority assigned by Mendelssohn to the two terms of his dichotomy, Hamann undermines the dichotomy itself by pointing out that the "instruments of the will" are "representations of good and evil" which must, as he says in an ironic parentheses, be "true or untrue." It is the will, in Hamann's view, that provides either true or untrue representations of good and evil as tools for the understanding. Whether those representations are in fact true or untrue depends upon whether the will is grounded in belief or in doubt.

Hamann then alludes to the biblical basis for the argument he is advancing. In 1 Cor. 13:9 Paul writes that "our knowledge is imperfect." Hamann's quotation of that phrase alludes not to Mendelssohn's concept of "imperfect" (*unvollkommene*) rights and duties but to the fragmentary nature of human knowledge. The word he uses here for "imperfect" is *Stückwerk*," which is the word found in Luther's translation of 1 Cor. 13:9. It means "patchwork," and it is this piecemeal and incomplete quality of our knowledge which Hamann is emphasizing. Since all human knowledge is incomplete or imperfect, it cannot stand alone. The "human grounds of reason" are to be found in the will, which orients a person either toward "belief in truth and doubt in untruth" or toward the contrary. In support of his argument, Hamann ironically quotes Garve's statement of the priority of faith to all systems, since Garve was a thinker much admired by Mendelssohn.

Hamann's next sentence combines in a manner typical of his style several strands of his thinking about the nature of human understanding. As we have seen, the capacity to know is analogous to an instinctual appetite, and Hamann expresses that opinion

by describing the understanding in terms of the sense of taste
-- saying that scepticism will find lies "tasty" and truths
"sickening like bad food." A second strand, completely compatible in Hamann's view with this imagery of the senses, is the
spiritual importance of believing the truth. When scepticism
displaces faith, "then the light in us is darkness," just as the
body is full of darkness when its eye is not sound (Mt. 6:23);
and "the salt has lost its savor," which means it is due to be
thrown away (Mt. 5:13). The result of this physical and spiritual death will be the loss of true meaning from all that men do
and think. Religion will become a "pure church parade" and
philosophy "an empty display of words." Outdated opinions will
take the place of meanings which are alive and relevant to the
times. In short, the effects of scepticism on morality, language and understanding will be devastating.

Following Mendelssohn, Hamann describes scepticism as a
disease. To be sceptical of the truth necessitates being gulli-
ble with regard to lies and self-deception, just as a fever has
alternating chills and warmth as symptoms. Where there is one,
the other is not far away. In his use of this metaphor, Mendelssohn admonishes the reader not to think him a sceptic, for he
is "perhaps among those who are farthest removed from this sickness of the soul." Furthermore, he exclaims, "I fervently wish
I could cure my fellow-men of it." It is, however, the warning
he then issues that particularly impresses Hamann. Mendelssohn
admits that he has "so often" tried to cure himself and others
that he knows "how difficult it is and how small the chances of
success are."[65] To Hamann, this statement is a confession. He
sees in such confession the only possible cure for one who has
succumbed to the disease of scepticism. The sceptic must confess
his illness and his need for restored faith, rather than try to
use his reason to cure himself. With a final ironic poke, Hamann
metaschematically affirms Mendelssohn's confession of the dangers
of scepticism by quoting his own warning against connecting sentiments with specific words (!) at the end of the *Jerusalem*:
"the unfortunate wretch" who has different sentiments and therefore "dares to find fault with these inoffensive, purified words,
will be in terrible trouble."[66] Hamann is no advocate of sepa-
rating words from sentiments. But he does consider Mendelssohn's

confession of the difficulty he has had curing scepticism to be,
in contrast with the rest of the *Jerusalem*, "inoffensive, purified words." The path to restored faith and redeemed language
is *via* the confession of sin.

Hamann closes the *Golgotha*[67] with a collage of texts from
the New Testament. With Pilate, he asks "What is truth?" (Jn.
18:38). With Jesus, he answers that the truth is the Spirit of
God, which this world can neither know nor receive (Jn. 3:8; 1:
11). Peace from God sanctifies the whole man -- spirit, soul
and body. The peace of the world will lead only to disaster.
The basis for faith in God's promises is trust in the words of
the biblical witness. The last sentence of the *Golgotha* is also
the last declarative sentence of the Bible (Rev. 22:20): "He
who testifies to these things says, 'Surely I am coming soon.'
Amen."

*   *   *

The Bible provides Hamann with the language of faith, with
which he discerns the meaning of history and the proper use of
human reason. Because language is "given" to man, and not subject to arbitrary manipulation, it has a "positivity" which gives
it both priority and authority in relation to the possibilities
of thought. Thought must conform to the limits laid down by
language, and resist the temptation to imagine dichotomies and
dialectics according to its own fancy. Language is given by
God to His highest creature -- man -- whom He created "in His
own image." Language is the foundation of man's moral relations
with God and with other men. Hamann sees throughout the Bible
an implicit presupposition of a covenant of language. Language
is also the means by which the gap caused by sin between the
moral law and the individual moral will can be bridged: the
Word of God condescends to come to man in the flesh and in words
which he can understand and receive. It is faith in this Word,
rather than in law or reason, which reconciles man to God. It
is standing on the promises of those biblical words, rather than
on the dictates of the law or the principles of reason, which
constitutes the life of faith. Whereas law and reason see themselves as based upon a revelation in the past or in the future,

faith is grounded in the present, for the one who came and will
come again is the Risen Lord whose Spirit sustains and guides
all who believe in Him.

CHAPTER VI

HISTORY, LANGUAGE AND FAITH

This final chapter is a systematic criticism of Hegel and
defense of Hamann with regard to their respective understandings
of the relation of history and language to the life of faith.
In the first section I discuss faith as an historical identity,
drawing on the materials presented in Chapters II and III. The
second section deals in a similar way with the question of language, recapitulating and interpreting the results of Chapters
IV and V with reference to the self-understanding of personal
faith. In conclusion, I argue that the dilemma of contemporary
theology, as outlined in Chapter I, can be understood in terms
of some of the presuppositions and convictions which account
for the difficulties in Hegel's philosophy; and that Hamann's
concept of a theological reason based on faith provides an alternative that expresses the truth and integrity of the life of
faith without sacrificing intellectual coherence.

Faith as Historical Identity

For Hegel, the self-understanding of the individual Christian within history should be determined by his identification
in his own particular will with the will of the universal. In
fact, "history" for Hegel is precisely that in which the universal attains concrete reality in the lives and consciousness of
individuals. It is when men become aware of themselves as historical moments of the universal that history becomes genuinely
significant for them. This knowledge of their own connection
with the universal is what Hegel understands as "freedom." According to him, freedom is spirit's self-knowledge in each individual of its own essential universality. Such a consciousness
was available in the Orient only to the despot and in Greece
and Rome only to the aristocratic elite. In the modern world,
however, by virtue of the decisive influence of Christianity,
there is an awareness of the fact that all men are essentially
free. This means that all men can have knowledge of the universal; the mediation between particular and universal which was

175

formerly available only to despots and nobility is now accomplished by each individual's self-conscious knowledge.

The decisive role which Hegel assigns to Christianity in
his philosophy of history is based upon his philosophical appropriation of the doctrine that God is Trinity. The theological
notion of God the Father and God the Son being joined in love as
God the Holy Spirit is translated by Hegel into a philosophy of
the Idea, nature and spirit. The universal Idea of thought produces the empirical and particular forms of nature, and is then
united with nature in a new reality which reconciles the universality of thought and the particularity of nature. Hegel calls
that reality spirit. Spirit is the dynamic process of the abstract Idea becoming concrete nature in history, just as the
Holy Spirit is, for western theology, the love which binds God
the Father and God the Son and makes them present in the world.
At the same time, spirit as history preserves within itself both
the pure thought of the universal and the empirical particularity
of nature. It transforms them into a higher unity in the self-
knowledge of men as "moments" in the progress of the universal
toward total freedom and immanence in the historical world.

As that which embraces the moment of nature, spirit in history must accept the particularity of the events which are given
to it as fundamental historical facts. Philosophy is not free
to interpret history without regard for those facts. But as
that which embraces the moment of the Idea, spirit must also
strive to understand in thought the ultimate purpose of history.
Only thought can grasp the self-relatedness of spirit's consciousness of its own freedom and reality in individual men, for
thought, like spirit, is a process of *Aufhebung*. Thus the understanding of history will be a task, even for the Christian, of
philosophical reflection. Spirit (*Geist*), in Hegel's use of
the term, means both "mind" and "spirit." It can be adequately
represented only when it is fully comprehended in terms of the
inherent reason which guides it.

"Reason" functions as Hegel's philosophical equivalent for
the theological concept of providence. To speak of divine providence is to focus attention upon God's power to govern the
events of world history according to His sovereign will. Likewise, to speak of "reason in history" is to indicate that history

proceeds according to its goal -- freedom -- and according to
the dynamic structure of the Idea which opposes itself to nature
and then unites itself with nature in spirit. Hegel describes
reason as infinite power, a term reserved by theologians for God
Himself. His rationale for identifying reason with God's will
in this way is his conviction that Christianity is the religion
in which God has revealed Himself fully. Christians need no
longer believe in providence only abstractly, or trivialize it
by relating it to personal matters which are ruled by chance
rather than reason. This means that the course of world history
is no longer to be understood as either unknowable or a matter
of chance and contingency. Indeed, Hegel sees himself as defending the objective knowledge of Himself given by God in Christianity against theologians who would reduce that knowledge to
a merely individual and subjective consciousness of God. Philosophy is in no way bound to accept Christian doctrines, but it
is sometimes called upon to help Christians achieve a better
understanding of the truth of their own faith.

One task of the philosophy of history will therefore be the
justification of the presence of evil in world history as the
will of God. If God is Lord of history, and history is really
one of the "systems" in which God "unfolds" Himself, then the
understanding of history will have to be a "theodicy," a justification of the ways of God. Hegel's analysis implies that the
gradual decline of religious faith and the church as major mani-
festations of God's power in the world requires such justification. The modern world is one in which the self-understanding
of men has become increasingly secularized, and Hegel justifies
this process as a necessary result of the universality of the
freedom toward which the Idea is striving in history. In order
for the truth of Christianity to be able to expand and embrace
the entire reality of world history, it must realize itself not
only in particular individuals or in one religion but in all
men. Thus Hegel defends the process of secularization as the
universalization of Christian truth.

The secular language which Hegel proposes for the understanding of history includes not only such philosophical terms as
Idea, nature and spirit, but also the political language of state
and constitution. The individual subjects of world history are,

in his view, nation-states. The concrete reality of freedom in
those states is expressed by their "constitution," which is the
structure of relations between those who rule and those who are
ruled. Here again Hegel emphasizes the need for the individual
citizen to identify his own personal will with that of the state
in which he participates. The state provides the context in
which he can come to realize his own relation with the universal
spirit in his times. It also provides a social foundation for
that consciousness of freedom, which is realized subjectively in
religious worship, objectively in artistic representation, and
comprehensively -- that is, both subjectively and objectively --
in philosophical thought. Only within this totality of socio-
political relations which Hegel calls the "state" can freedom
become concretely real.

Hegel also realizes, however, that it is very rare for an
individual to identify his particular will with the universal
will in the manner he describes. This realization in no way
undermines his belief that the unity of universal and particular
is the goal of history, for that belief is not based upon empirical study of historical persons but is presupposed as a result
of reflection on the development of national "constitutions."
Nevertheless, the obvious disparity between particular wills and
the universal will is in tension with Hegel's claim that knowledge of the will of God or the universal is available (at least
to Christians) in the secular self-consciousness of spirit. In
order to present a coherent notion of how Christians are to live
in history on the basis of faith, Hegel must show how the philosophical understanding of reason in history can inform their
historical consciousness and behavior as individual persons.

Here the startling self-contradiction within Hegel's philosophy emerges. On the one hand, he is very critical of any tendency toward "particularism" (for example, in religious piety),
which he seems to blame for much of the irrationality in the
world. He considers the belief that providence works in the
lives of individual persons trivial and degenerate. The personal
dimension of life remains, in his view, at the mercy of chance --
cut off from reason and understanding. The same is true for the
moral dimension of life: although it is inherently noble to
resist evil in the world, this nobility can also involve ignorance

of the course of history. Books such as the Bible are good for
moral instruction but useless for the interpretation of history.
The particularism of personal and moral concerns is, for Hegel,
simply not of historical significance. On the other hand, the
very people who make a difference in the course of political history do so, by Hegel's own account, precisely because they pursue their own particular passions rather than consciously sur-
render to the universal will. These world-historical leaders
are not thereby religious or moral men. Indeed, Hegel thinks
that their political power derives from their indifference to
conventional morality and even to any desire for personal happiness and a life of peace and security. What distinguishes the
particularism of these historical leaders from that of religious
folk is their total involvement in politics. Here Hegel contradicts his advocacy of self-identification with the universal and
his condemnation of particularism with his theory that a man's
actions in history are inevitably governed by his personal ambitions. The "cunning of reason" manages to exploit human passions for its own purposes, but the individual can have no knowledge of the higher purpose he is serving in the present.

This individual ignorance of the universal will in history
clearly contradicts Hegel's initial theoretical claim that a
"theodicy" is possible because God reveals Himself fully in history. It is a profound logical and philosophical difficulty in
his program, and it is also a religious dilemma for the Christian.
On the one hand, God is portrayed by the Bible and Christian
tradition as a God who encourages only those historical actions
which are consistent with piety and morality; on the other hand,
Hegel's reason disdains personal piety and suspends moral concerns whenever they conflict with its political purposes in history. In one stroke, Hegel undermines both his claim to preserve
Christian faith in a philosophical *Aufhebung* and the possibility
for a coherent personal identity within history. For all its
theoretical sophistication, Hegel's opposition of the moral
"imperative" to the historical "indicative" makes serving God
in the world virtually impossible not only for Christians but
for all men.

Turning to Hamann, striking similarities to Hegel's philosophy of history are evident. With his insistence upon the

historical nature of all truths and the temporal nature of man, Hamann stands over against philosophical traditions which teach the possibility of knowledge of "eternal" truths apart from their historical contexts. This position adumbrates Hegel's criticism of all philosophy which fails to see the need for the universal Idea to be united with particular nature in concrete historical Spirit. In other words, they share the opinion that truth does not simply exist: it happens. Thus they are agreed that any adequate understanding of truth must deal with historical events as the basic facts and empirical data which are, so to speak, "given" to men simply on the authority of the historical reports which have been received. To use a term drawn from the discussion of faith and language, the data of history have a "positivity" which both Hamann and Hegel acknowledge.

A second broad area of agreement is that of the relation of Christianity to history. Just as Hegel sees the advent of Christianity as a decisive turning-point in the development of philosophical knowledge of God and the understanding of historical providence which such knowledge makes possible, Hamann thinks of Christianity as the center of history, toward which all prophecies point and by which they are fulfilled. Without the revelation of Himself which God granted in Christianity, there could be no understanding of history at all.

Finally, there is a third major area of agreement between Hamann and Hegel in their understanding of history: the relation of God's will to the will of individuals. Although Hegel fails to understand Hamann's emphasis upon the transcendence of God over human institutions and doctrines, it is very similar to his own theory of the "cunning of reason." The will which determines the course of history is the will of God for Hamann and the will of spirit or reason for Hegel. Neither perceives the individual person as capable of imposing his personal will on the course of events. Hegel identifies God with the historical process to the extent that he calls the philosophy of history a theodicy, and Hamann affirms Lessing's effort to deal with moral issues within the context of a theodicy. Hamann is not especially concerned to "justify" God in relation to historical evil, but he is very much convinced that all claims for the primacy of individuals in history or morality are false.

Nevertheless, the very center of Hamann's theology of history is an affirmation of particularity as the mode of God's presence and activity in the world. Whereas Hegel says that the individual should identify with the universal, Hamann recites again and again the story of how God chose the people of Israel and prepared them to receive His Son as their promised Messiah. Their particular history is the sole textbook by which other histories can be understood. The truth of other nations can therefore be determined only by analogy to the prophecies and fulfillments recorded in the Bible. Although Hamann stresses that the Bible offers an account of the origins and destiny of all men, for it speaks in detail of both the creation and the End of the world, he never suggests that the universal truths contained in Scripture could or should be given a more universal expression. They are adequate, in Hamann's view, in their biblical context and language, which means in all their particularity.

The exegetical method which Hamann employs to interpret the Bible reflects his conviction that it is a particular book about particular people with universal implications. That method involves discerning events and persons in the Old Testament as "types" of events and persons in the New Testament and in all other history. Thus Judaism is held up by him as a prophetic type of the Christian church, and the figures of Jewish history illuminate the truth of situations which arise many centuries later. Typological interpretation cannot, however, be pinned down to a single meaning. It is possible only if the Holy Spirit guides the believer in the task of discerning the appropriate connections between prophetic words and the events which fulfill them. For example, a literalistic exegesis would understand Moses simply in terms of explicit biblical statements about him. Hamann, however, sees him as both a type of faith -- for he was the instrument of grace by which God let the Israelites out of Egypt, and as a type of unbelief -- for he disobeyed God in the wilderness and therefore was denied entrance into the promised land of Canaan. Literalistically, it is hard to understand how Moses can be a type of both faith and unbelief. Only by the Holy Spirit is it possible to discern which prophetic interpretation of the type explains the meaning of a given historical event in the present.

Although Hegel's dialectical method is also non-literalistic, for it involves thinking through all oppositions encountered in texts or in history until they are transformed by thought into a higher unity which embraces them both as moments within itself, Hamann's typological interpretation of history through the Bible has no such *Aufhebung*. For him, there is no unity of type and event or universal and particular. The Bible presents a picture of God as standing over against human history and ruling it without in any way becoming subject to it. His transcendence can never be compromised by any alleged overcoming of the gap which divides man from Him.

Consistent with this transcendence, Hamann does not believe that humans can attain to knowledge of God or the meaning of history by the exercise of unaided reason. He disagrees with Hegel's claim that Christianity has already unveiled God's full truth in the world. On the contrary, Christianity is the event by which the possibility for discerning God's truth in His continued self-veiling in the world is given. This means that historical understanding requires not only a textbook for the interpretation of events but also an authoritative record of what God has already done in the world, what He promises to do in the future, and generally what His ways of working in history are. Once again, the Bible is the medium for understanding these matters. Only by accepting the authority of the Bible as *the* account and interpretation which God has given of his own self-revelation in and to the world is there any possibility of an adequate historical understanding.

The Bible provides more than just the means for understanding biblical history: it is the instrument by which all world history is to be interpreted. Here the extent to which Hamann offers a radical alternative to modern theology is apparent. There is, in his view, no such thing as a valid "secular" historical understanding based upon non-biblical principles. The truth of the entire history of the world can be understood only in terms of God's truth, to which the Bible is the sole authoritative witness. This position implies that the entire issue of "secularization" is really a non-issue. If the Bible provides the language by which world history can be explained, then there is no initial division between the sacred and the secular. And

what has not been divided is surely not in need of reconciliation.
The world is indeed a fallen world, and far from being "sacred"
in itself. But the only way it can come to understand that fact
is through the Bible. Any separate or autonomous self-understanding the world may have is as "useless" for faith's understanding
of history as Hegel declared the Bible to be for rational comprehension. Thus Hamann appeals to the historical and moral significance of covenants given by God to man in order to criticize
Mendelssohn's philosophy of moral laws based upon a social contract. His point throughout in appealing to "covenant" is that
men exist only by virtue of God's love and according to His will.
As His servants, the moral and political relationship with Him
is more important than any other in their lives. Only within
the context of a right relation with God can the morality and
politics of human relations be worked out. Consequently, freedom is not located in the relation between the individual and
society, but in the relation between the individual and the
transcendent God. Men are "free" only to obey or disobey their
Lord. As the sole Creator, He has exclusive rights to all goods
and property. This applies to kings no less than to peasants.
In Hamann's view, all are equally subject to the sovereignty of
God, as his contrasting of Nimrod with Solomon and Nebuchadnezzar shows.

Although Hegel would certainly agree with Hamann's protest
against all theories of primeval freedom, his reason for doing
so would be very different. For Hegel, freedom is the goal of
history rather than its origin. Furthermore, if "obedience"
can be described as a relation in which one person submits to
the will of another person, then the notion of obedience to God
makes no sense at all to him, for he does not conceive of God
as a person. The path to freedom, in Hegel's terms, might better
be described as one of "resignation." His doctrines of the passions and of the cunning of reason serve to underscore this
point. Since the actions of individuals in history are governed
by the passions rather than by knowledge of God's will, there
is no possibility of personal knowledge of and obedience to
God's will for oneself. Furthermore, because the private passions
of some individuals are for public or political goals, they can
be exploited by the cunning of reason, thereby granting in effect

greater "freedom" or power for self-realization to those individuals rather than to others. This leads to Hegel's concept of
"world-historical" individuals, an idea that implicitly condones
the very elitism which Hamann explicitly repudiates. Once again,
no reconciliation seems to be possible between the moral and personal view of historical meaning offered by Hamann's understanding of biblical faith and the trans-moral and impersonal view
suggested by Hegel.

The centrality of this personal dimension is also emphasized
by the other aspect or "structure" of historical meaning which
is discernible in the argument of the *Golgotha* -- the concept of
God's condescension to man. As God's way of initiating and re-
establishing a personal relationship with men and therefore as
the best model for moral relations among men, the notion of condescension leads Hamann to criticize Mendelssohn's moral philosophy for its impersonal portrayal of social relations. Since
it is based upon property, it implies two classes, those with
and those without property. Over against this approach, Hamann
says that morality is a matter of personal relations. Thus the
duty which every man has toward every other man is to respond
actively to his needs. Theories of human rights not only ignore
the fact that all rights belong to God; they also encourage indifference to the personal needs of others. They presuppose a
moral individualism which ultimately results in the justification
of egoism. If all people were to claim such rights and act upon
them, says Hamann, a state of anarchy would be the result.

In both his concentration upon the totalities of nation-
states and his criticism of the anarchical tendencies of democracy, Hegel agrees with Hamann's attack upon moral individualism
and social atomism. But once again the foundations of their
agreement appear to be totally different. Hegel espouses a
theory of the state as the totality, and explicitly denies historical significance to the moral conscience of individuals.
Hamann, in contrast, calls for "condescension" not only from
privilege and indifference, but also from abstract theories.
In his view, it is precisely the abstract nature of philosophical thought that renders it incapable of solving the moral dilemmas posed by Mendelssohn. The entire matter can be understood,
he maintains, only in terms of the consciousness and conscience

of individual moral persons as they engage with one another in
conflict situations. In short, moral questions are not to be
solved from the top down, by the application of abstract theories,
but from the bottom up, by starting at the complex and ambiguous
level of the will and knowledge of those persons who are involved
in the question. It is this demand for working from the bottom
up in all humility that shows the influence on Hamann of the
concept of God's condescension to man.

The concepts of covenant and condescension are two examples
of how Hamann tries to understand the meaning of contemporary
and allegedly "secular" history in the terms of the biblical witness. In this effort, he is radically at odds with Hegel's self-
conscious program to translate Christian beliefs into the secular
language of philosophy and politics. Whereas Hegel speaks of
progress from one culture or nation to the next, Hamann interprets present events by means of people or events which happened
millennia ago, but are recorded in the Bible and are illuminated
as prophetic types for the believer by the Spirit of God. The
Bible provides him with a way of understanding the world without
submitting to its values, its criteria for judgment, and its
belief in itself. Questions raised by secular philosophers can
be answered only by turning to biblical language and imagery.
Indeed, the personal identity of the Christian is constituted
in the language of the Bible. Thus the question of whether
secular or biblical language is better able to express the truth
of Christianity and the faith of individual Christians is the
second major area of "discussion" between Hegel and Hamann.

Faith as a Covenant of Language

In Hegel's opinion, Hamann's allusions to and quotations
from the Bible do not constitute a language at all. In his comments on the "Metacritique," which is Hamann's most complete
statement on the relation of reason to language, Hegel makes it
clear that he does not understand, let alone agree with, Hamann's
analysis. Because he dismisses allusions to the biblical tree
of knowledge as efforts on Hamann's part to conceal the lack of
content and substance in his thought, Hegel fails to perceive
that the problem of knowledge, as Hamann understands it, is a
problem of sin. By seeking greater knowledge than God intends

him to have, man sins against his Creator and dooms himself to confusion. God placed a limit on man's knowledge, and man transgressed that limit. Hamann's concept of the role of reason in philosophy depends heavily upon this biblical story.

Since he ignores the implications of Hamann's allusion to the biblical tree of knowledge, Hegel can more easily overlook the fact that Hamann states explicitly that the task of reason is both to extend knowledge *and* to determine its limits. The means by which Hamann would carry out this second task is by an analysis of the nature of language. As the sole means by which knowledge can be acquired or expressed, language is, in Hamann's view, the prerequisite for any extension of knowledge as well as its greatest limiting factor. Hegel appreciates that Hamann tries to solve the question of the nature of reason by an appeal to language, but he distances himself from that approach and the limitations on reason which it entails.

Hegel is fully aware of the vital connection between language and thinking. His criticism of Hamann for failing to achieve a "spiritual form" or language is paralleled by his often-repeated charge that Hamann resisted all inducements to think about his subject matter. Although Hegel frequently endorses the content of Hamann's statements -- for example, his belief in the Trinity of God and the principle of the coincidence of opposites -- he also insists that, in a strict sense, Hamann's writings have no real content. They consist, in Hegel's view, of subjective particularities, and therefore are incapable of standing as works of either philosophical science or creative art. They express Hamann's formless vitality, but they do not indicate that he is capable of moving beyond his concentrated, abstruse intelligence to the point of thinking the presence of God in the world.

For Hegel, language expresses the self-relatedness of thought. He believes that all thinking is ultimately self-related; this means that, in order to understand the "otherness" of its object, thought can and must internalize that otherness. Thus thinking about God as other to the thinker leads to the awareness that God can be known as other only within consciousness. If this is so, then both the thinker and God are part of the totality of consciousness.

Hegel accepts the fact that this is not the way in which the religious consciousness normally uses language about God. At its most primitive level, this consciousness is aware of God only in "feeling," not as the object of the universal activity of thinking. Consciousness as feeling may have some dim sense of God's universality, but it has no sense at all of its own role in thinking God as universal. It simply knows God as the Absolute and as that which is both other and immediately present to it. To call this level of religious consciousness "feeling" is to indicate not that it occurs in the emotions but that it maintains this subjective sense of God's immediate presence; it fails to think about what God might be objectively or in Himself.

The stage of feeling, however, cannot last. In his analysis of religious language, Hegel argues that the sense of God's immediate presence is not constant, and that therefore feeling must ultimately lead to doubt. This sort of doubt is not scepticism about God's existence; it is only doubt that one can, as a believer, have certain knowledge of Him on the basis of feeling alone. A sense of ignorance about God enters into the religious consciousness, and with it an awareness of a need for some means of mediation between itself and God. Since God is no longer immediately available to knowledge, He must make Himself available through some sort of image (which could be a doctrine or a book). The believer will understand this image as given or revealed to him by God, and therefore as a positive authority for the knowledge of God. He will claim to "know" God through it not in feeling but by intuition, that is, by consciousness of the image through which the knowledge of God is mediated. Since the image is external to him in a sense that feeling is not, he will claim that his intuition is superior to feeling, for it offers an objective picture or concept of God not previously available. Nevertheless, the religious consciousness cannot remain at the stage of intuition, for its merely "mediated" faith remains in tension with the "immediate" faith of the stage of feeling.

The unity of the subjectivity of feeling and the objectivity of intuition is first achieved, according to Hegel, in a form of religious thinking which he calls "representation." It is representation which he thinks Hamann should have carried through but

did not. Whereas Hamann, according to Hegel, remained at the
level of extreme tension between feeling and intuition, in representation the subject thinks -- for the first time -- about the
universality of God. Once God's universality is grasped in
thought, it is seen that He can never be bound to any particular state of consciousness (feeling) or to any specific image
(intuition). The natural and historical images and stories by
which the religious consciousness understands itself are comprehended as symbolic rather than as literal representations of
God's truth.

Within representational thought, Hegel sees a development
from natural images like "Father" and "Son" to historical images
like the Cross and Resurrection of Jesus. The unity and fulfillment of representational consciousness comes only when it is
genuinely "spiritual," that is, when the subject understands God
in terms of His predicates rather than in terms of His relations.
Once again, Hegel's concept of thought as the internalizing of
otherness is evident. Representation becomes spiritual by advancing from the notion of God as a Father or as intervening in
history to the notion of God's internal or essential being as
all-wise, all-merciful, etc. God is no longer portrayed by imagination in relation to others; He is defined by thought as He
is in Himself. The language used by faith for this advance is
speculative rather than biblical: however helpful the imagery
of the Bible may have been for the primitive religious consciousness, it is not adequate for understanding God. It must be replaced by philosophical language, through which thought pursues
its goal of ever more comprehensive knowledge, culminating in
the realization of the unity of God with those who think Him.
Only then is the last shred of otherness internalized and the
universal activity of thought adequate to its universal object.
what Hegel calls natural and historical images. Rather than
interpret those images, however, Hegel simply chastises Hamann
for failing to develop them into spiritual or philosophical for-
mulations, which is the work of thought. Since thinking is, by
Hegel's definition, a universal activity, it follows that any-
one who resists it is locked into his own particularity. That
this is Hegel's verdict on Hamann is clear from his judgment on
Hamann's style as completely dominated by his own eccentricity.

He is "religious" in the sense of considering his personality to
be superior to all the objects of his attention and to those with
whom he is in conversation. Thus he makes no real effort to communicate. He uses writing and language to conceal rather than
to reveal himself and his meaning. He hides behind humor, trivialities, smugness and mystifications, none of which are helped
by his biblical allusions. His "originality" is ultimately only
his total unclarity and failure to think through the objects on
which he discourses in such a desultory manner.

These judgments by Hegel are very unbalanced. On the matter of the meaning of history alone, he himself apparently makes
no effort to think about Hamann's language long enough or deeply
enough to penetrate and understand it. To be sure, Hamann's
language is obscure, for it does not proceed by logical progres-
sions and it presupposes that the reader is thoroughly familiar
with both the Bible and whatever other works Hamann discusses.
But, as a language, it is impenetrable only when cut off from
its biblical roots. Given Niethammer's urging and the degree
to which Hegel himself was impressed by the *Golgotha*, it is
strange that he did not study it carefully enough to discern
the role of biblical language in it. Because of this failure,
Hegel misses the point of even the most obvious passages in the
Golgotha. When Hamann writes about the transcendence of God
over human institutions in tones which are reminiscent of Hegel's
own doctrine of the cunning of reason, the philosopher perceives
only a claim for God as a "simple presence," that is, as present
to the believer in feeling. Likewise, Hegel fails to grasp the
typological significance which biblical figures have for Hamann
in his use of the Bible for interpreting the significance of
contemporary history. According to Hegel's analysis, Hamann expresses only the subjective side of the truth of reason, ignoring
entirely the objective interests which are necessary for a comprehensive science. Thus he represents the extreme wing of the
movement of spirit in his time, for he subjectivizes everything
positive and thereby avoids a rigid orthodoxy as well as the
anti-religious prejudice of the Berlin Enlightenment. Yet this
subjectivity serves him and his readers simply as a refuge from
despair over the present course of history.

It is to his Christian faith as a form of subjective freedom
that Hegel credits Hamann's extraordinary genius. The very fact
that prevents him from communicating -- his lack of interest in
objective thought and language -- also protects him from the
social restrictions on his freedom which more ordinary men might
have accepted. Hegel sees Hamann's resistance to thought and
disciplined work as the dominant characteristic of his life and
personality. Therefore the major part of his analysis of Hamann
is *ad hominem* argumentation, or explanation of his statements
not in terms of what he says but in terms of who he is. In
Hegel's eyes, Hamann is a dabbler and a man who is alienated
from his life and work. His boredom leads him to seek friendship with a wide variety of people and to read prolifically on
every conceivable subject simply to escape the tedium of his own
life. His interest in people and books bears no relation to his
own beliefs and thoughts. He writes reviews sharply attacking
the works of his closest friends, and then refrains from publishing them for fear of offending those friends. He uses his piety
as a shield from personal and social responsibilities, excusing
himself from sins and debts alike on the grounds of God's mercy
and forgiveness. In short, Hamann's faith is, in Hegel's opinion, a lamentable self-deception by which he gives himself a
sense of peace but forsakes all effort to engage in the demand-
ing work of critical and constructive thinking. He has no interest in ideas, except as words and symbols which he uses to dis-
tract unsuspecting audiences from the lack of content in his
words.

There is, Hegel acknowledges, a better side to Hamann's
personality, one which he attributes to several causes. It is
the "worldly righteousness" of his character. One of the basic
causes for Hamann's worldliness is his genius, which is manifest
in his love for and use of symbols to appropriate subjectively
everything he confronts in the objective world. Thus bread and
wine have symbolic value for him in themselves, and not simply
as part of a sacramental ritual. Another cause is Hamann's capacity for friendship. In an age when friendship was highly
valued in general, Hamann stands out as unusually devoted to
his friends. However arbitrary Hegel may consider his choice
of friends, he sees this capacity as one root of Hamann's worldly

righteousness. The third cause is somewhat surprising, given
Hegel's criticisms of Hamann's piety. It is what Hegel calls
"the positive element" by which Hamann freed himself from the
obstinacy of his post-conversion proselytizing attitude toward
his friends.

According to Hegel, Hamann understands the positive element
or "otherness" of God and religious authority as a creation of
his own thought, as an aspect attributed to God by his own religious consciousness. In Hegel's terms, this means that Hamann
realized that his knowledge of God is a matter of feeling and
intuition, that the tension between them is his own doing, and
that he can, if he so desires, take the next step and begin to
think about God in the terms of spiritual or speculative representation. Hamann chooses not to use that language. While rejecting the rigid positivity of otherworldly Pietism, he remains
totally without focus in his life and thus open to encountering
the positive element (God) at any time and in any place. His
ability to subjectivize everything positive enables him not only
to ignore the objective side of the world in which he lives but
also to remain free of any external or positive authority over
his inner life and faith.

By this conclusion, Hegel shows how profound his misunderstanding of Hamann really is. He not only fails to grasp the
specific ideas of history and language which Hamann presents:
he does not see that Hamann's thought and style are shaped by
his conviction that the Bible is God's positive authority in
the world, and that it alone contains the statement and example
of how Christians are to understand history and use language as
they engage with the world. In Hamann's view, Christian faith
is based upon a covenant of language, a covenant which should
govern all thinking and historical action. This covenant is
given by God to man, and requires of every individual total
honesty in the use of words. The morality of language involves
the relation of words to intentions on the one hand and to deeds
on the other. To keep the covenant, a person must say what he
means and do what he says. The model for the right relation
between words and deeds is the way in which God fulfills the
prophetic promises He makes in the Old Testament in Christ and
the events of the New Testament.

All human reason is predicated upon the capacity to use language. Without words, there could be no reason at all, for only by words can consciousness think about anything, whether its own intentions or the actions which result from them. Language and reason together constitute the outer and inner bond of society, the basis upon which moral and social relations are possible. Thus all the rights and duties which Mendelssohn tries to organize into a system of moral philosophy must be examined in relation to the limits imposed upon them by human language before they can be defined according to the theoretical demands of philosophy.

Although the covenant of language is first made explicit in the Bible when God charges Adam with the task of naming the animals, a deeper theological basis for this covenant is God's creation of man "in His own image." Just as God spoke and all creation came to be, so also He created man as a creature of the word, having the power to govern His creation for Him by the use of language. Before man fell into sin, all his words fit reality, and God accepted the names he assigned to the animals. Man's words were adequate to the definiteness of concrete objects. Only with the Fall did words cease to have this precision and reliability. With the loss of his close relationship with God, man lost the clarity of His image, and thus also clarity in speech and thought. This is symbolized biblically by the story of the tower of Babel and the confusion of tongues, but Hamann clearly believes that the seed of all confusion was the original sin of Adam. Nevertheless, even that sin cannot change the fact that man is created as a being capable of using language, and that capacity, more than any other, is what likens him to God. Therefore, every abuse of language constitutes perjury -- the falsification of words while "under oath" before God.

Up to this point, Hegel might well agree with Hamann that language is the means by which reality is mediated to consciousness and that this implies both a moral responsibility to language and an indication of its special relationship with reason. Yet Hegel does not endorse Hamann's philosophy of language in the "Metacritique" or comment on it in the *Golgotha*, and the reason for this is clear. In his view, language can serve

reason as a tool for the expression of the ultimate unity-in-
otherness of everything. There is no practical limit on the
capacity of the religious consciousness to rise above feeling
and intuition to spiritual representation. In contrast, Hamann
believes that language is severely limited due to the fact of
sin, and that limitations on language are also limitations on
thought. His conviction that sin is the lust for greater knowledge than God has given is a sentiment which Hegel rejects as
pious agnosticism. According to his speculative approach, sin
is a necessary evil, the negative element which serves as a
vehicle for progress. Thus the sins of world-historical leaders
are really steps forward by the cunning of reason. For Hamann,
sin is the loss of the image of God and a close relationship
with Him -- not a stage of development toward more comprehensive
and adequate knowledge of God.

In relation to the question of language, Hamann's emphasis
on sin as the cause for the misuse of words follows from his
conclusion that the real problem concerns not the relation of
words to objects but the relation of thinkers to their words.
His charge that Mendelssohn fails to understand the real relation between his own language about moral laws and his personal
will (and knowledge) as a theorist applies equally to Hegel.
Whereas Mendelssohn tries to integrate the individual moral
agent into his theory by means of a concept of justice, Hegel's
device for attempting the same thing is a doctrine of the passions. The concept of justice fails to reconcile individuals
with the law because it is too abstract; and the doctrine of
passions fails because it undermines the abstract ideal of
spirit's self-knowledge in thinking men. In neither case is
the problem of the individual's sinful will solved in such a way
that the individual is empowered to live up to the law which he
tries to know and to obey.

The solution proposed by Hamann involves neither abstract
concepts nor psychological doctrines, but the historical claim
that man is redeemed from sin by the body and blood of Jesus
Christ. In Christ, God condescended to come to man in human
form, in order to heal the breach between them and restore His
image in His creatures. This could be accomplished only by a
purification of the will of men in relation to their words and

deeds. The will had to be restored to obedience, a task that
could be accomplished only if the will can be governed by faith.
There is no dispute here over the need for mediation: in his
interpretation of Hamann as defending the knowledge of God as a
"simple presence," Hegel is utterly mistaken. The debate is,
rather, over what can adequately perform the necessary mediation.
If the will is dominated by instinct, as Mendelssohn thinks, or
by the passions, as Hegel says, then law and reason are left offering a mediation that the individual can never appropriate.
But if the will is governed by faith, as Hamann thinks, then
the need is not for a mediation between personal wills and impersonal truth, but for a mediator between the sinful will of
man and the holy will of God. Thus faith really offers something different than the law or reason. According to Hamann,
law and reason promise a permanent mediation and thus an equalization of the relation between God and man. In contrast, faith
receives a mediator upon whom it will always depend for any
access to or knowledge of God.

Since language was initially given to Adam by God, and was
then restored to man by Christ, it can be said to have a double-
positivity in relation to its users. Therefore, man is not free
to exploit the ambiguities of language, or, like Hegel, to "develop" thought as far as he can. There is a model for the use
of language, and it is to be followed. Just as the Bible is
the "chains on belief" for the understanding of history, it is
also the sole authority for the proper use of words.

To call for an examination of words prior to their use in
theories, as Hamann does in response to Mendelssohn's discussion
of church, state and freedom of conscience, is to point to this
positivity of language and the need for receiving the correct
meanings and use of words from God through the Bible. If this
is not done, there is the possibility of misusing words in the
effort to construct theories to explain realities which in fact
can be understood only by using the lens of the Bible. For
example, Mendelssohn attempts to explain rights and duties, as
well as physical and moral realities, in terms of dichotomous
relations. Although rights and duties are said never to contradict each other in Mendelssohn's system, neither can they ever
be united (in the sense of ascertaining how rights are duties

and duties are rights). Hamann discerns in Mendelssohn's discussion of these matters a tendency to set rights and duties
over against one another as if they belonged to two different
groups of people. The same problem arises with such distinctions
as church from state and sentiment from action. In all these
cases, says Hamann, Mendelssohn sets up false dichotomies, and
in the process ignores his own stated principle of the close connection of concepts which appear to exclude each other.

Hegel applauds Hamann's protest against the practice of
thinking only in terms of dichotomies, but suggests an alternative which is equally unacceptable to Hamann. The claim to accept dichotomies as necessary evils or negative stages on
thought's way toward a new, transformed unity of opposites, which
Hegel calls the process of *Aufhebung*, is denounced by Hamann as
little more than "cleverness" at making concepts appear to divide
into two and then be reunited. The error in this dialectical
method of thinking is not its presupposition that all concepts
are inter-connected, a presupposition which Hamann shares.
Rather, the error is in the initial step away from concrete complexity toward abstract definition and clarification. The "divisions of reflection" which Hegel accepts and then tries to
overcome are simply rejected by Hamann as false. It is impossible, in his view, to extrapolate logical dichotomies from relations among words that are steeped in the "original sin" of linguistic confusion. Likewise, in the case of those "dichotomies"
which can be validated on the basis of ordinary usage, it is
impossible to rejoin them by philosophical theories. For example,
the eucharistic unity of Christ's body with bread is to be believed on the basis of faith in his verbal affirmation of that
unity, not because of the "hocuspocus" of a theory of transubstantiation.

In addition to his criticism of dialectical reason as untrue
to the meanings of words, Hamann finds that it is morally questionable. It implies a virtually unlimited capacity for the
development of thought by language, very much as Nimrod founded
the city of Babel, where man's pride in his unlimited powers
would force God to "confuse" human language. Dialectical reason
exploits words for the purposes of its own theories rather than
to discern the truth. Mendelssohn's exploitation of the words

"God" and "providence" involves using those words to bolster his theory of natural law but ignores their positive meanings as given by biblical tradition. Likewise, Hamann would say, Hegel's claim that Christianity provides a religious foundation for specu- lative thought is a similar exploitation of Christian language for the purpose of giving support to a theory which is essentially humanistic. Such theories, he believes, are vessels of wicked- ness that hover between earth and heaven, human and sinful but pretending to offer divine truth. The way in which they win people over to dialectical thinking is by constantly changing their perspective on the subject matter, a technique by which they seem to be comprehensive but in fact are only confusing. Thus Mendelssohn posits both eternal truths and merely temporal knowers of those truths, and Hegel proposes that the Idea of philosophy is both God and totally free of religious understand- ings of God. To find one point of view which provides a basis for such shifts in thought and a personal identity for the think- ers seems to be impossible.

In contrast to the shifting perspectives of dialectical reason, Hamann suggests what he takes to be a firm foundation for faith. He believes that the attempt to employ reason inde- pendently of Christian revelation is, like the attempt to attain salvation by one's own success at keeping the law, a means for self-equalization with God. Thus the New Testament portrayal of the Old Testament law serves as a type for the interpretation of the plight of modern philosophical reason. Like the law-bound Jews, the devotees of reason fail to acknowledge the fact of sin and man's separation from God, even though all their efforts to encompass or control God by means of reason -- or by keeping the law -- consistently fail. Only faith in God's gift of His only Son for the salvation of the world from sin can overcome the impasse into which autonomous reason and moral legalism lead.

Hamann suggests that the practitioners of philosophical reason and the followers of the law have in fact joined ranks in unbelief and doubt: Mendelssohn, the Jew, has become a rabbi of divine reason; and Hume, the philosopher, judaizes and pro- phesies. This exchange of roles between Jew and Greek is not the unity promised to them in Christ; it is the darkness shared by those who reject Christ. The Jew has stopped looking for a

Messiah, having refused to accept the one God already sent. The
Greek is looking for a new revelation, supposedly on the basis
of his scepticism about human reason. Although Hamann prefers
"Greek" ignorance to "Jewish" indifference, he considers both
to be trapped in idolatry. They worship a dead law of Moses or
a dead queen of a science (Jezebel) still to come, rather than
the living Word of God in Christ, as attested in the living
words of the Bible, through which the Holy Spirit speaks to men.

Prior to all use of reason or obedience to the law is a
person's basic attitude toward God's truth: to believe in it or
to doubt it. In Hamann's view, doubt is no more "necessary"
than sin, for belief is based not upon rational argumentation
but upon submitting one's own will to the will of God. Such
submission requires acceptance of the fragmentary nature of
human knowledge and of the fact that reason is not autonomous
with regard to either history or language. Reason conforms to
a person's fundamental attitude of faith or doubt, which it
presupposes and tries to defend as the truth. It is both false
and arrogant to claim that one's thought is non-circular. To
be delivered from the sin of this arrogance, man needs not better thinking but the humility to receive God's grace and submit
to the authority of the Bible for faith.

Biblical Faith and Theological Method

In conclusion, what are the implications of this study of
Hegel and Hamann for the dilemma of contemporary theology? According to my interpretation in Chapter I, the root cause of
that dilemma is the apparent presupposition of most theologians
that the methods of secular historians cannot be questioned in
relation to secular history, and that therefore the task for
Christian theology is to define itself in relation to those
secular approaches. Accordingly, those theologians who are
committed to reconciliation between faith and the secular world
try to define and defend the historical claims of Christianity
in terms of essentially secular arguments, while those who perceive faith as in tension with the world prefer to try to protect it from all dependence upon secular judgments. Between
these two camps there are many disputes, but no one ever seems
to question the validity of the way in which they have all

initially stated the problem. In general, it is fair to say
that modern theology has followed Hegel, for secularity is the
one fact upon which everyone agrees, whether that fact is applaud-
ed, with Hegel, or taken to be a problem, as by Barth and more
reactionary theologians. The possibility suggested by Hamann --
that the Bible provides the key to understanding all history,
without regard to any alleged dichotomy between "sacred" and
"secular" -- does not, in our times, receive much attention.
Yet it provides a coherent alternative to the dilemma of contemporary theology, and a perspective which sheds new light on
the problems posed by those theologians whose programs I examined
in the Introduction.

Of those theologians, only Troeltsch, Harvey and Pannenberg
unequivocally accept secular methods of historical interpretation
as authoritative for modern Christians. Troeltsch's claim that
faith can be given "certainty" by a "purely historical consideration" set the tone at the beginning of the twentieth century.
Harvey defends the historical-critical method of biblical interpretation on the grounds that it can distinguish the "memory-
impression" of Jesus from the "Biblical Christ" of later theological imagination. Despite his qualification that this Biblical
Christ was once a viable avenue to faith, Harvey is clearly per-
suaded that only secular exegetical methods can have authority
for contemporary Christians. By far the most philosophical of
the three, Pannenberg argues for a concept of God based upon his
secular "ontology of the future," and defends the resurrection
of Jesus as demonstrable by the methods of secular historical
research. The rejection of biblical authority as such for historical judgments, which is implicit in the writings of Troeltsch
and Harvey, is made explicit by Pannenberg. In short, all three
of these theologians share Hegel's belief that faith can be developed and strengthened by secular interpretation of its own
historical foundations.

On the basis of my interpretation of Hegel's philosophy of
history, several implications of such secular presuppositions
can be stated. In the first place, secular Christian faith
seems to be a highly intellectual faith. It is not just that
it is based upon certain philosophical considerations, or that
it requires a fair degree of theological sophistication in order

to be understood as faith at all. Most important is the way in
which secular faith understands itself as having a potential for
universal comprehension, and on that basis tries to justify itself as superior to the particularism of more traditional understandings of faith. That this claim breaks down is clear, I
argued, from Hegel's doctrine of the passions: the secular man
of history is every bit as particularistic and unaware of the
universal purposes of reason in his time as the Christian who
attempts to live a moral and devout life based upon the teachings
of the Bible. Nevertheless, secular theologians continue to
assume that their methods have greater intellectual integrity
than the methods of non-secularists. In fact, they have sacrificed the integrity of the individual as a unity of intellect,
emotion and will for the sake of a merely intellectual sophistication. To put my point as bluntly as possible: they pride
themselves on their secular justifications of faith, but those
justifications succeed only in validating a faith that no person could ever live. Ultimately either their claim to faith
will dissolve entirely into non-Christian secularism, as has in
fact happened in many quarters in the twentieth century; or they
will be forced to abandon their secular presuppositions and establish a more adequate foundation for their Christian faith.

The role of the Bible in this debate is ambiguous. While
Hegel justifies it for moral instruction but calls it useless
for the understanding of historical truths, Troeltsch and Harvey
want to discern in it the truth about Jesus without accepting
in toto its understanding of him, and Pannenberg tries to prove
its claims about the resurrection in terms which are utterly
alien to it. Although all these programs differ in significant
ways, they share the assumption that the Bible is nothing more
than a human record which is available to historical research.
The notion that it might have any special status, by virtue of
divine inspiration and authority, is utterly foreign to them.
The Bible, in their view, participates in and is limited by its
own historical context just like everything else. They reject
its understanding of history as a dynamic process of prophecies
and fulfillments given by God to man, and therefore find a great
deal of the biblical witness unintelligible. The difficulty
they have discerning the full truth of what the Bible says about

Jesus and his resurrection corresponds to the fact that they do
not turn to it to gain a deeper understanding of their own historical circumstances.

This alienation from biblical language is, if Hamann's
theology may be taken as correct in this regard, closely connected with the inability of secular theologians to develop a coherent
concept of the individual believer. All four of these thinkers
agree that the individual alone is not an adequate starting point
for theological reflection on the meaning of history. Historical
or moral individualism, such as that of Mendelssohn, is rejected
by them all on the grounds of its privatism and anti-social implications. It is this sort of privatism which Hegel thinks he
sees in Hamann, and which he criticizes so severely. If the
individual is the foundation for truth, then no methods -- whether
secular or religious -- can ever be trusted to lead the believer
out of himself to an appreciation of God as God, or the truth as
the truth. To accuse Hamann of defending such a private form
of faith, however, is to misread him entirely. Hamann's theology
is determined not by a theory of individualism, not even by his
eccentricity and "subjective freedom," but by his conviction
that faith must be based upon the Bible and nothing else. The
reason he concentrates upon the individual and personal side of
faith is his conviction that the Bible does: it is his model,
and its preoccupation with the personal relationship between
God and His people becomes his preoccupation. On the basis of
biblical authority Hamann believes that individual men, women
and children are the primary purpose of God's creation, that He
created them and redeemed them from their sins in order to have
a relationship with them in which He would love them and they
would worship Him. In contrast, Hegel and secularists in general
begin their reflections by consideration of ideas, methods and
institutions, and have no basis on which to proceed from those
abstract or general concerns to an understanding of the concrete
truth of individual Christian life and faith.

The question of the possibility of a "biblical" understanding of history and human existence brings me to the question of
secularization with regard to the uses of and presuppositions
about language. The two theologians upon whom I wish to concentrate at this point are H. R. and R. R. Niebuhr. In my brief

discussion of their work in Chapter I, I argued that their commitment to secular theories of historical meaning leads them to
interpret the language of Christian faith so as to adapt it to
their theories as much as possible. H. R. Niebuhr presents his
notion of internal and external history as a modern version of
the Chalcedonian paradox. In so doing, however, he portrays
that concept of Christ as an abstract theory of unity-in-duality,
rather than as an effort to articulate that in Jesus God condescended to unite the divine nature with human nature in one
person. Furthermore, by saying that external history serves as
both medium and judge for internal history, Niebuhr succeeds in
avoiding an "extreme dualism" but implicitly reverses the Chalcedonian relation by subordinating faith to secular knowledge.
In this way he shows that his thought is shaped more by secular
than by Christian presuppositions. R. R. Niebuhr is more suc-
cessful in demonstrating that the relation between internal and
external history is reciprocal, insofar as he declares that the
resurrection can serve as a basis for a "critique of historical
reason." As he executes this critique, however, it turns out
to be based not upon a biblical understanding of the resurrection
but upon the resurrection as a convenient paradigm for an essentially secular theory about historical events. In trying to
connect this theory with the New Testament in terms of his concept of recognition, Niebuhr shows that he, too, is exploiting
the texts to support his theory rather than doing a "critique"
of historical reason on the basis of a biblical Christian understanding of historical meaning.

Although it would surprise both Niebuhrs to find themselves
accused of theological "Hegelianism," their practice of imputing
new meanings to Christian language is a major aspect of Hegel's
philosophical program. He assumes that biblical language is not
capable of expressing conceptual thought, and that therefore it
is the task of the Christian thinker to translate thoughts which
may come to him through such imagery into more intelligible or
"spiritual" representations. Hegel's deepest misunderstandings
of Hamann stem from his lack of regard for the biblical allusions
in which Hamann expresses himself. So great is this misinterpretation that Hegel reads into Hamann a secular bias much like
his own. Given the fact, which I have argued with regard to both

history and language, that Hamann uses biblical language to present a highly intelligible position, it seems fair to conclude
that Hegel's sensitivity to that language is rather limited.
Although he frequently alludes to the Bible to support his own
speculative theories, Hegel shows very little ability to understand it in its own terms, much as the Niebuhrs present idiosyncratic interpretations of Chalcedonian doctrine and the biblical
accounts of Jesus' resurrection appearances.

When there is no "positive" authority over language and
thought, one possibility is to fall back upon a sort of thinking
which involves dichotomies and dialectics similar to those Hamann
criticized in Mendelssohn. Despite his approval of Hamann's
protest against the "divisions of reflection" proposed by Mendelssohn, divisions such as church from state and eternal from temporal, Hegel endorses such reflection as a necessary -- although
inadequate -- stage of thought. In Hegel's scheme, dichotomous
thinking is the stage of criticism, negativity and opposition,
such as when concrete nature stands over against the abstract
Idea, prior to their mutual *Aufhebung* into spirit; or like the
opposition within the religious consciousness between feeling
and intuition, which can be overcome only by spiritual representation.

Certainly this sort of language is very different from the
tenor of the Niebuhrs' theologies. A closer examination, however, shows that they are both really much closer to Hegel's
way of thinking than to that of Hamann. H. R. Niebuhr's entire
theology of history begins with the claim that knowledge of the
past can be divided into two categories -- internal and external
-- and that the task of theology is to comprehend them as distinct and yet related to one another. Likewise, R. R. Niebuhr
sets out from the problem of the already-existing dichotomy or
"divorce" between internal and external history, and defines his
task as their reconciliation in some more adequate vocabulary
than either offers by itself. H. R. Niebuhr remains at a level
that is, relative to the others, dichotomous (his "two-world"
presupposition) without falling into what he calls an "extreme
dualism." R. R. Niebuhr moves much closer to what I call a
"dialectical" reconciliation of the opposing terms from which he
sets out, although even he would not endorse Hegel's explicit

and programmatic effort to transform every opposition of thought into a higher unity.

The point that I want to stress, however, is the extent to which the differences between the Niebuhrs and Hegel are quantitative rather than qualitative with regard to theological method. All three think in terms of dichotomies and dialectical reconciliations. They disagree only about the extent to which reconciliation is possible or even desirable. Hegel's somewhat mystical belief that the poles of an opposition are preserved as "moments" in a new unity does not seem to be shared by the Niebuhrs, and they show a corresponding reluctance to abandon the tension between separate aspects of history as they understand it. Nevertheless, this methodological difference is slight compared to that between them all and Hamann. Rather than accepting all dichotomies proposed by philosophical reflection, Hamann insists upon criticizing them in terms of the words used to state them. If a proposed dichotomy is not clearly justified, then Hamann rejects it rather than play what he calls a game of "cleverness" in manipulating the words back into the appearance of unity. Hamann by no means rejects all dichotomies. He clearly thinks of God and fallen man, goodness and evil, and the like as logical and real oppositions. But he understands those oppositions in biblical terms, and the corresponding solution he proposes for overcoming them is a method not of philosophical or theological development toward reconciliation, but of looking to Scripture to see what God has done and is doing about them. Reconciliation is not the work of men at all: it is God's gift to His prodigal children.

What are the methodological consequences of basing theological reflection upon a concept of faith? Of those theologians surveyed in Chapter I, only Bultmann and Barth even attempt to do this, and they both define faith as somehow removed from secular methods of interpretation. Both are historians in secular terms, Bultmann in the field of New Testament studies and Barth in the history of Christian thought. But neither builds his constructive theology upon his historical work. For Bultmann, the task of systematic theology is to translate the mythical and historical language of the Bible into the existentialist language of contemporary self-understanding. Neither myth nor history can express the real, spiritual truths of faith, he insists; both are only attempts to give the appearance of objective truth to ideas which can be known to be true only subjectively. Barth also understands myth and history as an opposition and refuses to allow biblical truth to be identified with either of them. Rather than treat the language of the Bible as a merely human product which needs demythologization into contemporary form, however, he says that biblical language is neither mythical nor merely historical in the secular sense. The Bible, in Barth's view, includes "historical sagas" which are accurate accounts of historical people and events but not subject to historical research and confirmation. They are to be believed by Christians on the basis of faith -- because they are in the Bible. There are no historical means by which their accuracy can be explained or judged.

There is a sense in which Bultmann and Barth could be included in the preceding two discussions of contemporary theologians in relation to history and language. Bultmann is radically committed to secularization of the biblical witness, as are Troeltsch, Harvey and Pannenberg. But his preferred language is existentialist rather than, for example, the historical-critical terms used by Harvey to judge what is "true" in the New Testament. Likewise, Barth is hardly less guilty of exploiting Christian language for his own purposes than the Niebuhrs, although his theological program is explicitly "Biblicist" and antisecular in a way they both reject. Be that as it may, the way in which the Hegel-Hamann debate is most relevant to Bultmann and Barth is with regard to their efforts to make faith itself a methodological point of departure.

One decisive question for theological method is how the relation between God and man is to be conceived. In Hegel's view, the task of faith is to lead the believer to knowledge of God. Due to the phenomenon of "pious agnosticism," men deny that God can or ought to be known, thus making mature faith and comprehensive philosophy impossible. It is Christianity which has overcome this problem, for it teaches that God reveals Himself to men. Therefore men can know Him, and, by knowledge of Him, be reconciled to Him. Mediation between God and the individual is achieved by the knowledge of God which He makes available in Christianity. Although the word "God" is normally used as a proper noun for the deity, understood as a divine person, Hegel says it is the religious equivalent for the philosophical notion of the Idea. That is why he speaks in terms of mediation rather than about a mediator.

With Hamann it is just the reverse. He understands God as a person, and the goal of faith not as knowledge of God but a deeper relationship with Him. This is possible only on the basis of God's personal condescension to man in Jesus Christ, not by any theoretical or dialectical formulation which claims to be adequate to God. Man and human thought are never, in Hamann's view, adequate to God, but always depend upon His mercy and will for every provision in life and every insight into His will and being. Thus the mode of the Christian's relationship to God is obedience, an obedience that is possible by virtue of the Cross of Christ, who remains, in Hamann's view, the only mediator between God and man.

I have not presented enough materials to go into detail on this issue with regard to Bultmann and Barth. But the brief analysis I did offer of their thought should be sufficient to show that Barth is strongly in agreement with Hamann on this matter, while Bultmann has little basis at all for such agreement. Since biblical language about a God who speaks to men and listens to what they say to Him, who suffers over them and sends His representatives to them when they turn away from Him, who punishes them in anger and forgives them in love, is all highly "mythological," Bultmann cannot accept it as immediately intelligible in the way that Hamann and Barth do. Barth may try to justify such language as "saga" or some other special literary form, but this is primarily a device intended to protect the Bible from secular efforts to criticize or verify it. By his insistence that all mythological language be translated into existentialist terms, Bultmann deprives himself of any theological basis for speaking of a personal relationship between God and men. If the standard of truth is contemporary self-understanding, then it makes no sense to speak of man's sin against God and redemption in Christ, for this sort of talk is alien to the world of today. Demythologization as a theological and hermeneutical method undermines the personal relationship between the condescending God and the believer who worships Him, and will accordingly have a far-reaching influence on Bultmann's entire program.

A second decisive question for theological method is that of the individual's self-understanding. Here, ironically, Bultmann is actually closer to Hamann than is Barth, although that closeness is strictly "formal," for their differences over language ultimately lead them in very different directions. The issue with regard to self-understanding can be put briefly, the more so because it was discussed in the first part of this section: what is the power that rules the human self? For Hegel, it ought to be reason but in actuality is normally the passions. For Hamann, it is either faith or doubt, which in turn determine the character of reason and passion alike.

Even from the brief discussions of Bultmann and Barth in Chapter I, it is possible to see where they stand on this question. Because Bultmann believes that contemporary self-understanding occurs in existentialist language, he subordinates both mythical and historical language to it, and thereby avoids suggesting any division within the religious consciousness of the individual. The fact that the Christian finds himself in an alien world, where both mythical and historical beliefs abound, in no way undermines the integrity of that position. The sense of alienation from the world is basic to the New Testament and to Hamann's interpretation of it. Thus Bultmann is, in this formal sense, expressing in his demythologized language the biblical conviction of the primacy and unity of faith. In contrast, Barth presents a Christian self-understanding which seems to imply an internal division from oneself no less than Hegel's. He speaks of accepting the historical claims of the Bible even though they are not "'history' in our sense of the word." He admits that they will therefore have a "corresponding obscurity." Such language is not that of a man who stands squarely in his biblical faith and surveys the world on the basis of it. Barth's individual seems doomed to an inner alienation from himself -- a lack of confidence as a Christian in the world -- which is also certain to influence the character of all his theological thought.

* * *

What would be the major characteristics of a theological method as radically biblical as Hamann demands? It would turn to the Bible for a conceptual framework within which to understand not only biblical history but the history of the world. In this way it would presuppose and support the historical identity of the Christian as a person who is in but not "of the world" (Jn. 17:16-18). The language of this method would adhere as closely as possible to the language of the Bible, not in a literalistic sense but in terms of fundamental biblical categories. On this basis, faith would not be opposed to reason but its foundation. Finally, such a theological method in the twentieth century would have to be predicated upon the fact that the Bible is no longer readily understood by modern men -- even by many who count themselves Christians. This indicates that the first task of contemporary theology must be biblical hermeneutics. In a sense, Hamann seems to be saying the same thing with his extremely obscure style. It has a homiletical purpose, for it drives the unbelieving layman either to despair or to the Bible in search of some understanding of his allusions. And it carries a message for theologians, for it illustrates that the purpose of Christian theology is to facilitate understanding of the Bible, not by complex doctrines which satiate the mind, but by helpful directions for those who are hungry to hear and understand the words of God and to be transformed by them into the mind of Christ.

APPENDIX

As an aid to the reader, I include my own "working translation" of Hamann's *Golgotha und Scheblimini*. I have not attempted
to render it in idiomatic English, but rather to preserve Hamann's involuted syntax and much of his archaic punctuation in
my own version. I present it here not as a polished translation
but as background to this dissertation. Unfortunately, it is
not possible to include any notes other than Hamann's own (see
Schreiner's commentary for an excellent critical apparatus).
The text from which the translation has been made is Nadler's,
and the page references in the margin refer to vol. III of his
edition of Hamann's works. I should note, however, that Schreiner
has suggested corrections to that text at a number of points.
Because those points are very minor, and Nadler remains the most
widely available critical edition, I adhere to his text for the
sake of simplicity. For those who wish to consult Schreiner on
specific points, that task is facilitated by the fact that he,
too, keys his text to Nadler's pagination.

The title page (p. 291 in Nadler) reads as follows:

Golgotha and Scheblimini!

———————

by a

Preacher in the Wilderness

———————

Moses.

Who said of his father and mother,
'I regard them not';
He disowned his brothers,
And ignored his children....
They shall teach Jacob thy ordinances,
And Israel thy law;
They shall put incense before thee,
And whole burnt offerings upon thy altar.

Jeremiah.

Behold, I will feed them with wormwood,
and give them poisoned water to drink;
for from the prophets of *Jerusalem* un-
godliness has gone forth into all the land.

1784.

293   "I, too, cannot neglect to mention the pleasurable[1]
sentiments, free from all influence of benevolence or compulsion, which have been produced in me toward Herr Moses
Mendelssohn by reading his *Jerusalem*. It combines (according to one expert's judgment) everything which can win for
a writing entry and applause in the minds of the readers,
and by which all good writings since time immemorial have
gotten them: perfect clarity in the individual thoughts
with progression from one to the next within a smooth and
illuminating context; plausible and profitable truths in
many places, and expressions of the author's noble and
virtuous sentiments." But as for the theory of rights,
duties and contracts: the manner of rationally arbitrating
conflicts of interest satisfies me less than the common
opinion of old Cicero and his newest and excellent translator and expositor. On this issue and some similar matters
I will converse with my devoted reader at length and in
breadth, at the summit and in depth, inside and out, and
short but sweet.

     But since a great gap has been established between
our religious and philosophical principles, fairness requires that we compare the author with himself alone and
judge him only by his own professed standards. Herr Mendelssohn believes in a state of nature, which he relates
to society as the dogmatists relate it to a state of grace
-- partly as presupposition and partly in opposition. I
grant to him and to every dogmatist their conviction, even
though I am not capable of making either a proper concept
or use of this hypothesis, which is so current among most
men-of-letters in our century. With the social contract
I do no better! The divine and eternal covenant with Abraham and his offspring must be all the more important to us
both, on account of the blessing based on this documented
solemn contract and promised to all peoples of the earth.

     Since the author went to so much trouble for the specu-
lative friends of natural law, to define with their philosophical and juridical assistance its first principles, in
order to be able ultimately to explain rationally some
claims of the rabbis, the Gordian knot of the cancelled
ecclesiastical law also probably seems to be a consequence
of that vain and fruitless trouble. On account of its use
for the distinction between church and state, from which
294 Herr Mendelssohn set out and to which he returns, this
theory is so to speak the golden hip of the master, whose
metal must be tested. For the privilege conceded to the
speculative taste of twelve pages, which the dissident is
given freedom to skip over, is a double bribery, and with
these first principles the real issue is whether they can
be acknowledged or called into question before they are
put to use.

     Without composing out of state, religion and freedom
of conscience three moral beings or persons, whose immoral
dissension and feuding must appear all the more astonishing
if the moral order refers to laws which cannot contradict
one another, state religion and freedom of conscience are
first and foremost [three] words, which at first glance
say everything, or rather nothing. Therefore these words
are to other words as the indefiniteness of man is to the
definiteness of animals.

"Very well! let the quarrel be settled by an explanation of words." Yet the words to be explained stand immediately in the forecourt of the theory. It appears to me (*in
parenthesi*) to be as clearly the case with the moral capacity as with a moral being. The capacity is called moral if
it is compatible with the laws of wisdom and goodness:
therefore wisdom coupled with goodness should also be called
morality. But this coupling is actually called justice:
thus a faculty which is compatible with the laws of wisdom
and goodness should by rights be called just. Furthermore,
might and right are heterogeneous concepts even in the state
of nature; thus capabilities, means and goods appear to be
too closely related to the concept of might, if they are
not soon to lose their heterogeneity. -- But where do the
laws of wisdom and goodness come from? Are there such laws?
Why is it still necessary to search for a light and right
of nature? Were these laws not already implicitly the best
law of nature? Least of all do I grasp how the conclusion
follows out of the aforementioned explanations of law, morality and goods, that therefore man has a right to certain
goods or means, if one does not arbitrarily assume a right
to happiness, whose universality can be claimed just as
little as a universal right to divine legislation and immediate revelation.

295   Since for the definition of his basic principles the
theorist needs two classes, the privileged and the duty-
bound, he instantly creates them for himself, the first
out of a moral capacity and the second out of a moral necessity. Once more a seesaw of philosophical indefiniteness! -- The privileged are regarded only in relation to
the state of nature, but the duty-bound are regarded at
the same time in relation to the state of society; and,
through a sly expression, not-doing and passive suffering
could all the more carelessly be confused.

But for every right there is a corresponding duty:
thus for the moral capacity to use a thing for the pursuit
of happiness there is a corresponding incapacity; [it is]
a need rather than a necessity. Therefore there are in
the state of nature no other duties than those of omission,
no doing but a pure not-doing.

If I have a right to use a thing for the pursuit of
happiness, then everyone in the state of nature has an
identical right, just as a soldier has the right to kill
the enemy in time of war, and the enemy may kill him. Or
are the laws of wisdom and goodness as manifold as my and
every other ego? Or does even the metaphysical law of
royal self-love and self-concern belong to the law of nature?

Admittedly, the laws of wisdom and goodness cannot
contradict one another; yet are not cases of conflict between them just as conceivable as between self-interest
and benevolence? Is there no clash, no battle between
moral qualities as there is between moral beings? -- and
does not freedom there as here become a victim of moral
necessity and of the frightful imperative of the laws of
wisdom and goodness, in which accordingly there already
lurks a right of coercion.

But is it wisdom and goodness to circumcise and muti-
late with laws our -- I know not whether perfect or imperfect -- right to the means of happiness, and the meagre

capacity of our holdings? Or are these laws also already
such that through them all conditions under which things
might receive the predicate "a means of happiness" are
given to both classes? Now these laws, upon which our moral
capacity and incapacity depend, are presupposed as notorious
and revealed to the entire human race; or, since they are
296 supposedly related to inner sentiments, does their perfection consist in that they do not need to be expressed, and
thus also no speculative reader may be expressly held ac-
countable for it?

Nonetheless, for all the bantering words of the theorist's every explanation, the matter seems to come down to
this: that man in the state of nature is privileged, insofar as his use of a thing as a means of happiness is compatible with the laws of wisdom and goodness; conversely,
he will become duty-bound as soon as the use of a thing as
a means to happiness contradicts the laws. The former therefore may enjoy himself with an active natural law, but the
latter must be consoled for a passive, suffering natural
law. -- In spite of all the Pharisaical hypocrisy with
which the men-of-letters in our enlightened century mouth
the principles of contradiction and sufficient proof, they
are the most wicked disgrace upon their own house!

On account of these conflicts of interest between positive and negative powers, between self-interest and disa-
greeable dependence upon the benevolence of someone of wiser
self-interest in the state of natural independence, there
appears out of the brain of the theorist, like a mechanical
Pallas, the law of justice! -- What pomp of mystical laws,
in order to raise up a miserable law of nature, which is
scarcely worth the words and is suited to neither the state
of society nor the stuff of Judaism! "Whatever it is they
are building," an Ammonite would say, "whatever it is they
are building, if a fox climbs up their stone walls, it will
break them down." But all that is attempted is to give a
rational explanation of certain claims of the rabbis of
divine reason, without explaining the principles of reason
employed.

As a duty-bound reader I voluntarily resign myself to
the fact that I can dispute no privileged scribe's power
to use an obsolete Leibnizian definition of a word as an
aid to the discussion of the first letters of his natural
law, all the less since the laws of wisdom and goodness
which never contradict each other have a covert falling
out with the knowledge and will of the theorist, and need
to be brought together anew through justice.

But as a privileged man-of-letters I would wish for
myself devoted readers of better science and conscience,
to whom I might submit only the question: "How should jus-
297 tice, which gives to each his own, be able to stop being
what it is, to renounce its own being, to rob from wisdom
and goodness their own, and to give over its own unchangeable oneness for two, which are as different from each
other as it is from them both."

Is it wisdom and goodness to give and to leave to
everyone his own? Certainly, in the unique case where
there is no other right to property than the wisdom and
goodness of the giver. But this case is the only one of
its type. How now is a generic term to do justice to a

unique thing which adjusts itself to nothing and is not to
be brought under one rubric with anything?

Thus Leibniz was right for that single case which can
be discussed only in a theodicy. Our beautiful and sweet
spirits who, intoxicated by the strong drink of their omni-
science and love of man, blurt out all feeling of justice
in edicts and sermons and Aphtonian themes, are also right,
according to the continuous and systematic conclusiveness
of Roman and metaphysical-catholic despotism, whose transcendental understanding prescribes for itself its own laws
of nature.

But the law of justice is so constructed that, by its
own testimony, it depends upon conditions and upon a relation of the predicate to the subject. To be sure, a law
loses some of its categorical perfection through conditions;
and the relation of the predicate to the subject seems to
be an attribute abstracted from the logical truth. Meanwhile, I don't want to stand on niceties with the patchwork
of philosophical justice, since I never can figure out which
subject and predicate in this whole law are really in question. Is it that all conditions under which a right occurs
are given to the privileged? Then the duty-bound man is
perfectly robbed of his consciousness and conscience and
of all moral capacity. But a part of imperfect rights,
namely, the conditions which were not given, still depends
upon the consciousness and conscience of the duty-bound:
for, where the privileged are concerned, duties and conscience appear to be totally dispensable concepts, unknown
quantities and *qualitates occultae*. Who may condemn his
own conscientiousness? Who will press him to weigh such a
critical decision? The right is indeed in his hand! With
such a law of justice that funny gloss of the commentators
does agree, and with more decency and propriety: Break the
barrel, but don't let the wine run out! Or, as the Muses
298 of the fishmarket sing: Wash my back, but don't get it
wet!

Circulated through the serpent's deception of language,
under just as various as manifold verbal forms, in the whole
Jerusalem [there is] the eternal *petitio* of one and the same
hypocritical *principii* of outward perfection of rights and
actions, of inner imperfection of duties and sentiments --
Indeed everything does depend upon both those questions,
which I must repetitiously touch upon.

     I.   "According to the law of reason, are there
          rights to persons and things which can be
          connected with doctrines, and can be earned
          by assent to them?

As worms pass through children, laws, which are the
golden hemorrhoids and nymph Egerie of many a philosophical
government, also pass through the craven men-of-letters.
If a connection between the physical and the moral cannot
be denied, and the different modifications of writing and
kinds of marking also must have had different effects on
the progress and improvement of concepts, opinions and
knowledge, then I don't know why it should be so difficult
to imagine a connection between moral capacities and doctrines. According to the law of reason, i.e. of the unchangeable connection and essential bond between concepts

which presuppose or exclude one another, doctrines are as closely connected with a moral capacity in general as with the special right of decision in cases of conflict. Doctrinal agreement has an effect on our sentiments, which in turn influence our moral judgment and corresponding behavior.[2]

> II. "Can perfect rights be produced by contracts without [there being] imperfect duties prior to the contract, and are compulsory duties based upon duties of conscience?"

With perfect rights physical force takes the place of moral capacity, and with perfect duties physical necessity extorts actions with force. With such a perfection the whole speculative law of nature is ripped, and spills over into the highest non-law -- until the end of the fading splendor. In short, all glorified laws of wisdom and goodness, the law of justice and the law of reason are lost in the all-merciful will and *bon plaisir* of that Romish marionette player and virtuoso, and in his swan song: *Heu quantus artifex pereo*! -- Your end has come, the thread of your life is cut!

There is however a social contract; thus there is also a natural contract, which must be older and more authentic, and on whose conditions the social contract must be based. Thereby all natural property now becomes once more conventional, and man in the state of nature becomes dependent upon its laws, i.e. positively obligated to behave according to those very same laws which all nature and especially man have to thank for the preservation of his existence and the use of all means and goods which contribute to it. Man, as duty-bound to nature, has accordingly least of all an exclusive right to and odious monopoly on his capacities, or their products, or the fruitless mule of his labor and the more forlorn bastards of his usurping, violent overpowering of the creatures subjected against their will to his vanity.

Not even to him, not to him alone is the moral capacity subordinate in using things as means, but to those laws of wisdom and goodness which are our beacons in the immeasurable kingdom of nature; and all conditions under which the predicate of happiness belongs to the subject of one who is duty-bound are given to him as such, and not as one who is privileged, through the law of nature and the law of her justice and of his own reason. He has, therefore, neither a physical nor a moral capacity for any other happiness than that intended for him, and to which he was called. All means which he uses for the attainment of a happiness which is not given to and shared with him are heaped up abuses of nature and distinct injustices. All lust for well-being is the spark of a hellish uproar.

For no Solomon, to whom the God of the Jews gave very great wisdom and understanding and a steady heart, like the sand, which lies on the shore of the sea; -- for no Nebuchadnezzar, to whom the God of the Jews has given the wild animals to serve him, in spite of their definiteness: but only for a philosopher without sorrow and shame, only for a Nimrod in the state of nature would it be becoming to proclaim as though he had horns on his forehead: "To me and me alone

belongs the right of decision, whether? and how much? to
whom? when? under which circumstances? I am bound to benevolence." But if the ego, even in the state of nature, is
so unjust and uncircumcised, and if every man has an identical right to me! and me alone! -- then let us rejoice in
the We of God's grace, and be thankful for the crumbs which
their hunting- and house-dogs, greyhounds and bulldogs leave
over for orphaned waifs! "Behold, if the river is turbulent
he is not frightened; he is confident though Jordan rushes
against his mouth. -- Who has leave to force him to throw
a tip to poor sharecroppers! Who has leave to resist his
appropriating the phooey! phooey! of poor sinners!"

Since, therefore, if everybody wants to establish his
unphilosophical ego as the royal referee in cases of conflict, neither a state of nature nor a state of society is
possible; rather, in both states the decision about natural
or appointed laws must devolve upon One universal Lord and
Heir. So it is scarcely worth it to poke about at greater
length in the speculative and theoretical rubbish of the
right to use property for self-interest, the right to decide issues of benevolence, and the totality of logical
conditions necessary for the perfection of the rights of
compulsion; rather, all social contracts are based, according to the law of nature, on the moral capacity to say "Yes"
or "No", and on the moral necessity to make good that spoken
word. The moral capacity to say "Yes" or "No" is grounded
in the natural use of human reason and language. The moral
necessity to fulfill one's given word [is grounded] in the
fact that our inner declaration of intention cannot be expressed, revealed or recognized other than orally or in
writing or by our actions; and our words, as the natural
signs of our sentiments and no less of our deeds, must stand.
Therefore reason and language are the internal and external
bond of all social life, and through a divorce or separation
of that which nature by its appointment has joined together
belief and trust are abolished; lies and deceit, shame and
vice are confirmed and stamped as means of happiness. Fun-
damentum est iustitiae FIDES -- dictorum *constantia* et
veritas. -- Est enim *primum*, quod cernitur in universi
generis humani societate, eiusque autem vinculum est RATIO
et ORATIO, quae conciliat inter se homines coniungitque
naturali quadam societate. -- *Res a natura copulatas er-
rore diuellere*, fons est fraudium, maleficiorum, scelerum
omnium.[3]

Therefore every Sophist is not only a liar but also a
hypocrite, and uses language as an empty puppet-show, [in
order] to present his idol, the vain fabrication of human
art, as an out-flowing of divine reason and a corporeal
daughter of her voice,[4] to trick superstitious readers by
the blind word of a golden hip or golden calf, and to worm
his way like a thief or murderer into their confidence at
the expense and to the peril of unrecognized living truths.

"If a ruler listens to falsehood, all his officials
will be wicked." For all his claims to a royal monopoly
on injustice, for all his whimsical attempts to circumscribe
or spoil through edicts threatening the gallows or disgrace
for subjects who challenge that monopoly by imitating him,
the only effect is to make the sophistry of his lordship
all the more hateful and ludicrous in the eyes of posterity.

For he spoke, and it came to be! -- "and whatever the man called every living creature, that was its name." According to this image and likeness of definiteness, every word of a man was supposed to be and remain the event itself. On this similarity of the impression and the inscription to the model of our race and the master of our youth; on this right of nature, to make use of the word as the most real, noble and powerful means of revelation[5] and communication of our innermost declaration of intention; on these is the validity of all contracts based, and this mighty fortress of the truth in the inward being is superior to all French practice, tax-machinery, pedantry and bartering tactics. Therefore, the misuse of language and its natural testimony is the grossest perjury, and it turns the transgressor of this first law of reason and its justice into the most wicked enemy of mankind, traitor, and adversary of German uprightness and sincerity, on which our dignity and happiness are based. A Punic preacher, not in the wilderness, found that nature made man German, and that all *Oeuvres diverses* in a cynical-sodomistic dialect which stinks of b.. and f.. as of pitch and brimstone are nothing but black arts of a f.. *Diable* of the darkness.

302　　　In a valley of vision full of vague and vascillating concepts, it is not good to boast of a greater Enlightenment! -- of a better development! -- of a more accurate distinction! -- all by means of a more sophisticated use of language and common sense! -- over against the times and the system of a Hobbes. I have already denounced the relationship with what the one calls a right and the other calls might. Compulsory duties, whose perfection consists in the fact that they can be extorted by force, seem to border just as closely on the obligatory nature of fear. Furthermore, when just as much is won through the expression of benevolence as is lost through sacrifice: then cases of conflict between benevolence and self-interest, or between duties to oneself and to one's neighbor, are just as much fruits of a miserable sophistry as of a simulated conflict between the rights of the deity and of mankind, the conflict on which the theorist blames all evil which has been practiced since time immemorial under the philsophical and political cloak of truth and justice. Love of man is a congenital weakness, and benevolence little more than a foppery into which and right away out again one is always trying to talk oneself, which pesters the reader with school jargon and lives like a lord, indulging itself on the side by guzzling the contents of concepts and making fun of the partisan public with the empty skins. Soon the whole Penelope's web comes down to cleverness at making every other untorn unity appear as two which then instantly fall back into one another, that through the same hocuspocus under both aspects the standpoint and perspective are every now and then distorted, and the speculative man-of-letters becomes dizzy from twirling -- meanwhile the epah of theory [is] hovering between heaven and earth in the land of Shinar, and *Jerusalem* shall not still be inhabited in its place, in Jerusalem, but will come to the same end as Babel.[6]

　　　Really, it is a confusion of concepts and just as little in accordance with truth in the strictest sense, as to the greatest advantage of the readers, to oppose state and church, to cut off so sharply inner happiness from outer calm and security, like the temporal from the eternal. The child of the one mother was smothered by her while sleeping, and the child still living already struggles under the up-303 lifted sword of the Solomonic executioner, about to be cut in two, one half to the one and the other half to the other --

For the true fulfillment of our duties and for the perfection of man, actions and sentiments are necessary. State and church have them both as their object. It follows that actions without sentiments and sentiments without actions are a bisection of duties which are whole and alive into two dead halves. When grounds for acting may no longer be grounds of truth, and grounds of truth are moreover not fit as grounds for acting; when being depends upon necessary understanding and reality upon accidental will; then all divine and human unity in sentiments and actions stops. The state becomes a body without spirit and life -- a carcass for vultures! The church becomes a ghost, without flesh and bone -- a scarecrow for sparrows! With the immutable connection of concepts which either presuppose or exclude one another, reason stands still, like sun and moon at Gibeon and in the valley of Aijalon.

Yet the theorist still thinks that, if need be, the state may be given just as little responsibility for the sentiments of its subjects, as dear God may be given for their actions. In this way he contradicts not only his own scheme of Judaism, but -- again agreeing with Hobbes -- locates the greatest happiness in outer calm and security, no matter how they come about or how perfectly frightful they may be, like that evening calm in a fortress which expects to be taken during the night; so that they, as Jeremiah says, "shall sleep a perpetual sleep, and not wake." Through such word games of physiognomical and hypocritical indefiniteness, every letter- and phrase-monger in the midnight of our enlightened times can earn a triumph over the most expert master, to whom he really owes the gratitude for his triumph. But a linguistic confusion of concepts does not remain without practical consequences.

*   *   *

Without wearing myself and you out, devoted reader! with the even more speculative application, I would, for the sake of our mutual safety in the upper floor, wish no such loose foundation and sandy ground under the new and harsh theory of Judaism.

Since I too know of no eternal truths except those which are unceasingly temporal, I have no need to soar up into the cabinet of the divine understanding, nor into the 304 sanctuary of the divine will; neither do I need to tarry over the difference between immediate revelation through word and writing, which is comprehensible only here and now, and mediate revelation through thing (nature) and concept, which is said to be legible and comprehensible at all times and in all places, by virtue of its soul-writing.

"Always to struggle against all theories and hypotheses, and to speak of facts, to want to hear of nothing but facts, and to look for facts least of all precisely at that point where it is most important." -- Yet I have neither hunger for consecrated bread, nor leisure and strength for labyrinthine walks and peripatetic labyrinths: rather, I hurry to the issue, and totally concur with Herr Mendelssohn that Judaism, precisely as he understands it, knows nothing of revealed religion, i.e. that to them nothing has really been made known and entrusted by God through word and writing, with the sole exception of the material vehicle of the mystery, the shadow of the good things to come instead of the true form of these realities, whose real communication God had reserved to himself through a higher Mediator, High Priest, Prophet and King than were Moses, Aaron, David and Solomon. -- Just as Moses, therefore, did not himself know that his face had a shining brightness which struck fear into the people: so also was the entire legislation of this divine minister a mere veil and curtain of the old covenant-religion, which still to this day remains unlifted, swaddled and sealed.

The characteristic difference between Judaism and Christianity concerns, therefore, neither immediate nor mediate revelation, as understood by Jews and Naturalists -- nor eternal truths and doctrines -- nor ceremonial and moral laws: rather merely temporal truths of history, which have come to pass at one time and never recur -- *facts*, which have become true through a connection of causes and effects at one point in time and in one place, and therefore can be thought of as true only from that point in time and that place, and which must be confirmed by authority. Authority can, to be sure, humble; but it cannot instruct. It can knock reason down, but it cannot keep it down. Nevertheless, without authority the truth of history disappears with the event itself.

305   This characteristic difference between Judaism and Christianity concerns truths of history of not only past but also future times, which are proclaimed and stated beforehand through the Spirit of a providence as universal as it is particular, and which, due to their nature, cannot be received in any other way than through faith. Jewish authority alone gives them the necessary authenticity; these memorabilia of ancestry and posterity were also confirmed by miracles, proven by the credibility of the witnesses and transmitters of the tradition, and supported by evidence of real fulfillments which are sufficient to catapult faith over all Talmudic and dialectical doubts and pitfalls.

Hence is the revealed religion of Christianity with right and reason called faith, trust, confidence, firm and childlike reliance on divine pledges and promises, and on the splendid progress of its life as it develops itself in representations from one degree of glory to another, until the full uncovering and apocalypse of the mystery which was kept hidden and believed for long ages, in the fullness of seeing face to face: just as the father Abraham believed in the Eternal, and rejoiced that he was to see His day, saw it and was glad; for no distrust made him waver concerning the promise of God, but he grew strong in his faith as he gave glory to God. That is why his faith was reckoned to him as righteousness. But to the law-giver Moses was entry into the promised land flatly denied; and through a similar sin of unbelief in the spirit of grace and truth, which should have been preserved in the hieroglyphic practices of symbolic ceremonies and actions of pristine significance, until the times of refreshing, out-pouring and anointing, this earthly vehicle of a temporal, figurative, dramatic, animal legislation and sacrificial worship degenerated into the corrupted and deadly creeping poison of a childish, slavish, literalistic, idolatrous superstition. Accordingly Moses' entire Pentateuch together with all the Prophets constitute the rock of Christian faith, and the cornerstone chosen and precious, which the builders rejected, has become the cornerstone for them also, but to make them stumble, a rock that will make them fall, so that they may stumble out of unbelief over the Word on which their entire building rests. Moses, the greatest prophet and the national law-giver, is only the smallest most transitory shadow of his office, which he himself confessed to be only the prototype of another prophet, whose raising up he promised to his brothers and their descendants, with the injunction and command to obey Him. The golden calf of Egyptian tradition and Rabbinic human ordinances, propagated under the appearance of divine reason by Aaron and the leaders of the synagogue -- (for the sake of the Eternal!) -- was the utter destruction of the law, in accordance with their own prophecy. Through this last abomination of desolation, Moses [was] turned into the pope of the desecrated nation, the corpse of his rotting legislation into the relic of superstition, houses of prayer into dens of thieves, Bethel into Bethaven, and the city of the bridegroom of blood, despite the heathen and anti-Christian Rome, into a Babylonian whore and school of the ruling accuser, slanderer, liar and murderer from the beginning.

Therefore, Christianity does not believe in doctrines of philosophy, which is nothing but an alphabetical scribbling of human speculation, and subject to the fickle changes of moon and mode! -- not in images and image-worship! -- not in animal- and hero-worship! not in symbolic elements and passwords or some black strokes which the invisible hand of Chance had painted on the white wall! -- not in Pythagorean-Platonic numbers!!! -- in no fleeting shadows of actions and ceremonies which neither remain nor endure, yet are believed to possess a secret power and inexplicable magic! -- in no laws, which must be obeyed even when not believed, as the theorist puts it somewhere, despite his Epicurean-Stoic word-mincing over faith and knowledge! -- No, Christianity knows and is acquainted with no other chains on belief than the sure prophetic word in the oldest of all documents of the human race and in the holy scriptures of authentic Judaism, without Samaritan segregation and apocryphal mishnah. That depository made even the Jews into a chosen race for His possession, instructed in divinity, anointed and called before all peoples of the earth for the salvation of mankind.

Admittedly, a hoard kidnapped for the iron furnace of Egyptian brick-making and forced labor needed chains on actions, and a task-master for the imminent building of a particular state. As the spirit of the leader of the host

307 was exasperated to the point of cursing and sanctioning killing: thus their vulgar vanity and childish impatience for a king grieved the spirit of the last judge to the point of patient revenge [as] all-wise love, which leads to moral improvement through physical suffering.

The extraordinary taste for legislation, and the Royal luxuriating in it, proves just as great an inability to govern oneself as one's equal, and is a common need for slaves and slave-like despots. One part of Mosaic wisdom was, like the people's possessions, booty from the Egyptians; Midianite cleverness contributed its share, and, in order to make the masterpiece of eternal permanence still curlier and more colorful, a Wolffian magic wand finally discovered the vein of a Chinese ceremony that was bound to transitory actions of pristine significance, but was abandoned to the unavoidable misunderstandings and unsocial misuses of oral propagation, just as the catechism of universal human religion, crafted and embossed in the days of preparation of the legislation, [was abandoned] to the loose gossip of Aaron, with which he intended to deck it out with finery.

As for the standard implicit in the two questions about the best form of government and the healthiest diet, rather did the heavenly politics have to condescend to the earthly "thére" and temporal "at that time", without thereby being chained to the here-and-now, in order, like the sun, to run through its luminous eternal cycle from the faith of Abraham *before* the law to the faith of his children and heirs of the promise *following* the law; for the promise, but no law, was given to the flesh of the righteous Abraham as the sign of the covenant. Precisely in this true politics do we behold, as that philosopher said, a deity, where common eyes see the stone. The pristine significance of transitory actions probably pointed, therefore, to the lost or distorted key of knowledge, which was so inconvenient to the heads of the synagogue that they took upon themselves the unauthorized permission to destroy utterly the whole lock of the law, thereby locking up the kingdom of heaven against men, not going in themselves and preventing those who wanted from entering; but the rabbis of divine reason became *literati III literarum*, the most perfect and masoretic men-of-letters in the holiest and most fruitful understanding.

308 By nature and the concept of the thing, the abolition of the Mosaic constitution, which was of necessity connected with land ownership and certain civil institutions and was related to the temple, priesthood and laws of purification, was reported more understandably and openly than that angelic affair was able to achieve on the mountain steaming with smoke and blazing with fire, moved by meteors of dark tempests in an Arabian desert, by means of the sound of trumpets and the voice whose words the listeners declined to hear, so that the word would not be spoken to them (for they could not endure the order that was given). With a soul-writing so audible, indelible and legible that it can be read while running, the kingdom of heaven was introduced -- and like a butterfly it escaped from the empty cocoon and dead pupa form of Judaism! Nevertheless, the ears of the Sophist with uncircumcised heart and senses are buzzing with so many doubts and musings, hypotheses and theories, that he neither discerns nor can discern the soft

voice of common sense for all the uproar! -- Without fire
and hearth one is not a citizen, without land and people
not a prince, and the priestly nation of a merely book-bag
religion remains, in the words of Scripture, a derogation
of God and of divine reason. To be sure, it would be a
greater miracle than happened to their shoes and clothing
if that legislation, given to a hoard of fugitive bondsmen
wandering in the desert, who were to build the first church-
state, could be appropriate for a rabble without state and
religion, scattered by the four winds, as their mummy right
down to the present day and here and there and everywhere
throughout the earth. No, the entire mythology of the
Hebrew economy was nothing but a type of a more transcendent history, the horoscope of a heavenly hero, by whose
appearance everything is already complete and yet is still
to come, as it is written in its law and its prophets:
"They will perish, but thou dost endure; they will all wear
out like a garment. Thou changest them like raiment, and
they pass away" --

Infinitely more valuable than that shadow-figure of
the Jewish church-state and its exclusive rights of citi-
zenship is, to the philosopher and world-citizen, the oldest
of all documents, since it concerns the whole human race,
whose true relations to his people Moses explains without
309 egotistical prejudices; at the same time, just as much
through the individual fragments of the earliest ancestry
as through the extensive plan of providence which elected
him as the instrument of its public institutions, he brought
immortal honor upon himself even unto the latest posterity.
For what are all the *miracula speciosa* of an Odyssey and
Iliad and their heroes in comparison with the simple but
richly significant phenomena of the venerable patriarchal
walk? What is the gentle, loving soul of the blind Maeonian
ballad-monger in comparison with the spirit of Moses, which
glows *a priori* and *a posteriori* from its own deeds and
higher inspirations!

Thus the newest etymology for the word "nobility" from
an Arabic root may also be very favorable for the European
centaur-knighthood[7]: for certainly the Jew always remains
the real original nobleman of the whole human race, and the
prejudice of their pride in family and ancestors is more
deeply grounded than all titles of the ludicrous heraldic
chancery style. Even the disproportion of their little
order, scattered over the whole world, to the rabble of all
other peoples is part of the concept of the thing; just as
the caricature of the documents speaks for the authenticity
and remote antiquity of their charter, and shouts down the
wittiest mockery. The duration of their legislation is
fully the strongest proof of the power of its author, of
the superiority of his ten words over the twelve scrounged
tablets, water-addicted monsters and pumpkin plants, which
came into being in a night and perished in a night, so that
the shade and joy are gone. Moses remains the great Pan,
in comparison with whom all pharoahs and their practitioners
of the "Black Arts" are totally *servum pecus*.

An Egyptian priest scolded the Greeks for being children. Among their games, through whose invention and practice they made a name for themselves, is the *Globe aspirant*
of philosophy also to be found. Although the ignorance of

their age is neither suitable to nor respectable in our century, the little foxes and masters of Greek wisdom affect the pure nakedness and hobby of heathen ignorance with such a naïveté of taste that they, as the prophet says, "know neither their Lord nor their Lord's manger". Systematic atheism thus belongs principally to the Atticism by which the common sense of some of their babblers distinguishes itself from the unavoidable and equally universal
310 superstition of popular idolatry, although they are unable to fill out the appearances of indefinite objects with anything better than a few transcendental fads, which quite often had no other accreditation or sufficient foundation than the *relationes curiosas* of oriental myths and rumors, indigenous folktales, premonitions, dreams, puzzles and more of the same old childishness.

But since the gods of the earth have made themselves the most high philosophers, Jupiter (once *summus philosophus*) had to creep into the cuckoo-form of a pedagogue; and although Herr Mendelssohn appears to some extent to take it amiss that his deceased friend let who-knows-which historian suggest to his fancy the idea of the divine education of the human race, he himself not only cast the concept of religion and church in the mould of a public educational institution, but also in this school-masterly respect he has parroted and spelled out so many trivialities about the leading-strings of language and writing and their natural parallelism with the religious power of masoretic literalism and scholastic verbiage that a devoted reader can scarcely suppress a yawn at least once during this speculative slumber. For him [Mendelssohn] it is a completely ungrounded article of faith to view "the alphabetical language as mere signs of sounds". According to his grounds of reason, *inuita Minerua experientiae*, the way in which writing refers to things is not less than necessarily by and through language: yet he claims with an almost incredible and unexcusable conviction that writing is the immediate designation of things. It is only a pity that born-deaf philosophers alone can claim this privilege! -- With such a crab-gait of the understanding and without soaring ingenuity, it is just as easy to think of the immeasurable as measurable, and vice versa -- just as easy by immediate designation of things for all of German literature to be not only surveyed but also improved by an Emperor in Peking as by a born-deaf Johann Ballhorn! --

But if all human knowledge can be reduced to a few fundamental concepts, and if the same sounds occur quite frequently in the spoken language, as do the same pictures in different hieroglyphic tablets, but always in different connections through which they multiply their meaning:
311 then this observation may also be applied to history, and the whole range of human events with all their changes may just as well be grasped and divided into sections, as the starry heaven is into constellations, without knowing the number of stars. -- Therefore the entire history of the Jewish people seems, according to the parable of their ceremonial law, to be a living, spirit- and heart-awakening elementary text of all historical literature, in heaven and on earth and under the earth -- a permanent, progressive leading toward the year of the Jubilee and the governmental plan of the divine regime for the whole creation from

its beginning up till its exit, and the prophetic puzzle of a theocracy is mirrored in the pieces of this smashed vessel, like the sun "on the dewdrops on the grass, which tarries for no one, nor does it wait for men". For yesterday the dew from the Lord was only on Gideon's fleece, and all the ground was dry; today the dew is on all the ground, and only the fleece is dry.

The entire history of Judaism was not only prophecy; rather, its spirit was occupied more than that of all other nations, to whom one perhaps cannot deny the analogy of a similar dark divination and anticipation, with the ideal of a savior and judge, a man of power and miracles, a lion's whelp, of whom it was said that his descent according to the flesh was out of the tribe of Judah, but that his departure from heaven was from the bosom of the Father. Moses' Pentateuch, the Psalms and the Prophets are full of hints and glimpses of this appearance of a meteor over the pillar of cloud and the pillar of fire, of a star out of Jacob, a sun of righteousness with salvation under its wings! of the signs of the contradiction in the ambiguous form of his person, his message of peace and joy, his works and pains, his obedience unto death, even death on a cross! and of his elevation out of a worm's dust of the earth to the throne of immovable majesty -- of the kingdom of heaven, which this David, Solomon and Son of Man would plant and complete as a city with a foundation, whose builder and creator is God, as a Jerusalem above, which is free and the mother of us all, as a new heaven and a new earth, without sea and temple within --

These temporal and eternal truths of history about the King of the Jews, the messenger of their covenant, the first-born and head of his church, are the Alpha and Omega, the foundation and tip of our wings of faith: but the end and grave of the Mosaic church-state became the occasion and workshop of metamosaic chains on actions, and of a more than Egyptian bondage and [a more than] Babylonian captivity.

312

Therefore, unbelief in the most real, historical sense of the word is the only sin against the Spirit of the true religion, whose heart is in heaven and whose heaven is in the heart. The mystery of Christian holiness consists not in services, sacrifices and vows, which God demands of men, but rather in promises, fulfillments and sacrifices, which God has done and achieved for the benefit of men; not in the great and huge commandment that He imposed, but in the highest good, which He gave as a gift; not in legislation and moral doctrines, which concern merely human sentiments and human actions, but in execution of divine decrees by means of divine deeds, works and institutions for the salvation of the whole world. Dogmatics and ecclesiastical law belong solely to the public educational and administrative institutions, and as such are subject to the arbitrariness of the authorities,[8] an outward discipline that is sometimes coarse and sometimes refined, according to the elements and degrees of the dominant aesthetic. These visible, public, common institutions are neither religion nor wisdom, which come down from above, but earthly, unspiritual and devilish, according to the influence of foreign cardinals or foreign ciceroni, poetic confessors or prosaic pot-bellied priests, and according to the changing system of

statistical balance and preponderance, or of armed tolerance
and neutrality -- church and school affairs have, as creatures and miscarriages of the state and of reason, often
prostituted themselves for both just as sordidly as they
have betrayed them. Philosophy and politics have needed
the sword of superstition and the shield of unbelief for
all their common deceptions and violence, and so probably
as much through their love as through their hatred they
have mishandled dogmatics more wickedly than Amnon did the
sister of his brother Absalom.

313   Next to the infinite mis-relation of man to God, "public educational institutions dealing with the relation of
man to God" are noisy unrhymed sentences of dry words which
infect the inner sap, the more a speculative creature gets
to suck in of them. In order, first of all, to lift up the
infinite mis-relation and clear it out of the way, before
there can be any talk of relations which are said to serve
as the basis for connecting public institutions, either man
must become a partaker of a divine nature, or else the godhead must take on flesh and blood. The Jews through their
divine legislation, and the Naturalists through their divine
reason, have seized upon a palladium for equalization: consequently, no other mediating concept remains for Christians
and Nicodemuses than to believe with all their heart, with
all their soul, with all their mind. For God so loved the
world -- This is the victory which has overcome the world,
our faith.

A similar mis-relation of man to man appears to adhere
just as naturally to all public institutions of the state;
therefore the mis-relation of double fees is neither striking
nor surprising in a system *de convenance*, which ennobles
all the first-born children of the kingdom to the *deterioris
conditionis* of bondsmen by means of a Jewish and Turkish
circumcision of their salt bread and bread of affliction,
which changes into fleshpots and roasted quail for foreign
Galileeans, windbags and adventurers of philosophical in-
dustry. Indeed, according to another dogmatics, getting a
little and giving double are neither sentiments nor actions
deterioris conditionis --

Exclusive self-love and envy are the inheritance and
trade of a Jewish naturalism, contrary to the royal law to
love one's neighbor as oneself. A being which needs our
benevolence, demands our assistance, makes immoral claims
on anything whatsoever from our physical capacities in his
own self-interest, extorts with force, and needs the service of his serfs all the more, the greater he wishes to
appear -- Such a being is nothing but a dead god of the
earth, similar to the one who had to thank, for the tolerance of his wise maxims and heroic experiments in skin for
skin, the decree of the highest judge: He is in your power!
The only true God of heaven and the Father of men sends his
rain and sunshine without respect of persons. But the Jews
were against His good deeds, and especially those institutions which should have through their mediation contributed
314 to the palingenesis of the creation; in just the same sense
our *illustres ingrats* and desperate Sophists also make all
regalia of nature, luck and providence into idols of their
vanity and a net of their avarice; and, like the dumb car-
rier of sacred tools in the fable, they do not think it

robbery stridently to appropriate, to usurp for their Midas-
profits and ear-earnings, under the yoke of animal definiteness, the devotion of their kindred mob. Through base and
hostile sentiments, full of lies and anger, the whole mecha-
nism of religious and political legality is propelled with
a hellish ardor, which consumes itself and its own work, so
that at the end nothing at all is left except a *caput mortuum*
of the divine and human form. -- A kingdom which is not of
this world can therefore claim no other right for the church
than to be tolerated and suffered with more precise need;
since all public institutions of merely human authority cannot possibly exist next to a divine legislation, but run the
risk of, like Dagon, losing head and hands, so that the trunk
alone remains lying on his own threshold, *turpiter atrum
desinens in piscem* of the beautiful Philistine nature.

State and church are Moses and Aaron; philosophy, their
sister Miriam, the leprous prophetess. The younger brother
is a god to the firstborn, who in turn is his mouth; for
Moses was slow of speech, with heavy tongue, had heavy,
weary hands and an even heavier rod, of which he himself
was once afraid, and with which he sinned unto death in the
desert; but the Urim and Thummim, the "light and right" of
the state, were based upon Aaron's wave offering, and joined
to both his thigh offerings --

Herr Mendelssohn had quoted an addition of the commen-
tator, who defames the decree of the highest judge in the
oldest of all legal affairs as ridiculous nonsense. He
deals almost just as rabbinically with a decree of the
founder of our religion. To give everyone his due, to the
emperor his taxes and to God the honor of his name: this
in his eyes is "an obvious contradiction and conflict of
duties". But was it Jesuitical foresight to call the hypocrites and tempters by their right name? The blind guides
who abused Moses' seat and laid heavy, unbearable burdens
on the shoulders of others did not lift a finger themselves;
they tithed mint and dill and cummin with mathematical conscientiousness but abandoned the weightiest matters of the
315   law, justice, mercy and trust; they strained out the gnats
and swallowed the camels. That just decree full of wisdom
and goodness, to give to the emperor his taxes and to God
the honor, was therefore not Pharisaical advice to serve
two masters[9] and to carry the tree on both shoulders, in
order to be able, as a free Naturalist-nation without religion and state, to nourish and enjoy the pride of beggars
and the luck of knaves at the expense of the human race.

                    *   *   *

Devoted reader! let me, an old Marius, rest a little
on the debris of the philosophical-political *Jerusalem*,
before I give you a parting blessing. -- In the desert there
are pipes that the wind moves back and forth; but no patri-
otic Catos -- "What are you doing here, Elijah?" Religion
and pay! For Heaven's sakes! Oaths and the Sermon on the
Mount -- Has not the theorist shown to us reverend (not to
mention famous) clergymen, while looking us straight in the
eye, that we have become his business-brothers according to

the flesh; just as he himself, alas! by being decadently
seduced by Greek tradition and wordly dogmas, turned into
a circumcised brother in the spirit and essence of heathen,
naturalistic, atheistic fanaticism; for no one who denies
the Son has the Father, and whoever does not honor the Son,
he also does not honor the Father. But he who has seen the
Son has seen the Father. He and the Son are a unique Being
who admits of no divisions or plurality in the political or
metaphysical spheres and no one has seen God; only the only-
begotten Son, who is in the bosom of the Father, has realized
his fullness of grace and truth.

To be sure, it is a cause for grief not to know what
one is oneself, and almost ludicrous to be just the opposite
from what one wants and intends to be. Thus the Jew was
without any other god than that over which the archangel
Michel contended three thousand years ago; the Greek has
expected for two thousand years a science and queen, who
is still said to be coming, and of whom one will one day
be able to say: this is Jezebel! The Jew, without any
other anointed one than the one raised up by his own people,
with the assistance of the Roman caretaker and in collusion
316   with his friend Herod, as Moses raised up a brazen serpent
-- in place of temples, schools, which are similar to the
birthplace of the one raised up! -- without any other sacrifice than his eloquent blood -- Instead of Joseph's dream
of a universal monarchy, [the Jew is] cursed like Canaan;
a slave of all slaves shall he be to his brothers. The
philosopher à la Grecque, a king of peace and of justice!
His circumcision knife extends to everything which carries
a purse, his priests and Levites do not bathe in the blood
of calves and goats, or skin their fur, but are Maitres des
hautes oeuvres & basses oeuvres toward their own natural
species -- The capitol is a Bedlam, and Coheleth a Calvary!

It befalls even a David Hume that he judaizes and prophesies, like Saul the son of Kish. When Philo, the Pharisee, finally confesses to the hypocrite Cleanthes a fit of
astonishment and melancholy from the greatness and obscurity
of the unknown object, and his contempt of human reason,
that it can give no solution more satisfactory with regard
to so extraordinary and pompous a question as that of his
own existence: then indeed is the entire devotion of the
natural religion lost in the Jewish anachronism of a longing
desire and expectation that Heaven would be pleased, if not
to abolish the disgrace of so great an ignorance, at least
to alleviate it through another Gospel than the Cross, and
through a Paraclete who is said to be coming (adventitious
Instructor).

This adulterous philosophy, of which one half speaks
Asdodic and not pure Jewish, does not deserve to be rebuked
and have its hair plucked, as Nehemiah did, so that it would
seek to spoil for us not only all the work of the vineyard
-- ("You, O Solomon, may have the thousand, and the keepers
of the fruit two hundred") -- but also every vow of life,
since no one can swear in good conscience to the permanence
of sentiments any more than to the duration of love and its
earnings before enjoying it, which admittedly appears to be
a very superfluous evil in a state where judgments and opinions and sentiments are privileged and usable small change
without corresponding actions.

Yes, notwithstanding it is written in the law of Moses: you shall not muzzle an ox; consequently the philosopher thinks as though this would have been said out of a divine predilection for Israelite bulls and oxen, and not for our own sake, for our sake alone. Are, then, teaching and comforting and preaching not actions which tire the body? Or is a pure, light tongue of the learned, which knows how to sustain with a word him that is weary,[10] not worth as many silver pieces as the pencil of the most ready and vigorous writer, who does nothing but sign his name, and often scribbles it so idiotically that one understands neither how to digest the content nor read the signature without special grace and inspiration and assistance from a Scheblimini.[11] Does not even Melchizedek receive as alms for his blessing a tenth of everything?

317

I, too, conclude with the broken, lingering tone of an already-mentioned solemn protest against every miserable sophistry and hateful consistency, which so many infectious subjects may have forced or wheedled out of me -- and yet with the result -- *reparabilis adsonat Echo*![12]

Belief and doubt affect man's capacity to know; as fear and hope affect his instinctual appetite. Truth and untruth are tools of the understanding: (true or untrue) representations of good and evil are tools of the will. All our knowledge is imperfect, and all human grounds of reason consist either in belief in truth and doubt in untruth or in belief in untruth and doubt in truth. "This (partly negative, partly positive) belief is prior to all systems. It has produced them first, in order to justify itself,"[13] says the venerable friend of Herr Moses Mendelssohn. But if the understanding believes in lies and finds that tasty, and doubts truths and finds them sickening like bad food, then the light in us is darkness and the salt has lost its savor -- Religion is a pure church parade -- philosophy, an empty display of words, superannuated opinions without meaning, obsolete rights without power! Therefore scepticism with regard to the truth and gullibility about self-deception are just as inseparable symptoms as chills and warmth in a fever. The one who believes himself to be farthest removed from this sickness of the soul and fervently wishes to be able to cure it in all his fellow-men himself confesses to have so often performed this cure on himself and tried it on others that he has become aware of how difficult it is and how small the chances of success are. -- Woe to the unfortunate wretch who dares to find fault with these inoffensive, purified words!

318

What is truth? A wind that blows where it wills, whose sound one hears, but does not know: whence? and whither? -- A spirit whom the world cannot receive, for it does not see him, and does not know him.

Devoted reader, what does the peace which the world gives have to do with you and me? We know for certain that the day of the Lord will come like a thief in the night. When people say, "There is peace and security," then sudden destruction will come upon them -- May the God of the peace which passes all understanding sanctify us wholly; that our spirit and soul and body may be kept blameless in the time to come --

"He who testifies to these things says, 'Surely I am coming soon!' Amen!"

NOTES

CHAPTER I

[1]Ernst Troeltsch, *The Absoluteness of Christianity and the History of Religions*, trans. David Reid (London: SCM Press Ltd., 1972), p. 123.

[2]Loc. cit.

[3]Rudolf Bultmann, "New Testament and Mythology," in *Kerygma and Myth: A Theological Debate*, ed. Hans Werner Bartsch, trans. Reginald H. Fuller (New York: Harper Torchbooks, 1961), pp. 1-44.

[4]Ibid., pp. 34-35.

[5]Ibid., pp. 3-5.

[6]Ibid., p. 13.

[7]Ibid., pp. 15-16.

[8]Ibid., pp. 34-40.

[9]Ibid., p. 36. My italics.

[10]Ibid., p. 42.

[11]Ibid., p. 43.

[12]Karl Barth, "Man in his Time," Article 47 in *Church Dogmatics*, vol. III: *The Doctrine of Creation*, Part Two, trans. and ed. G. W. Bromiley et al. (Edinburgh: T. & T. Clark, 1960), p. 442.

[13]Ibid., p. 452.

[14]H. Richard Niebuhr, "The Story of Our Life," in *The Meaning of Revelation* (New York: The Macmillan Company, 1941; reprint ed., 1962), pp. 43-90.

[15]Ibid., pp. 59-73.

[16]Ibid., p. 76.

[17]Ibid., pp. 68-73; 81-82.

[18]Ibid., p. 90.

[19]Ibid., p. 83.

[20]Ibid., p. 84.

[21]Richard R. Niebuhr, *Resurrection and Historical Reason: A Study in Theological Method* (New York: Charles Scribner's Sons, 1957).

[22]Ibid., p. vi.

[23]Ibid., p. 90.

[24]Ibid., p. 70.

[25]Ibid., p. 171.

[26]Ibid., p. 148.

[27]Ibid., p. 173.

[28]Ibid., p. 175.

[29]Ibid., p. 178.

[30]Van Austin Harvey, *The Historian and the Believer: The Morality of Historical Knowledge and Christian Belief* (New York: The Macmillan Company, 1966).

[31]Ibid., p. 63.

[32]Ibid., pp. 266-268.

[33]Ibid., p. 270.

[34]Ibid., p. 274.

[35]Ibid., pp. 280-281.

[36]Ibid., p. 283.

[37]Wolfhart Pannenberg et al., *Revelation as History*, trans. David Granskou (New York: The Macmillan Company, 1969), pp. 3-21.

[38]Wolfhart Pannenberg, *Theology and the Kingdom of God*, ed. Richard John Neuhaus (Philadelphia: The Westminster Press, 1969), p. 60.

[39]Ibid., p. 68.

[40]Wolfhart Pannenberg, "Focal Essay: The Revelation of God in Jesus of Nazareth," in *New Frontiers in Theology: Discussions among Continental and American Theologians*, vol. III: *Theology as History*, ed. James M. Robinson and John B. Cobb (New York: Harper & Row, 1967), pp. 114-117.

[41]Ibid., "Response to the Discussion," p. 227.

[42]Space does not allow adequate discussion of the historical influence of Hegel or Hamann, nor of the people and historical events which shaped their own thought. For an analysis of Hegel's decisive role in the secularization of Christian theology of history, see Karl Löwith, *Meaning in History* (Chicago: The University of Chicago Press, 1949). The best book on the historical developments in theology which were responsible for the secularization and general misunderstanding of Hamann's thought is Hans W. Frei, *The Eclipse of Biblical Narrative: A Study in Eighteenth and Nineteenth Century Hermeneutics* (New Haven: Yale University Press, 1974).

[43]Georg Wilhelm Friedrich Hegel, *Vorlesungen über die Philosophie der Weltgeschichte*, Vol. I: *Die Vernunft in der Geschichte*, ed. Johannes Hoffmeister (Hamburg: Felix Meiner Verlag, 1955). *Lectures on the Philosophy of World History: Introduction*, trans. H. B. Nisbet, with an Introduction by Duncan Forbes (Cambridge: Cambridge University Press, 1975). Hereafter: *LPH*.

[44]In taking this position, I am consciously criticizing an opposing trend in American interpretation of Hegel. See, for example, Walter Kaufmann, "Hegel on History," in *Hegel: A Reinterpretation* (Garden City: Doubleday Anchor, 1966), pp. 249-297; George Dennis O'Brien, *Hegel on Reason and History: A Contemporary Interpretation* (Chicago: The University of Chicago Press, 1975); and Burleigh Taylor Wilkins, *Hegel's Philosophy of History* (Ithaca: Cornell University Press, 1974).

[45]Johann Georg Hamann, *Golgotha und Scheblimini*, in *Sämtliche Werke*, ed. Josef Nadler (Vienna: Herder Verlag, 1951), vol. III, *Schriften über Sprache/Mysterien/Vernunft, 1772-1788*, pp. 291-320. Translations mine. Hereafter: *G & S*.

[46]Moses Mendelssohn, *Jerusalem, oder über religiöse Macht und Judenthum*, in *Gesammelte Schriften*, ed. G. B. Mendelssohn (Hildesheim: Verlag Dr. H. A. Gerstenberg, 1972 [1843], vol. III, pp. 257-362. Translations mine. Hereafter: *Jerusalem*.

[47]Georg Wilhelm Friedrich Hegel, "Hammans Schriften," in *G. W. F. Hegel: Werke in zwanzig Bänden*, vol. 11: *Berliner Schriften, 1818-1831*, ed. Eva Moldenhauer and Karl Markus Michel (Frankfurt/M.: Suhrkamp Verlag, 1970), pp. 275-352. Translations mine. Hereafter: *HS*.

[48]Ibid., p. 321.

[49]Two contemporary spokesman for this line of interpretation are Bruno Liebrucks, *Sprache und Bewusstsein* (Frankfurt/M.: Akademische Verlagsgesellschaft, 1964), vol. I, pp. 286-340 *et passim*; and Josef Simon, ed. and author of the Introduction to *J. G. Hamann: Schriften zur Sprache* (Frankfurt/M.: Suhrkamp Verlag, 1967). The extent to which this tendency can be exaggerated is illustrated by the way Hamann's name is hyphenated with Herder's, to make "Hamann-Herder," by Frank E. Manuel, *The Eighteenth Century Confronts the Gods* (New York: Atheneum, 1967), pp. 281-309. One indication of how this interpretation is often not even questioned is the effort of one of Hamann's few English-language interpreters to refer to him in a defense of secularization: see Ronald Gregor Smith, *Secular Christianity* (London: Collins, 1966), p. 157.

[50]The two who are most relevant to this study and whose work is presupposed throughout it are Karlfried Gründer, *Figur und Geschichte: Johann Georg Hamanns 'Biblische Betrachtungen' als Ansatz einer Geschichtsphilosophie* (Freiburg/Munich: Verlag Karl Alber, 1958); and Lothar Schreiner, Introduction and Commentary to *Golgotha und Scheblimini*, vol. 7 of *Johann Georg Hamanns Hauptschriften Erklärt*, ed. Fritz Blanke and Lothar Schreiner (Gütersloh: Carl Bertelsmann Verlag, 1956).

CHAPTER II

[1]Nisbet's translation follows Hoffmeister in putting all passages from Hegel's manuscripts in italics. I shall distinguish them in the footnotes by the designation (MS), as opposed to (N) for those passages taken from students' notes.

[2]*LPH*, p. 25 (MS). Translation modified. The German text may be found in Hoffmeister's edition (hereafter cited as: Hoff.), p. 25.

[3]Ibid., pp. 25-26 (MS); Hoff., pp. 25-27.

[4]Ibid., pp. 27-28 (MS); Hoff., pp. 28-29.

[5]Ibid., p. 29 (MS); Hoff., p. 31. Translation modified.

[6]Some of these connections are traced by O'Brien, *op. cit.*, and Wilkins, *op. cit.*

[7]*LPH*, pp. 34-35 (MS); Hoff., pp. 37-38.

[8]Ibid., p. 36 (MS); Hoff., pp. 40-41.

[9]Ibid., p. 35 (MS); Hoff., p. 38. Translation modified.

[10]Ibid., p. 37 (MS); Hoff., p. 41.

[11]Ibid., p. 40 (MS); Hoff., p. 45. Translation modified.

[12]Ibid., p. 41 (N); Hoff., p. 46.

[13]Ibid., pp. 42-43 (MS); Hoff., p. 48.

[14]Ibid., p. 42 (N); Hoff., p. 48.

[15]Ibid., p. 44 (MS); Hoff., p. 50.

[16]Ibid., pp. 60-61 (N); Hoff., pp. 70-71.

[17]Loc. cit.

[18]Ibid., p. 44 (N); Hoff., p. 50.

[19]Ibid., p. 46 (N); Hoff., p. 53. Translation modified.

[20]Ibid., p. 46 (MS); Hoff., p. 53.

[21]Ibid., p. 54 (MS); Hoff., pp. 61-62.

[22]Ibid., p. 55 (MS); Hoff., pp. 63-64.

[23]Ibid., p. 51 (N); Hoff., pp. 58-59.

[24] Ibid., p. 144 (MS); Hoff., p. 175.

[25] Ibid., p. 54 (MS); Hoff., p. 62. Translation modified.

[26] Ibid., p. 36 (MS); Hoff., p. 40.

[27] Ibid., p. 93 (N); Hoff., p. 111.

[28] Ibid., p. 96 (N); Hoff., p. 114.

[29] Ibid., p. 99 (MS); Hoff., p. 117.

[30] Ibid., pp. 99-100 (MS); Hoff., pp. 118-119.

[31] Ibid., p. 103 (MS); Hoff., p. 123.

[32] Ibid., pp. 116-117 (MS); Hoff., pp. 138-139.

[33] Ibid., pp. 117-119 (MS/N); Hoff., pp. 139-142.

[34] See above, pp. 43, 45.

[35] *LPH*, p. 36 (MS); Hoff., p. 40. Translation modified.

[36] Ibid., p. 60 (N); Hoff., p. 70.

[37] Ibid., p. 66 (N); Hoff., p. 77.

[38] Ibid., p. 85 (N); Hoff., p. 100.

[39] Ibid., pp. 78-79 (N); Hoff., p. 92.

[40] Ibid., p. 141 (MS); Hoff., p. 171.

[41] Ibid., pp. 90-91 (MS); Hoff., pp. 107-108.

[42] Ibid., p. 66 (N); Hoff., p. 77.

[43] Ibid., p. 21 (N); Hoff., p. 18.

[44] Ibid., p. 43 (N); Hoff., pp. 48-49.

[45] Ibid., p. 68 (MS); Hoff., p. 79.

[46] Ibid., pp. 72-73 (N); Hoff., p. 85.

[47] Ibid., p. 73 (MS); Hoff., p. 85.

[48] Ibid., p. 74 (MS); Hoff., p. 87.

[49] Ibid., p. 76 (MS); Hoff., p. 90.

[50] Ibid., p. 89 (N); Hoff., p. 105.

NOTES

CHAPTER III

[1] *G & S*, p. 319.

[2] See Chapter I, footnote 7. There are two similar studies in English which attempt to interpret just one major text by Hamann. In both cases that text is the *Socratic Memorabilia*. See Albert B. Anderson, "Ignorance and Enlightenment: A Study in the Religious Philosophy of Johann Georg Hamann (1730-1788)" (Ph.D. dissertation, Harvard University, 1964); and James C. O'Flaherty, *Hamann's Socratic Memorabilia: A Translation and Commentary* (Baltimore: The Johns Hopkins Press, 1967).

[3] *G & S*, p. 303. I have not reproduced Hamann's extensive underscoring, on the grounds that it is often more confusing than helpful. In this decision I am following the practice of O'Flaherty (see note 2) and Ronald Gregor Smith, *J. G. Hamann, 1730-1788: A Study in Christian Existence, with Selections from his Writings* (New York: Harper & Brothers, 1960).

[4] See, for example, W. M. Alexander, *Johann Georg Hamann: Philosophy and Faith* (The Hague: Martinue Nijhoff, 1966), pp. 152-155.

[5] *Jerusalem*, p. 309. A new translation of Mendelssohn's *Jerusalem* is available in: Moses Mendelssohn, *Jerusalem and Other Jewish Writings*, trans. and ed. Alfred Jospe (New York: Schocken Books, 1969). Although I find Jospe's translation unreliable, in the sense that he often seems to "polish" Mendelssohn's meaning to make him appear contemporary, I have found it helpful to consult, and will include page references to it, using the abbreviation: Jos. Thus, for this passage: Jos., p. 58.

[6] Ibid., pp. 281ff.; Jos., pp. 32ff.

[7] Ibid., p. 312; Jos., p. 61.

[8] *G & S*, p. 305.

[9] Ibid., pp. 303-304.

[10] *Jerusalem*, pp. 348-350; Jos., pp. 97-99.

[11] Ibid., p. 311; Jos., p. 61.

[12] Ibid., p. 263; Jos., p. 17.

[13] *G & S*, p. 304.

[14] *Jerusalem*, p. 318; Jos., p. 68.

[15] Ibid., p. 337; Jos., p. 87.

235

[16]*G & S*, p. 304.

[17]*Jerusalem*, p. 311; Jos., p. 61.

[18]Ibid., p. 313; Jos., p. 62.

[19]Ibid., p. 349; Jos., p. 98.

[20]Ibid., p. 307; Jos., p. 57.

[21]Ibid., p. 315; Jos., p. 64.

[22]*G & S*, p. 305.

[23]*Jerusalem*, p. 349; Jos., p. 98.

[24]*G & S*, p. 306.

[25]*Jerusalem*, p. 322; Jos., p. 72.

[26]Ibid., p. 350; Jos., pp. 98-99.

[27]Ibid., p. 355; Jos., pp. 103-104.

[28]Schreiner, op. cit., p. 114.

[29]*G & S*, p. 305.

[30]For a general study of typology in relation to Hamann, see Gründer, op. cit., pp. 93-158.

[31]*G & S*, pp. 305-306.

[32]Ibid., p. 308.

[33]Ibid., p. 305.

[34]Loc. cit. Cf. Rom. 9:33, 1 Cor. 1:23 and 1 Pet. 2:6-8.

[35]See above, p. 94.

[36]*G & S*, p. 311.

[37]Ibid., pp. 310-311.

[38]*Jerusalem*, p. 323; Jos., p. 73.

[39]Ibid., p. 330; Jos., p. 80.

[40]Ibid., p. 331; Jos., p. 80.

[41]*G & S*, p. 308.

[42]*Jerusalem*, p. 353; Jos., pp. 101-102.

[43]Micah 5:6 in the New American Bible. See 5:7 in the RSV.

[44]See Schreiner's discussion, op. cit., pp. 131-134.

[45]Pp. 106-107.

[46]*G & S*, p. 312.

[47]Ibid., p. 307.

[48]*Jerusalem*, p. 266; Jos., pp. 19-20.

[49]See Gründer, op. cit., pp. 21-27. According to Gründer, Hamann's understanding of the concept is trinitarian rather than merely christological.

[50]*G & S*, p. 293.

[51]Ibid., p. 297.

[52]*Jerusalem*, pp. 270-271; Jos., pp. 23-24.

[53]Ibid., p. 305; Jos., p. 55.

[54]*G & S*, p. 299.

[55]*Jerusalem*, p. 271; Jos., pp. 24-25.

[56]*G & S*, p. 299.

[57]*Jerusalem*, pp. 269-279, 305; Jos., pp. 23-31, 55.

[58]*G & S*, pp. 298-299.

[59]Ibid., pp. 299-300.

[60]*Jerusalem*, p. 272; Jos., p. 26.

[61]*G & S*, pp. 294-295.

[62]*Jerusalem*, p. 270; Jos., pp. 23-24.

[63]*G & S*, p. 295.

[64]Ibid., pp. 297-298.

[65]*Jerusalem*, p. 270; Jos., p. 24.

[66]Ibid., pp. 270-271; Jos., p. 24.

[67]Pp. 156-161.

CHAPTER IV

[1]See Karlfried Gründer, "Geschichte der Deutungen," in
Die Hamann-Forschung, Vol. 1 of *Johann Georg Hamanns Hauptschriften Erklärt*, ed. Fritz Balnke and Lothar Schreiner (Gütersloh:
Carl Bertelsmann Verlag, 1956), p. 21. This essay is a detailed
history of Hamann scholarship up until 1955. Included in the
same volume is a complete (until 1955) bibliography of Hamanni-
ana, compiled by Lothar Schreiner. Hereafter: *HH I*.

[2]*Hamanns Schriften*, ed. Friedrich Roth (Berlin: G. Reimer,
1821-1825).

[3]Quoted in *HH I*, p. 22.

[4]*HS*, p. 297.

[5]Gründer reports in *HH I*, p. 26, that Goethe invited Hegel
to tea in October, 1827, and was entertained by his extensive
knowledge of Hamann. After Hegel's article appeared the following year, Goethe professed to reading and re-reading it. "Hegel's judgments as a critic," he said, "have always been good."

[6]*HS*, p. 321.

[7]Loc. cit.

[8]Ibid., p. 324.

[9]Ibid., pp. 325-326.

[10]See above, Chapter III, pp. 83-84.

[11]*G & S*, p. 312. In Hegel's quotation of this passage (*HS*,
p. 323), its anti-institutional tone is considerably intensified
by the deletion of Hamann's qualification on the "arbitrariness
of the authorities" as "sometimes coarse and sometimes refined."
This omission makes Hamann appear unaware of the very real differences among human institutions, and thus increases the credibility of Hegel's criticism of him for readers who are not familiar with the text of the *Golgotha*.

[12]*HS*, pp. 323-324.

[13]See above, Chapter III, pp. 92-93.

[14]*HS*, p. 334.

[15]Ibid., pp. 334-335.

[16]Ibid., pp. 320-321.

[17]*LPH*, p. 92 (MS); Hoff., p. 109.

[18] *HS*, p. 277.

[19] See Chapter II, p. 51.

[20] *HS*, p. 278.

[21] Ibid., p. 279.

[22] Ibid., p. 280.

[23] Loc. cit.

[24] Ibid., p. 284.

[25] Ibid., p. 285.

[26] Ibid., p. 308.

[27] Ibid., pp. 308-309.

[28] Ibid., p. 293.

[29] Loc cit.

[30] Alexander, op. cit., p. 4.

[31] For details see the authoritative biography by Josef Nadler, *Johann Georg Hamann, 1730-1788: Der Zeuge des Corpus mysticum* (Salzburg: Otto Müller Verlag, 1949), pp. 71-81.

[32] *HS*, p. 293.

[33] Ibid., p. 294.

[34] Ibid., p. 296.

[35] Ibid., p. 297.

[36] Ibid., p. 312.

[37] Ibid., pp. 308-312.

[38] Ibid., p. 310.

[39] Ibid., p. 313.

[40] Loc. cit.

[41] Ibid., p. 295.

[42] Ibid., pp. 313-314. For a discussion of Hegel's view of positivity as a necessary stage of religious awareness, see George Rupp, *Christologies and Cultures: Toward a Typology of Religious Worldviews* (The Hague: Mouton, 1974), pp. 107-116.

[43] *HS*, p. 317.

[44] Ibid., p. 314.

[45] Ibid., pp. 316-317.

[46] Ibid., p. 294.

[47] Ibid., p. 281.

[48] Ibid., pp. 299-302.

[49] Ibid., pp. 319-320.

[50] Ibid., p. 332.

[51] Ibid., pp. 335-336.

[52] Ibid., p. 280.

[53] Ibid., p. 336.

[54] Ibid., pp. 343-344.

[55] Ibid., p. 337.

[56] Ibid., p. 315.

[57] The "Metakritik über den Purismum der Vernunft" is included in the Nadler edition of Hamann's *Sämtliche Werke*, vol. III, pp. 281-289. For a complete translation, see R. G. Smith, *J. G. Hamann*, pp. 213-221. A recent discussion of Hamann's criticism of Kant has been published by Oswald Bayer, "Selbstverschuldete Vormundschaft: Hamanns Kontroverse mit Kant um *wahre* Aufklärung," in *Die Wirklichkeitsanspruch von Theologie und Religion* (Ernst Steinbach Festschrift), ed. Dieter Henke et al. (Tübingen: J. C. B. Mohr, 1976), pp. 1-34.

[58] I am indebted for this felicitous term to Theodor Bodammer, *Hegel's Deutung der Sprache: Interpretationen zu Hegels Äusserungen über die Sprache* (Hamburg: Felix Meiner Verlag, 1969), p. 133.

[59] *HS*, p. 326.

[60] Ibid., p. 327.

[61] *Immanuel Kant's Critique of Pure Reason*, tr. Norman Kemp Smith (New York: St. Martin's Press, 1965), p. 61 (A 15).

[62] *HS*, p. 328. See also Smith, op. cit., pp. 217-218.

[63] In relation to this image, Josef Simon observes that the tree of knowledge in Paradise also had two "trunks" [knowledge of good and knowledge of evil] and one unknown root. See his note to this passage, op. cit., p. 262.

[64] See Smith's translation, op. cit., p. 218; cf. Nadler, III, p. 287.

[65] *HS*, p. 332.

[66] Ibid., p. 339.

[67] Ibid., p. 317.

[68] Ibid., p. 318.

[69] Ibid., p. 331.

[70] Ibid., pp. 330-331.

[71] *Werke*, ed. Ph. Marheineke et al. (Berlin: Verlag von Duncker und Humblot, 1840), vol. XI, pp. 85-252. The translations are my own, but see also those by E. B. Speirs and J. Burdon Sanderson, *Lectures on the Philosophy of Religion* (New York: Humanities Press, 1962), vol. I, pp. 89-258. Hereafter: Speirs. Several papers on Hegel's treatment of "Representation" within his *Lectures on the Philosophy of Religion* have been published recently. See in particular: George L. Kline, "Hegel and the Marxist-Leninist Critique of Religion," in *Hegel and the Philosophy of Religion: The Wofford Symposium*, edited, with an Introduction, by Darrel E. Christensen (The Hague: Martinus Nijhoff, 1970), pp. 157-177; Kenneth L. Schmitz, "The Conceptualization of Religious Mystery: An Essay in Hegel's Philosophy of Religion," in *The Legacy of Hegel: Proceedings of the Marquette Hegel Symposium, 1970*, ed. J. J. O'Malley et al. (The Hague: Martinus Nijhoff, 1973), pp. 108-136; and Louis Dupré, "Religion as Representation," also in *The Legacy of Hegel*, pp. 137-143.

[72] *Werke*, XI, p. 117; Speirs, pp. 120-121.

[73] Ibid., p. 120; Speirs, p. 124.

[74] Ibid., pp. 121-125; Speirs, pp. 125-129.

[75] Ibid., pp. 125-134; Speirs, pp. 129-138.

[76] Ibid., pp. 134-137; Speirs, pp. 138-141.

[77] Ibid., pp. 140-141; Speirs, p. 145.

[78] See the critical edition prepared by Georg Lasson, Georg Wilhelm Friedrich Hegel, *Vorlesungen über die Philosophie der Religion* (Hamburg: Verlag von Felix Meiner, 1966 [1925]), vol. I, p. 42.

[79] *Werke*, XI, pp. 141-142; Speirs, pp. 146-147.

[80] Ibid., pp. 143-144; Speirs, pp. 147-148.

[81] Lasson, op. cit., p. 39.

[82] Ibid., p. 42.

[1]The only thorough study of Hamann's philosophy of language
in English is James C. O'Flaherty, *Unity and Language: A Study
in the Philosophy of Johann Georg Hamann* (Chapel Hill: University
of North Carolina, 1952). Many of Hamann's writings on language
have been collected, with a commentary by Elfriede Büchsel, in
Volume 4 of *Hamanns Hauptschriften Erklärt: Über den Ursprung
der Sprache* (Gütersloh: Gerd Mohn, 1963). Also worthy of mention are Martin Seils, *Wirklichkeit und Wort bei Johann Georg
Hamann* (Stuttgart: Calver Verlag, 1961); Georg Baudler, *'Im
Worte Sehen': Das Sprachdenken Johann Georg Hamanns* (Bonn: H.
Bouvier u. Co., 1970); Heinz Georg Herde, *Johann Georg Hamann: zur
Theologie der Sprache* (Bonn: H. Bouvier u. Co., 1971); and
Josef Simon's "Einleitung," op. cit., pp. 9-80.

[2]*G & S*, p. 294.

[3]*Jerusalem*, p. 270; Jos., p. 24.

[4]Ibid., p. 296; Jos., p. 46.

[5]Ibid., pp. 333-335; Jos., pp. 83-84.

[6]Ibid., pp. 269-270; Jos., pp. 23-24.

[7]On the concept of positivity in relation to authority,
see Chapter IV, pp. 117-118.

[8]*G & S*, p. 298.

[9]*Jerusalem*, pp. 270-271; Jos., p. 24.

[10]Ibid., pp. 281-285; Jos., pp. 32-36.

[11]Ibid., pp. 325-326; Jos., pp. 74-75.

[12]Ibid., pp. 324-341; Jos., pp. 73-91.

[13]Ibid., p. 305; Jos., p. 55.

[14]Ibid., p. 313; Jos., pp. 62-63.

[15]*G & S*, pp. 302-303.

[16]See Chapter III, p. 70, note 22.

[17]Kant, op. cit., A 60 - A 61/B 84 - B 85, pp. 98-99.

[18]Nadler, vol. III, pp. 284-286; cf. Smith, op. cit., pp.
215-216.

[19]*G & S*, p. 302.

[20] *Jerusalem*, pp. 259-260; Jos., pp. 13-14.

[21] See Chapter III, pp. 129ff.

[22] *Jerusalem*, p. 282; Jos., p. 33.

[23] Ibid., p. 271; Jos., p. 25.

[24] Ibid., p. 287; Jos., p. 38.

[25] *The Odyssey of Homer*, trans, with an Introduction by Richmond Lattimore (New York: Harper Torchbooks, 1965), Book II, 85-128, pp. 41-42.

[26] See Schreiner, op. cit., p. 95.

[27] Nadler, vol. III, pp. 287, 289; cf. Smith, op. cit., pp. 218, 220.

[28] *Jerusalem*, pp. 263-264; Jos., p. 17.

[29] *G & S*, p. 301.

[30] Loc. cit.

[31] See above, p. 138 and note 5.

[32] *Jerusalem*, p. 355; Jos., pp. 103-104.

[33] See Chapter III, pp. 87-93.8.

[34] *Jerusalem*, p. 270; Jos., p. 24.

[35] Ibid., p. 292; Jos., pp. 42-43.

[36] *G & S*, p. 300.

[37] Ibid., p. 302.

[38] *Jerusalem*, p. 356; Jos., p. 105.

[39] See Schreiner, op. cit., pp. 167-168, for a helpful comment on Hamann's appreciation of pagan philosophers as prophets of Christianity. For Hamann's documentation of this quotation, see note 3 in the Appendix.

[40] *G & S*, pp. 296-297. The final period is Hamann's punctuation.

[41] *Jerusalem*, p. 269; Jos., p. 23.

[42] Ibid., p. 270; Jos., p. 24.

[43] *G & S*, p. 294; see above, pp. 137-140.

[44] *Jerusalem*, pp. 269-270; Jos., pp. 23-24.

[45] Schreiner, op. cit., p. 71.

[46] See Chapter III, pp. 87-88; and above, pp. 153-154.

[47] *G & S*, pp. 312-313.

[48] *Jerusalem*, p. 265; Jos., p. 19.

[49] Ibid., p. 282; Jos., p. 33, omits these phrases.

[50] Schreiner, op. cit., p. 143, traces this interpretation to Luther.

[51] *G & S*, p. 315.

[52] Schreiner, op. cit., p. 155, traces the phrase, "a queen ...coming," to Kant's *Metaphysics of Nature*.

[53] Ibid., p. 145.

[54] See the *G & S*, pp. 296, 307, for examples.

[55] Ibid., p. 316.

[56] David Hume, *Dialogues Concerning Natural Religion*, ed. with an Introduction by Henry D. Aiken (New York: Hafner Publishing Co., 1948), p. 94.

[57] Alexander, op. cit., p. 38.

[58] Although many interpreters identify Hume's own position with that of Cleanthes, Frederick Copleston, for one, agrees with Hamann. See *A History of Philosophy*, Vol. 5: *Modern Philosophy: The British Philosophers*, Part II, *Berkeley to Hume* (Garden City: Doubleday Image, 1964), pp. 111-113.

[59] Hume, op. cit., p. 93.

[60] Ibid., p. 94.

[61] *G & S*, pp. 317-318.

[62] See above, pp. 140-142.

[63] *Jerusalem*, p. 286; Jos., pp. 36-37.

[64] Ibid., p. 322; Jos., p. 72.

[65] Ibid., p. 290; Jos., p. 41.

[66] Ibid., p. 360; Jos., p. 109.

[67] *G & S*, p. 318.

NOTES

APPENDIX

[1] Garve, Notes on the first book by Cicero on duties, pp. 95-96. [See Schreiner, op. cit., p. 56.]

[2] See Adelung. [*Grammatisch-kritisches Wörterbuch*, 1796, p. 443; see Schreiner, op. cit., p. 75.]

[3] Cicero, *De Officiis*, Ch. I, VII, #6; XVI, #3; Ch. III, XVIII, #11.

[4] *Bath-Qol* [written by Hamann in Hebrew, the phrase means an imitation or echo of God's voice; see Schreiner, op. cit., p. 88].

[5] See Luther's Preface. [Viz., his Preface to the Psalter; see Schreiner, op. cit., p. 90.]

[6] Zech. 10:10-11; 12:6.

[7] See Köster's dissertation. [Reference obscure; see Schreiner, op. cit., p. 125.]

[8] According to A. L. Z., April, 1785, p. 48. [this reference to the *Allgemeine Literaturzeitung* was not in the original text; see Schreiner, op. cit., p. 140.]

[9] to limp on both sides, Luther on Ps. 35:15.

[10] Is. 32:4.

[11] [The word "Scheblimini" is Hamann's (and Luther's) transliteration of the Hebrew in Ps. 110:1, meaning "Sit at my right hand"; see Schreiner, op. cit., p. 47.]

[12] Persius I, v, 102. [See Schreiner, op. cit., p. 160.]

[13] "we have invented them." Garve on Ferguson, pp. 296-297. [This reference is to Christian Garve, *Adam Fergusons Grundsätze der Moralphilosophie*, translation with notes, Leipzig, 1772; see Schreiner, op. cit., p. 161.]

SELECTED BIBLIOGRAPHY

I.   General Works Consulted

Beck, Lewis White. *Early German Philosophy*: *Kant and His Predecessors*. Cambridge: Harvard University Press, 1969.

Becker, Carl L. *The Heavenly City of the Eighteenth-Century
Philosophers*. New Haven: Yale University Press, 1932.

Butterfield, Herbert. *Christianity and History*. New York:
Charles Scribner's Sons, 1950.

_____. *Man on His Past*: *The History of Historical Scholar-
ship*. Cambridge: Cambridge University Press, 1969.

Cassirer, Ernst. *The Philosophy of the Enlightenment*. Translated by Fritz A. Koelln and James P. Pettegrove. Boston:
Beacon Press, 1955.

Collingwood, R. G. *Essays in the Philosophy of History*. Edited
with an Introduction, by William Debbins. New York: Mc-
Graw-Hill Book Company, 1966.

_____. *The Idea of History*. New York: Oxford University
Press, 1970 (1946).

Collins, James. *The Emergence of Philosophy of Religion*. New
Haven: Yale University Press, 1967.

Copleston, Frederick. *A History of Philosophy*. 8 Vols. Revised ed. Garden City: Doubleday Image, 1962-1967.

Dilthey, Wilhelm. *Pattern and Meaning in History*: *Thoughts on
History and Society*. Translated and edited, with an Intro-
duction and notes, by H. P. Rickman. New York: Harper
Torchbooks, 1962.

Dray, William H. *Philosophy of History*. Foundations of Philosophy Series. Englewood Cliffs (N.J.): Prentice-Hall,
Inc., 1964.

Frei, Hans W. *The Eclipse of Biblical Narrative*: *A Study in
Eighteenth and Nineteenth Century Hermeneutics*. New Haven:
Yale University Press, 1974.

Hazard, Paul. *The European Mind*: *1680-1715*. Translated by
J. Lewis May. Cleveland: Meridian Books, 1963.

Kant, Immanuel. *On History*. Edited, with an Introduction, by
Lewis White Beck. Translated by Lewis White Beck et al.
The Library of Liberal Arts. New York: The Bobbs-Merrill
Company, 1963.

249

Krentz, Edgar. *The Historical-Critical Method*. Philadelphia: Fortress Press, 1975.

Löwith, Karl. *From Hegel to Nietzsche   The Revolution in Nine-teenth-Century Thought*. Translated by David E. Green. Garden City: Doubleday Anchor, 1967.

_____. *Meaning in History*. Chicago: The University of Chicago Press, 1949.

Mackintosh, H. R. *Types of Modern Theology: Schleiermacher to Barth*. London: Collins, 1964 (1937).

Mandelbaum, Maurice. *The Problem of Historical Knowledge: An Answer to Relativism*. New York: Harper Torchbooks, 1967 (1938).

Manuel, Frank E. *The Eighteenth Century Confronts the Gods*. New York: Atheneum, 1967.

Nisbet, Robert A. *Social Change and History: Aspects of the Western Theory of Development*. Oxford: Oxford University Press, 1970.

Oelmüller, Willi. *Die unbefriedigte Aufklärung: Beiträge zu einer Theorie der Moderne von Lessing, Kant und Hegel*. Frankfurt/M.: Suhrkamp Verlag, 1969.

Royce, Josiah. *The Spirit of Modern Philosophy: An Essay in the Form of Lectures*. New York: W. W. Norton & Company, Inc., 1967.

Schweitzer, Albert. *The Quest of the Historical Jesus: A Critical Study of its Progress from Reimarus to Wrede*. Translated by W. Montgomery, with a Preface by F. C. Bur-kitt. New York: The Macmillan Company, 1964.

Shelley, Bruce. *By What Authority? The Standards of Truth in the Early Church*. Grand Rapids: William B. Eerdmans Publishing Company, 1965.

Walsh, W. H. *Philosophy of History: An Introduction*. New York: Harper Torchbooks, 1957.

Welch, Claude. *Protestant Thought in the Nineteenth Century: Volume I, 1799-1870*. New Haven: Yale University Press, 1972.

II.   Works Consulted for Contemporary Theology

Altizer, Thomas J. J. *The Gospel of Christian Atheism*. Phila-delphia: The Westminster Press, 1966.

Baillie, John. *The Idea of Revelation in Recent Thought*. New York: Columbia University Press, 1964.

Balthasar, Hans Urs von. *The Theology of Karl Barth*. Translated by John Drury. Garden City: Doubleday Anchor, 1972.

Barth, Karl. *Church Dogmatics*. 4 Vols. Translated by G. W.
Bromiley and T. F. Torrance. Edinburgh: T. & T. Clark,
1936-1962.

_____. *Protestant Thought*: *From Rousseau to Ritschl*. SCM
ed. Translated by Brian Cozens et al. New York: Simon
and Schuster, 1969.

_____. "The Strange New World within the Bible." In *The Word
of God and the Word of Man*. Translated, with a new Foreword,
by Douglas Horton. New York: Harper Torchbooks, 1957.
Pp. 28-50.

Berdyaev, Nicholas. *The Meaning of History*. Translated by George
Reavey. Cleveland: Meridian Books, 1962.

Bultmann, Rudolf. *Existence and Faith*: *Shorter Writings of
Rudolf Bultmann*. Selected, translated, and introduced by
Schubert M. Ogden. Cleveland: Meridian Books, 1960.

_____. *History and Eschatology*: *The Presence of Eternity*.
The Gifford Lectures, 1955. New York: Harper & Row, 1957.

_____. *Jesus Christ and Mythology*. New York: Charles
Scribner's Sons, 1958.

_____ et al. *Kerygma and Myth*: *A Theological Debate*. Edited
by Hans Werner Bartsch. Translated by Reginald H. Fuller.
New York: Harper Torchbooks, 1961.

Buren, Paul M. van. *The Edges of Language*: *An Essay in the
Logic of a Religion*. New York: The Macmillan Company, 1972.

Cox, Harvey G. *The Secular City*: *Secularization and Urbanization
in Theological Perspective*. Rev. ed. New York: The Macmillan Company, 1966.

_____. "Tradition and Future: The Need for a New Perspec-
tive." In *On Not Leaving It to the Snake*. New York: The
Macmillan Company, 1969. Pp. 29-43.

Cullmann, Oscar. *Christ and Time*: *The Primitive Christian Conception of Time and History*. 3rd ed. Translated by Floyd
V. Filson. Philadelphia: The Westminster Press, 1963.

Ebeling, Gerhard. *Introduction to a Theological Theory of Language*. Translated by R. A. Wilson. London: Collins, 1973.

Frei, Hans W. "Niebuhr's Theological Background." In *Faith and
Ethics*: *The Theology of H. Richard Niebuhr*. Edited by Paul
Ramsey. New York: Harper & Brothers, 1957. Pp. 9-64.

Gilkey, Langdon. *Naming the Whirlwind*: *The Renewal of God-
Language*. Indianapolis: The Bobbs-Merrill Company, 1969.

Harnack, Adolf. *What is Christianity?* Translated by Thomas Bailey Saunders with an Introduction by Rudolf Bultmann. New York: Harper Torchbooks, 1957.

Harvey, Van Austin. *The Historian and the Believer*: *The Morality of Historical Knowledge and Christian Belief*. New York: The Macmillan Company, 1966.

Kaufman, Gordon D. "Can a Man Serve Two Masters?" *Theology Today* XV, no. 1 (April, 1958), pp. 59-77.

_____. *An Essay on Theological Method*. American Academy of Religion Studies in Religion, no. 11. Edited by Stephen D. Crites. Missoula (Mt.): Scholars Press, 1975.

_____. "History and Mysticism." *The Review of Metaphysics* X, no. 4 (June, 1957), pp. 675-689.

_____. *Relativism, Knowledge and Faith*. Chicago: The University of Chicago Press, 1960.

_____. "What Shall We Do With the Bible?" *Interpretation* 25, no. 1 (Jan., 1971), pp. 95-112.

McGill, Arthur C. *Suffering*: *A Test of Theological Method*. Philadelphia: The Geneva Press, 1968.

Macquarrie, John. *Twentieth-Century Religious Thought*: *The Frontiers of Philosophy and Theology, 1900-1970*. Study edition. London: SCM Press Ltd., 1971.

Montgomery, John Warwick. *History & Christianity*. Downers Grove (Ill.): Intervarsity Press, 1965.

Niebuhr, H. Richard. *The Meaning of Revelation*. New York: The Macmillan Company, 1962 (1941).

_____. *Radical Monotheism and Western Culture, With Supplementary Essays*. New York: Harper & Brothers, 1960.

_____. *The Responsible Self*: *An Essay in Christian Moral Philosophy*. Introduction by James M. Gustafson. New York: Harper & Row, 1963.

Niebuhr, Reinhold. *Faith and History*: *A Comparison of Christian and Modern Views of History*. New York: Charles Scribner's Sons, 1949.

Niebuhr, Richard R. "Archegos: An Essay on the Relation between the Biblical Jesus Christ and the Present-Day Reader." In *Christian History and Interpretation*: *Studies Presented to John Knox*. Edited by W. R. Farmer, C. F. D. Moule and R. R. Niebuhr. Cambridge: Cambridge University Press, 1967. Pp. 79-100.

_____. *Resurrection and Historical Reason*: *A Study in Theological Method*. New York: Charles Scribner's Sons, 1957.

Ogden, Schubert M. "What Sense Does It Make to Say, 'God Acts in History'?" In *The Reality of God and Other Essays*. New York: Harper & Row, 1966. Pp. 164-187.

Ogletree, Thomas W. *Christian Faith and History: A Critical Comparison of Ernst Troeltsch and Karl Barth*. Nashville: Abingdon Press, 1965.

Pannenberg, Wolfhart. "Focal Essay: The Revelation of God in Jesus of Nazareth" and "Response to the Discussion." In *Theology as History*. Vol. III in *New Frontiers in Theology: Discussions among Continental and American Theologians*. Edited by James M. Robinson and John B. Cobb. New York: Harper & Row, Publishers, 1967. Pp. 101-133 and 221-276.

_____. *The Idea of God and Human Freedom*. Translated by R. A. Wilson. Philadelphia: The Westminster Press, 1973.

_____ et al. *Revelation as History*. Translated by David Granskou. New York: The Macmillan Company, 1969.

_____. *Theology and the Kingdom of God*. Edited by Richard John Neuhaus. Philadelphia: The Westminster Press, 1969.

Pauck, Wilhelm. *Harnack and Troeltsch: Two Historical Theologians*. New York: Oxford University Press, 1968.

Robinson, James M. "Hermeneutic Since Barth." In *The New Hermeneutic*. Vol. II in *New Frontiers in Theology: Discussions among Continental and American Theologians*. Edited by James M. Robinson and John B. Cobb. New York: Harper & Row, Publishers, 1964. Pp. 1-77.

Rosenstock-Huessy, Eugen. *The Christian Future, or The Modern Mind Outrun*. New York: Charles Scribner's Sons, 1946.

_____. *Speech and Reality*. Introduction by Clinton C. Gardner. Norwich (Vt.): Argo Books, Inc., 1970.

Smith, Ronald Gregor. *Secular Christianity*. London: Collins, 1966.

Spiegler, Gerhard. "Overcoming History with History: Some Unfinished Old Business at the New Frontiers of Theology," In *The Future of Empirical Theology*. Edited by Bernard E. Meland. Vol. VII in *Essays in Divinity*. Edited by Jerald C. Brauer. Chicago: The University of Chicago Press, 1969. Pp. 269-281.

Stevenson, W. Taylor. *History as Myth: The Import for Contemporary Theology*. New York: The Seabury Press, 1969.

Tillich, Paul. *The Courage To Be*. New Haven: Yale University Press, 1952.

_____. *The Interpretation of History*. Translated by N. A. Rasetzki (Part I) and Elsa L. Talmey (Parts II, III, IV). New York: Charles Scribner's Sons, 1936.

_____. *The Protestant Era*. Abridged ed. Translated by James
Luther Adams. Chicago: The University of Chicago Press,
1957.

Troeltsch, Ernst. *The Absoluteness of Christianity and the History of Religions*. Translated by David Reid. London: SCM
Press Ltd., 1972.

Wink, Walter. *The Bible in Human Transformation: Toward a New
Paradigm for Biblical Study*. Philadelphia: Fortress Press,
1973.

III. Works Consulted for Hegel

Bodammer, Theodor. *Hegels Deutung der Sprache: Interpretationen
zu Hegels Äusserungen über die Sprache*. Hamburg: Felix
Meiner Verlag, 1969.

Cook, Daniel. "Language and Consciousness in Hegel's Jena
Writings." In *Journal of the History of Philosophy*, 10
(1972), pp. 197-211.

_____. *Language in the Philosophy of Hegel*. The Hague:
Mouton, 1973.

Crites, Stephen. "The Gospel According to Hegel." *Journal of
Religion* XLVI, no. 2 (April, 1966), pp. 246-263.

Dupré, Louis. "Religion as Representation." In *The Legacy of
Hegel: Proceedings of the Marquette Hegel Symposium, 1970*.
Edited by J. J. O'Malley et al. The Hague: Martinus
Nijhoff, 1973. Pp. 108-136.

Fackenheim, Emil L. *The Religious Dimension in Hegel's Thought*.
Bloomington: Indiana University Press, 1967.

Findlay, J. N. *The Philosophy of Hegel: An Introduction and
Re-Examination*. New York: Collier Books, 1962.

Gray, J. Glenn. *Hegel and Greek Thought*. New York: Harper
Torchbooks, 1968.

Gründer, Karlfried. "Nachspiel zu Hegels Hamann-Rezenzion."
In Vol. I of *Hegel-Studien*. Edited by Friedhelm Nicolin
and Otto Pöggeler. Bonn: H. Bouvier u. Co. Verlag, 1961.
Pp. 81-101.

Hegel, Georg Wilhelm Friedrich. *Enzyklopädie der philosophischen
Wissenschaften im Grundrisse (1830)*. Edited by Friedhelm
Nicolin and Otto Pöggeler. Hamburg: Verlag von Felix
Meiner, 1969. Part I: *The Logic of Hegel*. Translated by
W. Wallace. Oxford: Clarendon Press, 1894. Part II:
Hegel's 'Philosophy of Nature' and Part III: *Hegel's 'Philo-
sophy of Mind'*. Translated by A. V. Miller, with a Foreword
by J. N. Findlay. Oxford: Clarendon Press, 1970-1971.

_____. "Hamanns Schriften." In *Berliner Schriften*: *1818-1831*. Vol. 11 in *G. W. F. Hegel*: *Werke in zwanzig Bänden*. Edited by Eva Moldenhauer and Karl Markus Michel. Frankfurt/ M.: Suhrkamp Verlag, 1970. Pp. 275-352.

_____. *Hegels theologische Jugendschriften*. Edited by H. Nohl. Tübingen: J. C. B. Mohr, 1907. *On Christianity*: *Early Theological Writings by Friedrich Hegel*. Translated by T. M. Knox, with an Introduction, and Fragments Translated by Richard Kroner. Gloucester (Mass.): Peter Smith, 1970.

_____. *Phänomenologie des Geistes*. Edited by Johannes Hoffmeister. Hamburg: Verlag von Felix Meiner, 1952. *The Phenomenology of Mind*. Translated, with an Introduction and Notes by J. B. Baillie. Introduction by George Lichtheim. New York: Harper Torchbooks, 1967.

_____. *Die Vernunft in der Geschichte*. Vol. I in *Vorlesungen über die Philosophie der Weltgeschichte*. Edited by Johannes Hoffmeister. Hamburg: Felix Meiner Verlag, 1955. *Lectures on the Philosophy of World History*: *Introduction*. Translated by H. B. Nisbet, with an Introduction by Duncan Forbes. Cambridge: Cambridge University Press, 1975.

_____. *Vorlesungen über die Philosophie der Geschichte*. Vol. 12 in *G. W. F. Hegel*: *Werke in zwanzig Bänden*. Edited by Eva Moldenhauer and Karl Markus Michel. Frankfurt/M.: Suhrkamp Verlag, 1970. *The Philosophy of History*. Translated by J. Sibree, with a Preface by Charles Hegel and a new Introduction by C. J. Friedrich. New York: Dover Publications, Inc., 1956 (1899). *Reason in History*: *A General Introduction to the Philosophy of History*. Translated, with an Introduction, by Robert S. Hartman. The Library of Liberal Arts. New York: The Bobbs-Merrill Company, Inc., 1953.

_____. *Vorlesungen über die Philosophie der Religion*. 2 Vols. Edited by Georg Lasson. Hamburg: Verlag von Felix Meiner, 1966 (1925).

_____. "Vorrede zu Hinrichs' Religionsphilosophie." In *Berliner Schriften*: *1818-1831*. Vol. 11 in *G. W. F. Hegel*: *Werke in zwanzig Bänden*. Edited by Eva Moldenhauer and Karl Markus Michel. Frankfurt/M.: Suhrkamp Verlag, 1970. Pp. 275-352. "'Reason and Religious Truth': Hegel's Foreword to H. Fr. W. Hinrichs' *Die Religion im inneren Verhältnisse zur Wissenschaft* (1822)." Translated by A. V. Miller, with Introduction by Merold Westphal. In *Beyond Epistemology*: *New Studies in the Philosophy of Hegel*. Edited by Frederick G. Weiss. The Hague: Martinus Nijhoff, 1974. Pp. 221-244.

_____. *Werke*. Vols. 11-12. Edited by Ph. Marheineke et al. Berlin: Verlag von Duncker und Humblot, 1840. *Lectures on the Philosophy of Religion*. 3 Vols. Translated by E. B. Speirs and J. Burdon Sanderson. New York: Humanities Press, 1962.

_____. *Wissenschaft der Logik*. 2 Vols. Edited by Goerg Lasson. Hamburg: Verlag von Felix Meiner, 1969 (1934). *Hegel's 'Science of Logic'*. Translated by A. V. Miller, with a Foreword by J. N. Findlay. London: George Allen & Unwin Ltd., 1969.

Heidegger, Martin. *Hegel's Concept of Experience*. (n.t.). New York: Harper & Row, 1970.

Heinrich, Dieter. *Between Kant and Hegel: Post-Kantian Idealism --An Analysis of its Origins, Systematic Structures and Problems*. Lectures transcribed and edited by Stephen Dunning et al. Cambridge (Mass.): n.p., 1973.

_____. *Hegel im Kontext*. Frankfurt/M.: Suhrkamp Verlag, 1967.

Kaufman, Walter. *Hegel: A Reinterpretation*. Garden City: Doubleday Anchor, 1966.

Kline, George L. "Hegel and the Marxist-Leninist Critique of Religion." In *Hegel and the Philosophy of Religion: The Wofford Symposium*. Edited, and with an Introduction, by Darrel E. Christensen. The Hague: Martinus Nijhoff, 1970. Pp. 157-177.

Kojève, Alexandre. *Introduction to the Reading of Hegel: Lectures on the 'Phenomenology of the Spirit'*. Assembled by Raymond Queneau. Edited by Allan Bloom. Translated by James H. Nichols, Jr. New York: Basic Books, Inc., 1969.

Kroner, Richard. "System und Geschichte bei Hegel: eine Säkularbetrachtung." *Logos: Internationale Zeitschrift für Philosophie der Kultur* 20 (1931), pp. 243-258.

MacIntyre, Alasdair. "Hegel and Marx." In *A Short History of Ethics*. New York: The Macmillan Company, 1966. Pp. 199-214.

_____. "Hegel on Faces and Skulls." In *Hegel: A Collection of Critical Essays*. Edited by Alasdair MacIntyre. Garden City: Doubleday Anchor, 1972. Pp. 219-236.

Marcuse, Herbert. *Reason and Revolution: Hegel and the Rise of Social Theory*. Boston: Beacon Press, 1960 (1941).

Nadler, Käte. "Hamann und Hegel. Zum Verhältnis von Dialektik und Existentialität." *Logos: Internationale Zeitschrift für Philosophie der Kultur* 20 (1931), pp. 259-285.

O'Brien, George Dennis. *Hegel on Reason and History: A Contemporary Interpretation*. Chicago: The University of Chicago Press, 1975.

Rupp, George. *Christologies and Cultures: Toward a Typology of Religious Worldviews*. The Hague: Mouton, 1974.

Schmitz, Kenneth L. "The Conceptualization of Religious Mystery: An Essay in Hegel's Philosophy of Religion." In *The Legacy of Hegel: Proceedings of the Marquette Hegel Symposium, 1970*. Edited by J. J. O'Malley et al. The Hague: Martinus Nijhoff, 1973. Pp. 108-136.

Schrader, George. "Hegel's Contribution to Phenomenology." *The Monist* 48 (1964), pp. 18-33.

Simon, Josef. *Das Problem der Sprache bei Hegel*. Stuttgart: W. Kohlhammer Verlag, 1966.

Theunissen, Michael. *Hegels Lehre vom absoluten Geist als theologisch-politischer Traktat*. Berlin: Walter de Gruyter & Co., 1970.

Westphal, Merold. "Hegel's Theory of Religious Knowledge." In *Beyond Epistemology: New Studies in the Philosophy of Hegel*. Edited by Frederick Weiss. The Hague: Martinus Nijhoff, 1974. Pp. 30-57.

Wiedmann, Franz. *Hegel: An Illustrated Biography*. Translated by Joachim Neugroschel. New York: Pegasus, 1968.

Wilkins, Burleigh Taylor. *Hegel's Philosophy of History*. Ithaca: Cornell University Press, 1974.

IV. Works Consulted for Hamann

Alexander, W. M. *Johann Georg Hamann: Philosophy and Faith*. The Hague: Martinus Nijhoff, 1966.

_____. Review of Introduction and Commentary to *Golgotha und Scheblimini*. Vol. 7 in *Johann Georg Hamanns Hauptschriften Erklärt*, by Lothar Schreiner. *The Hamann News-Letter*, Vol. III, no. 1 (May, 1963), pp. 13-14.

Altmann, Alexander. *Moses Mendelssohn: A Biographical Study*. University (Ala.): University of Alabama Press, 1973.

Anderson, Albert B. "Ignorance and Enlightenment: A Study in the Religious Philosophy of Johann Georg Hamann (1730-1788)." Ph.D. dissertation, Harvard University, 1964.

Baudler, Georg. '*Im Worte Sehen*': *Das Sprachdenken Johann Georg Hamanns*. Bonn: H. Bouvier u. Co., 1970.

Bayer, Oswald. "Selbstverschuldete Vormundschaft: Hamanns Kontroverse mit Kant um *wahre* Aufklärung." In *Der Wirlichkeitsanspruch von Theologie und Religion: Ernst Steinbach zum 70. Geburtstag*. Edited by Dieter Henke et al. Tübingen: J. C. B. Mohr, 1976. Pp. 3-34.

Blanke, Fritz. *Hamann-Studien*. Studien zur Dogmengeschichte und systematischen Theologie, no. 10. Edited by Fritz Blanke et al. Zurich: Zwingli-Verlag, 1956.

Büchsel, Elfriede. Introduction and Commentary to *Über den Ursprung der Sprache*. Vol. 4 in *Johann Georg Hamanns Hauptschrift Erklärt*. Edited by Fritz Blanke and Karlfried Gründer. Gütersloh: Gerd Mohn, 1963.

Disselhoff, Julius. *Wegweiser zu Johann Georg Hamann, dem Magus im Norden*. Elberfeld: W. Langewiesche, 1871.

Gajek, Bernhard. *Sprache beim jungen Hamann*. Munich: Uni-Druck, 1959.

Gründer, Karlfried. *Figur und Geschichte: Johann Georg Hamanns 'Biblische Betrachtungen' als Ansatz einer Geschichtsphilosophie*. Freiburg/Munich: Verlag Karl Alber, 1958.

_____. "Nachspiel zu Hegels Hamann-Rezension." In Vol. I of *Hegel-Studien*. Edited by Friedhelm Nicolin and Otto Pöggeler. Bonn: H. Bouvier u. Co. Verlag, 1961. Pp. 81-101.

_____, and Schreiner, Lothar. *Die Hamann Forschung*. Vol. 1 in *Johann Georg Hamanns Hauptschriften Erklärt*. Edited by Fritz Blanke and Lothar Schreiner. Gütersloh: Carl Bertelsmann Verlag, 1956.

Hamann, Johann Georg. *Entkleidung und Verklärung: Eine Auswahl aus Schriften und Briefen des "Magus im Norden."* Edited by Martin Seils. Berlin: Eckart-Verlag, 1963.

_____. *Hamanns Schriften*. 8 Vols. Edited by Friedrich Roth and Gustav Adolph Wiener. Berlin and Leipzig: G. Reimer, 1821-1843.

_____. *Sämtliche Werke*. Edited by Josef Nadler. 6 Vols. Vienna: Herder Verlag, 1949-1957.

_____. *Sokratische Denkwürdigkeiten/Aesthetica in nuce*. Edited, with an Introduction, by Sven-Aage Jørgensen. Stuttgart: Philipp Reclam jun., 1968.

Hegel, Georg Wilhelm Friedrich. "Hamanns Schriften." In Vol. 11 in *G. W. F. Hegel: Werke in zwanzig Bänden*. Edited by Eva Moldenhauer and Karl Markus Michel. Frankfurt/M.: Suhrkamp Verlag, 1970. Pp. 275-352.

Herde, Heinz. *Johann Georg Hamann: zur Theologie der Sprache*. Bonn: Bouvier, 1971.

Herder, Johann Gottfried. "Essay on the Origin of Language." In *'On the Origin of Language': Two Essays by Jean-Jacques Rousseau and Johann Gottfried Herder*. Translated, with Afterwords, by John H. Moran and Alexander Gode. Introduction by Alexander Gode. New York: Frederick Ungar Publishing Co., 1966. Pp. 85-166.

Homer. *The Odyssey of Homer*. Translated, with an Introduction, by Richmond Lattimore. New York: Harper Torchbooks, 1965.

Hume, David. *Dialogues Concerning Natural Religion*. Edited, with an Introduction, by Henry D. Aiken. New York: Hafner Publishing Co., 1948.

Jørgensen, Sven-Aage. *Johann Georg Hamann*. Stuttgart: J. B. Metzlersche Verlagsbuchhandlung, 1976.

Kant, Immanuel. *Kritik der reinen Vernunft*. 2 vols. Frankfurt/ M.: Suhrkamp Verlag, 1968. *Immanuel Kant's 'Critique of Pure Reason'*. Translated by Norman Kemp Smith. New York and Toronto: St. Martin's Press and Macmillan, 1965.

_____, Hamann, et al. *Was ist Aufklärung? Thesen und Definitionen*. Edited by Ehrhard Bahr. Stuttgart: Philipp Reclam jun., 1974.

Koepp, Wilhelm. *Der Magier unter Masken: Versuch eines neuen Hamann-bildes*. Göttingen: Vandenhoeck & Ruprecht, 1965.

Leibrecht, Walter. *God and Man in the Thought of Hamann*. Translated by James H. Stam and Martin H. Bertram. Philadelphia: Fortress Press, 1966.

Liebrucks, Bruno. "Sprache als Bild." In Vol. I of *Sprache und Bewusstsein*. Frankfurt/M.: Akademische Verlagsgesellschaft, 1964. Pp. 286-340.

Lowrie, Walter. *Johann Georg Hamann: An Existentialist*. Princeton: Princeton Theological Seminary, 1950.

Lumpp, Hans-Martin. *Philologia crucis: Zu Johann Georg Hamanns Auffassung von der Dichtkunst*. Tübingen: Max Niemeyer Verlag, 1970.

Mendelssohn, Moses. *Jerusalem, oder über religiöse Macht und Judenthum*. In Vol. III of *Gesammelte Schriften*. Edited by G. B. Mendelssohn. Hildesheim: Verlag Dr. H. A. Gerstenberg, 1972 (1843). Pp. 257-362. *Jerusalem or on Religious Power and Judaism*. In *'Jerusalem' And Other Jewish Writings*. Translated and edited by Alfred Jospe. New York: Schocken Books, 1969. Pp. 11-110.

Metzke, Erwin. "Hamann und das Geheimnis des Wortes." In *Coincidentia Oppositorum: Gesammelte Studien zur Philosophiegeschichte*. Edited by Karlfried Gründer. Witten (Ruhr): Luther-Verlag, 1961. Pp. 271-293.

_____. *J. G. Hamanns Stellung in der Philosophie des 18. Jahrhunderts*. Schriften der Königsberger Gelehrten Gesellschaft, 10. Jahr, Heft 3. Halle (Saale): Max Niemeyer Verlag, 1934.

Nadler, Josef. *Johann Georg Hamann, 1730-1788: Der Zeuge des Corpus mysticum*. Salzburg: Otto Müller Verlag, 1949.

Nadler, Käte. "Hamann und Hegel. Zum Verhältnis von Dialektik und Existentialität." *Logos Internationale Zeitschrift für Philosophie der Kultur* 20 (1931), pp. 259-285.

Nebel, Gerhard. *Hamann*. Stuttgart: Ernst Klett Verlag, 1973.

O'Flaherty, James C. *Hamann's 'Socratic Memorabilia'*: *A Translation and Commentary*. Baltimore: The John Hopkins Press, 1967.

_____. "Some Major Emphases of Hamann's Theology." *Harvard Theological Review* 11, no. 1 (January, 1958), pp. 39-50.

_____. *Unity and Language*: *A Study in the Philosophy of Johann Georg Hamann*. Chapel Hill: University of North Carolina, 1952.

Salmony, H. A. *Johann Georg Hamanns metakritische Philosophie*. Vol. I: *Einführung*. Zollikon (Switzerland): Evangelischer Verlag, 1958.

Schmitz, F. J. "The Problem of Individualism and the Crises in the Lives of Lessing and Hamann." *University of California Publications in Modern Philology* 27, no. 3 (October, 1944), pp. 125-148.

Schreiner, Lothar. Introduction and Commentary to *Golgotha und Scheblimini*. Vol. 7 in *Johann Georg Hamanns Hauptschriften Erklärt*. Edited by Fritz Blanke and Lothar Schreiner. Gütersloh: Carl Bertelsmann Verlag, 1956.

Seils, Martin. *Theologische Aspekte zur gegenwärtigen Hamann-Deutung*. Göttingen: Vandenhoeck & Ruprecht, 1957.

_____. *Wirklichkeit und Wort bei Johann Georg Hamann*. Stuttgart: Calver Verlag, 1961.

Sievers, Harry. *Johann Georg Hamanns Bekehrung*: *Ein Versuch, sie zu verstehen*. Studien zur Dogmengeschichte und systematischen Theologie, no. 24. Edited by Fritz Blanke et al. Zurich: Zwingli Verlag, 1969.

Simon, Josef. Introduction and Notes to *J. G. Hamann*: *Schriften zur Sprache*. Frankfurt/M.: Suhrkamp Verlag, 1967.

Smith, Ronald Gregor. *J. G. Hamann, 1730-1788*: *A Study in Christian Existence, with Selections from his Writings*. New York: Harper & Brothers, 1960.

Unger, Rudolf. *Hamanns Sprachtheorie im Zusammenhange seines Denkens. Grundlegung zu einer Würdigung des geistesgeschichtlichen Stellung des Magus in Norden*. Munich: C. H. Becksche Verlagsbuchhandlung, 1905.

Wild, Reiner. *'Metacriticus bonae spei'. Johann Georg Hamanns "Fliegender Brief*: *Einführung, Text und Kommentar*. Frankfurt/M.: Peter Lang, 1975.